KNOCKING DOWN GINGER

For Pamela, my wife,
who shared a common childhood,
and for Ashley, our grandson,
that he might know something of how we lived.

John Gorman

KNOCKING
DOWN
GINGER

Caliban Books

Contents

Illustrations

Photo credits

Introduction

Knocking Down Ginger is a remembrance of working class life in Stratford, East London, from the 1930s to 1956, a watershed date in the history of the Communist Party, and the date of my own resignation from the Party. It is not a carefully researched, chronological autobiography, but rather a series of recollections which intertwine and overlap, abstracting the strongest memories from those formative years in my life. Early memories are invariably the most easily retrieved from the amazing databank of the mind, though I accept that recall is liable to be subjective. Memory can also be deceptive for we all remember things that did not happen exactly as we recapture them, and favourite stories tend to become embellished with the retelling. To avoid the worst excesses I have dipped into books and pamphlets on my shelves, to confirm a date, check a fact, or quote the written word. Whilst trying to be factual, I have changed the name of just one schoolboy, to give him a deserved anonymity.

I owe a special debt of thanks to Leonard Harrow, who read and edited my manuscript. Len offered friendly advice and gave encouragement throughout, usually over pints of real ale at the Traveller's Friend, Woodford. There was also the help of my wife, Pamela, who was always willing to discuss the past and tolerate the many hours that I spent writing in the isolation of my garden studio.

The story I tell is personal, but the past of each of us belongs to us all.

John Gorman
December 1994

CHAPTER 1
The Houses in Between

It was another Stratford, without swans and Shakespeare, the Stratford, east of Stratford-atte-Bow, in West Ham, the largest industrial borough in England, where I was born in the summer of 1930. Swans could not have survived the disgusting and foul industries that poured a chemical pot-pourri of filth into the river Lea. As early as 1614, one Lancelot Gamblyn, starchmaker of Stratford Langthorne, and nine others, all of West Ham, were arraigned because in their making of starch, 'a stenche and loathsome smell doth arise insomuch as the ayer is corrupted and His Majesty's subjects who are to passe and repasse by and through the highway ... leading to Bow Bridge ... are in great danger of being choaked and killed with the said stenche and loathsome smell.' Three centuries later, even the Yardley lavender factory in Stratford could not disguise the vile and pestilent odours created by the chemical works of Boake Roberts and the singular aroma arising from British Feeding Meals, who converted domestic refuse into animal foods. Peculiar smells from a warren of manufacturers of fertilisers, vitriol, soaps, inks, varnishes and paints, all blended with the fetid, nauseating stench of bone boiling, skinning, glue-making, pie-making and diverse smells of countless obnoxious industries. The sulphurous, putrid brew swirled upwards, clinging to the soot and smoke of the London and North Eastern Railway Company to choke the lungs, blacken the washing and coat the houses with a sticky patina of permanent grime. Lying beyond the boundaries of a 19th century slaughterhouse Act which placed restrictions on offensive trades, foul industries legally proliferated in Stratford, free from paying full rates, free to poison and pollute.

My paternal grandfather, John Elliot Gorman, had migrated from Devon to Stratford in 1913, to the house where I was born, as an escape from rural poverty, a poverty so biting that it too often saw kettle broth on the table to feed his six children. Kettle broth? Hot water seasoned with salt and pepper with a hunk of stale bread dropped in it. He was a cabinet maker, a fine and reliable craftsman who died of tuberculosis, at the bench – his employer's bench – coughing blood, at the age of fifty-seven. My grandmother, Adelaide Charlotte Gorman, was a charlady, still rising at five in the morning to scrub floors on her hands and knees for the Aerated Bread Company at the age of sixty-five, for sixpence (2.5p) an hour, after the Second World War. My mother, Lilian Buzzard, came from South Shields, Durham, the daughter of a miner, Thomas Buzzard, who had started work at Auckland Park colliery at the age of twelve. One of seven children, my mother had been put into service at fourteen as a servant to the manager of Westoe colliery. My father, John, known to many as Jack, was a carpenter; we were poor, but like many working class families, did not think of ourselves as poor. There were always those who were worse off.

'Our street', and it was always, our street, although it was St James Road, lay to the east of the epicentre of the infernal cauldron, nearer to the railway works which were the largest in Europe, employing more than four thousand workers. A narrow soot blackened stretch of late 19th century artisans' dwellings, the street lay sandwiched between the railway at one end and two cemeteries at the other, one Anglican, the other Jewish, the resting place of two Rothschilds, far from the Mount of Olives. Beneath a pall of smoke and smuts, the women slaved on their knees to whiten their front door-steps, scrub their own strip of pavement from front gate to kerb and to keep clean 'nets'. The nets were white lace curtains, designed to blur the view and curiosity of passers-by who were separated from the front rooms of the houses by a distance of one yard and a low brick wall topped with crudely cast iron railings mounted with spear-tops. A woman who did not maintain the outward signs of cleanliness was regarded as slovenly, to be despised and the subject of malicious gossip. Though time changed practice, the note of condemnation in my mother's voice was obvious, when, fifty years later she said of a newly arrived neighbour, 'She's very nice, but she doesn't clean her front.'

At the railway end of the street was an unnecessarily large church and an adjoining vicarage, a gloomy but substantial red-brick edifice with a high wall, a large front garden, many rooms and one vicar. All the other houses in the street were built of yellow bricks, had low walls, tiny back gardens, few rooms and many occupants. It was a social gap that the vicar seldom crossed, remaining incarcerated in ecclesiastical isolation unless it was to venture a few steps to his church or to walk the length of the street to the little Church of England elementary school that stood close by the Jewish cemetery. Opposite the school was a rag and bone yard and a tiny off-licence, while half way down the street was a corner shop and an estates office, the only other buildings which differed substantially from the two rows of facing terraces. My parents did not drink, but as a boy I used to accompany a friend to the off-licence to have a jug filled with ale for his mother. The licensee, Mrs Paddock, was short, as wide as she was tall, red faced, with red podgy arms to match, gingerish hair and dangly earrings. Her head barely reached the top of the pumps as her strong thick arms pulled them towards her bosom, the heady smell of the beer rising from the jug to fill our nostrils. Outside the shop, we surreptitiously sipped the froth, an introduction to one of the forbidden pleasures of adult life.

The houses opposite us backed onto the 'Sick Home', a barrack-like building with a gate-house and guarded with forbidding cast-iron railings, painted dark green. Built in 1854 as an industrial school for pauper children, it was the scene of a tragedy and scandal in 1890 when twenty-six children perished there in a fire, trapped in a locked and unlit dormitory. Early in the present century it became a workhouse for the Poplar Union. Just before the First World War it was re-opened as Forest Gate Sick Home, a home for 'imbeciles' and expectant mothers, a bizarre dual role that prevailed until well after the Second World War, my own son being born there in 1951. Although it was then known as Forest Gate Hospital and was part of the National Health Service, older inhabitants still referred to it as 'the workhouse.' To us however, it was always the Sick Home. Sometimes, a demented inmate would escape – the expectant mothers seemed happy to stay – and white coated attendants could be seen scurrying up and down our street looking for the escapee, an event always regarded with amusement, never alarm.

Neighbouring streets offered a few small shops selling the necessities for a hard life. 'Faithfull's' was an oil shop, another corner shop, this one surmounted by two plaster Ali Baba jars, symbolic of the trade, the dim shop interior dangerously lit by gaslight in an atmosphere that reeked of paraffin and mothballs. It was a poor man's Aladdin's cave, the floor piled with halfpenny bundles of creosoted firewood, open tins of dog biscuits, bunches of canes, some with curved ends to serve as grips for the beating of unfortunate children, and giant coarse bristled scrubbing brushes made for the back-breaking work of women with red raw hands. The floor of the shop was heaped with a profusion of jars and tins containing oils, varnishes, disinfectants, soda and turpentine, muddled with balls of string, mousetraps, white enamel bowls with blue rims and galvanised metal buckets that shone like silver and clanked like dustbins. Outside, hanging from large hooks, were bass brooms, cane carpet beaters, mops and tin baths – small oval ones for washing clothes and babies and long oblong ones with rounded ends for the ritual family bath night.

Nearby, was the fish and chip shop. A large window and a small door faced the pavement with an eternal queue that might have been part of the structure. The frying trays were heated by fires at floor level, stoked with wood and coal. In winter, the shop was warm and inviting, the fires casting a red glow, the tangy smell from the large tin salt-cellars complementing the sharp smell of vinegar and frying fish. In summer, it was like a ship's boiler-room in the tropics as the red-faced owner chopped wood on the floor behind the counter, shovelled coal and stirred boiling fat, sweat dripping from his chubby chin as he combined the roles of stoker and cook. Between fuelling the fires and battering the fish he would make chips, pulling with all his weight on the handle of a clumsy chip chopper that was clamped to the counter. It was fascinating to watch the pale, raw, peeled potatoes being pushed into the contraption with his thick fingers and see the evenly sliced chips emerge into a tin bowl. I was certain that one day his fingers would disappear into the machine and appear from the other end as chips, but it never happened. A scrawled notice hung in the window, 'Clean newspapers wanted'. How clean they were is a moot point, for reading newspapers in the lavatory was a common practice. A small square of greaseproof paper slapped into the middle of a page of newsprint left plenty of newspaper in direct contact with the contents. I soon learned the principles of off-set printing while reading the reverse type on a penn'orth of chips. The whole scene, the heat, smell, queue, is linked forever with the recall of two women fighting outside the shop, clawing, scratching, hair pulling, rolling, screaming and swearing, battling in the centre of the road encircled by enthused onlookers. What it was about, I never knew. How it ended, I never cared. My chips were ready and shocked by the primitive savagery I walked away, dipping repeatedly and compulsively into the paper, the din receding. Yet, the picture remains, the flimsy drab dresses, lank hair, thin faces and bone hard violence. It was, and is the only time, I have seen women fight.

Just across the road from the chip shop was Warman's dairy, and it was a real dairy, through the open door behind the counter you could see the cows in their stalls and breathe the sweet smell of fresh grassy milk. On some summer days the cows were herded to graze on Wanstead Flats, the nearest grazing-land to East London. The flats were part of Epping Forest, always described by my teacher as 'the lung of London.' Occasionally I would be sent to have a jug filled with milk if we had run short, but only then, for our allegiance was to the London Co-op who delivered daily by handcart, the milk coming in half-pint and pint size bottles sealed with cardboard tops.

I never passed the butcher's shop when it was closed, without experiencing pride and a sense of reflected glory, because the strong wooden shutters that secured the shop had been made by my father. They were framed and jointed, solid and varnished to a rich treacle colour, six tall panels slotted into place and fastened by a long black iron bar, padlocked at both ends. They were made during a period of unemployment, in his shed in the backyard of our house. If I felt pride each time I looked at them, my father felt robbed of just reward for his labour. He had persuaded the butcher to have new shutters by bargaining on the price until he agreed to make them for a few pounds, which after the cost of timber measured the profit in shillings. The handful of coins helped to eke out the dole, a starvation pittance that had already driven him to sell two sets of my cigarette cards to a second-hand bookshop for threepence, the price of two sausages and a few potatoes to provide a dinner for the family when we were faced with hunger. Half a sausage each with a boiled potato. The desperation that drove a kindly man and a skilled craftsman to sell his little boy's treasured but pathetic collection in order to provide food seared his pride. Means tested misery heaped humiliation upon helplessness, creating an anger stoked by poverty towards the absolute unfairness of capitalism. The hurt was suppressed and seldom revealed, but it remained with him until the end of his days.

Visits to the butcher were usually to buy mince, rabbit, stewing-beef, scrag-end or other cheap cuts. The floor was scattered with sawdust and I would scrape patterns with the toe of my shoe while I waited for my mother to be served. I would watch with fascination as the butcher weighed the meat on counter scales, skilfully selecting from an ascending row of gleaming brass weights that ran from ounces to pounds. Once, I was sent on an errand to buy some lamb chops, a luxury during a period of relative prosperity. Walking home, clutching the paper-wrapped meat, I had to pass the local builder's yard. The builder kept a yard dog, Rover, a pitiful mongrel whose fur was matted and yellow, soaked where he lay tethered in his own urine. For some reason the dog was loose that day and he came onto the pavement to confront me, sniffing the air, drooling at the smell of the meat. He barred my path and bared his teeth, a long low growl signalling his intent. It was a moment of decision. Terrified by the ravenous beast, I threw the chops straight in front of him and sped past to home, safety, and the awful despair of my mother, for the chops were irreplaceable.

The little shops were convenient but most food was bought from the stalls in Stratford market or Queen's Road, Upton Park. Though miles apart, my mother would walk the length of both markets, seeking to stretch her meagre budget by buying for a halfpenny cheaper. On Saturday nights, the stalls in Stratford market traded late, and the naphtha lamps hissed in the winter darkness, a warm yellow welcoming light shining through the wire-covered glass bowls. The atmosphere of the sissing oil and the banter of the costers created an ambience never to be matched by supermarkets, as the anxious bustling crowds sought broken biscuits, bruised apples and cut-price salmon and shrimp paste, farthings counted as carefully as pounds. At the kerb, competing with a barrel organ, shuffled small groups of unemployed, cloth-capped and pinched, singing as only the Welsh can sing, semi-circling the man selling matches and falling silent as they passed the blind ex-serviceman from the Great War, still rattling his cup above a tray of bootlaces, a plea written on cardboard hanging from his neck. A regular busker played the spoons, two large spoons gripped between his second and fourth fingers which he rhythmically rattled over his bones with amazing speed. The elbows of his jacket and the knees of his trousers were worn threadbare with his daily performance. There were few coppers to spare, but the poor gave to the poor. Pedlars and buskers could expect nothing from the rich, for their paths never crossed. Lawyers, bankers and landlords were as rare as eleven bob notes in Stratford market. From Angel Lane, a comic misnomer for a narrow street of dilapidated two-up, two-down cottages and ancient shops running from the railway works to the High Street, children made forays around the stalls, searching for fallen fruit. Just once, I remember that two of the children were barefoot. Bootless children were a rare sight, but this was a time of high unemployment with Salvation Army soup kitchens and riots outside the Labour Exchange, always referred to as the 'Unemployment Exchange'. The government of the comfortable, tweedy, pipe-smoking Baldwin pleaded for national economy, a plea observed by my father as being misdirected to people who had economised all their lives. We had known nothing else.

'Our street' was a cut above Angel Lane, Bridge Road and the turnings around Stratford Market – well my mother thought so. The houses in St James Road had been built for mechanics during the industrialisation of the area during the 1870s and were in a reasonable state of repair. They were certainly preferable to the decaying tenements in Windmill Lane and the older dwellings around Stratford market and Carpenters Road. Other streets, even those in nearby turnings, were considered less salubrious. We certainly regarded the south of the borough, Custom House, Canning Town and Silvertown, as rougher areas, with their large population of casual dockers, gasworks labourers and factory workers in the chemical, sugar and rubber trades.

Our house was narrow, just fourteen feet wide, with a passage leading to three rooms and a scullery. A tight staircase led to three bedrooms. The lavatory was in the backyard, it still is, and I did not see a bathroom until I was evacuated in 1939. Toilet paper was squares of cut newspaper, pierced with a hole in the corner and suspended diagonally from a piece of string hanging on a nail. The lavatory pan was covered with broad white wood planks, jointed together, with a hole cut in the middle. The seat was fixed down. For men and boys peeing in the darkness the skill was to hit the hole first time and be guided by the sound of splashing water. Inaccurate aim brought howls of complaint from the next woman to go 'to the lav.' We always called it the 'lav', but a friend's mother used to refer to it politely as, 'The Houses of Parliament'. 'Can Fred come out to play?' 'Hang on, he's in the Houses of Parliament.' Alternatively, 'He's on the throne.' Why was it so called? I don't know. During the war, a picture of Churchill hung in her lavatory, though whether it was an act of patriotism or an expression of contempt, I never found out.

The fixed lavatory seats were the cause of an hilarious incident a few doors along from us. A visitor to the house, a young man courting the daughter, was invited home for the evening to meet the family for the first time. Bottles of brown ale and milk stout were opened and mum, dad, a couple of brothers, the daughter and her boyfriend settled down to play cards on the kitchen table. The boyfriend, who had already had a few beers before he arrived, was woozily conscious that he had to be on his best behaviour to impress the parents. Inevitably the time came for him to go to the lav. Making his uncertain way out into the backyard, stumbling past the dustbins, he entered the lavatory thinking to himself, 'Be careful, don't piss on the seat, I must lift the seat, I must lift the seat.' He did. After a considerable struggle in the pitch blackness with a seat that seemed to be jammed, he succeeded in lifting the whole wooden board upwards, resting it against the back wall as though it was hinged, nails protruding as from a fakir's bed. Unfortunately, it was not long before his intended mother-in-law, a woman of stout proportions, also went out to the lav. Her screams resounded along the neighbouring backyards as she dropped directly onto the cold china bowl, impaling her back on the nails.

Our scullery, at the back of the house, had a brick built 'copper' in one corner for boiling water and washing clothes. Mondays were hell, a daylong Bedlam of steam and toil. It began at six in the morning when my mother twisted newspaper and chopped firewood to light the fire beneath the boiler, ready for the weekly wash. Sheets were stripped from the beds, dirty clothes collected and piled into a heap in the scullery. Soon, steam that was to fill the house began to drift from the gap around the circular wooden lid that covered the boiler. The scullery and adjoining kitchen – which was our living room – were gradually transformed into a sauna, though we had never heard of the word. In between firelighting, filling the boiler with buckets of water and collecting the clothes, my mother prepared breakfast while we all took turns to wash at the shallow, stone, fluted sink in the scullery. Washing was in cold water from the only tap in the house, the hard water refusing to produce lather from the pinky red bar of Lifebuoy soap. My father washed first, drank five cups of strong tea made with Libby's milk and left for work. Fed and washed, shoes polished, I would be packed off to school leaving my mother free to continue her battle with the washing, while at the same time looking after my baby sister, Dorothy.

Washing went on all day, stoking the fire, twirling the boiling clothes with a dolly stick bleached like driftwood, no soap powders, just soda and steam. Lifting the heavy scalding wet sheets from the copper with a wooden stick was a dangerous wrestling match as they were heaved into a tin bath of warm water, ready for the rubbing board, a fiendish device for racking the body. Made of corrugated zinc, held by a two legged wooden frame, the rubbing board stood in the bath, ready to batter and skin knuckles as the brick-hard lump of yellow Sunlight soap was rubbed furiously up and down, pounding dirt from cotton. As tired fingers wrung and squeezed, the next ordeal awaited. The mangle. Surely no machine was more aptly named. A cast iron monster, its giant wooden rollers mangled shirt buttons as surely as the treadmill turning of the great iron wheel racked my mother.

On Mondays, the tablecloth was 'in the wash'. Home from school for dinner – it was never called lunch – the plain wood kitchen table would be spread with newspaper. Monday dinner was always cold meat left over from the Sunday roast, with hot mashed potatoes as wet as the washing. Everything seemed soggy and my mother's hair, usually hairclipped and neat, was loose, dank and dishevelled.

Back to school for the afternoon, the wash day battle resumed, Robin's starch, Reckitt's blue and pegging out the clothes to dry on a rope line in the backyard, the sagging rope held high in the middle with a clothes-prop that kept the sail-like sheets just inches from the ground. Rain was a tragedy; a snapped line a disaster that brought tears. On rainy winter days sheets were draped on a clothes-horse in front of the kitchen range, hung from makeshift lines and slung over the backs of chairs, steam rising, renewing the sauna. Unsympathetic to the problem of trying to dry the family washing in the kitchen, the room in which we lived and ate, a room barely ten feet by eight feet in size, I hated the disruption, discomfort and chaos. Coming home from school in the afternoon it would be impossible to sit by the fire. The kitchen table, a surface for all purposes, would already be piled with half dry washing and commandeered for ironing and mending. All that was left was the floor, where I squatted as close to the fire as the clothes-horse allowed, lifting my head from a comic to peer through gaps in the washing at the glowing stove.

Solid black flat-irons were heated on top of the kitchen range and picked up by using an 'iron holder', a much scorched piece of rag as smooth and slippery as the iron itself. Sometimes the cloth would slide away, flesh searing against the hot iron. There were two irons, worked in relays, one left on the range to heat while the other was being used. The polished iron slid over shirts and sheets, guided by a dexterous and skilful hand, a clean, sweet warm smell rising from damp cotton. When the ironing was finished, my mother would fetch her work-box and button-box, two old biscuit tins, the patterns worn in parts to the bare metal. She would sit by gaslight late into the night, for socks had to be darned, leaving warm woollen lumps to be felt by curling toes, mangled buttons replaced and shirt collars turned. In hard times there were more darns than original socks, patches were patched and new collars made from shirt tails. During the war, we were urged by government to 'Make-do and Mend'. That was a laugh. Perhaps the campaign was conceived by people who talked of 'my tailor', bought their shirts by the dozen and whose wives burdened them with hat bills.

The copper had another purpose, to heat water for bath night, always a Friday. The long tin bath would be lifted from the nail where it hung on the fence in the yard, brought indoors and placed on the floor in front of the kitchen range. The hot water was then laboriously ladled from the copper into a galvanised bucket, carried into the kitchen and tipped into the bath. A few buckets-full, a handful of soda added and the bath would be ready. My sister was usually first in, followed by myself, then my mother. After each one was bathed, another dipper full of hot water would be added to freshen the lukewarm water left by the previous bather, but keeping the bathwater hot was impossible. To compound the discomfort, the side of the bath, nearest the fire, became too hot to touch while the other side remained freezing. Last one in, and sometimes it was me, slopped in a grey sludge that was almost cold.

I never saw my father bath. Most times he went to the West Ham baths, the slipper baths, rows of cubicles, each with a giant tap controlled by an attendant with a turnkey from outside in the corridor. Each cubicle had a number and you had to call out your instruction, 'More hot for number five' or whatever, until a suitable temperature was reached. If you stayed in for more than twenty minutes the attendant would bang on the door, calling out, 'Time's up'. When I was thirteen, modesty demanded that I too went to the baths, a Saturday morning escapade with a gang of my mates. We used to call out for hot water for a number belonging to another cubicle. Wallowing in the steaming luxury of number six, I would call out, 'More hot for number eight', and await the yells of the unfortunate occupant as he received an unexpected torrent of water. Retaliation would follow as number eight, wrongly guessing the number of the perpetrator, called out 'More cold for number five'. A shivering number five would respond in kind, escalating the conflict until the attendant, rushing from tap to tap, realised the game. He would go mad, cursing and threatening to box our ears. It was a miracle that no one was scalded.

West Ham baths was a municipal palace, only rivalled in contemporary splendour by the local Odeon. Built in the early thirties by order of the Labour Council, it filled a public need in a borough of houses without bathrooms. Furthermore, its construction had provided jobs for scores of unemployed building workers, including my father. He had a lasting civic pride for the building, not only as a craftsman who had helped with its creation, but as a Labour voter who saw it as a fundamental and tangible expression of Labour policy. When a 'Ratepayers' candidate – a conservative in disguise – was foolish enough to canvass our street in a local election, complaining about public expenditure, he suffered an informed and devastating rebuff on our doorstep from my father. Listening from the gloom of the passage, I heard my first political lecture.

Daily life in our home centred around the scullery and the kitchen. This was because the other two downstairs rooms and one bedroom were let to lodgers, an arrangement dictated by the purse. The house was rented, as were all the houses in the street, from a property company in the city. They were very rich. Our family alone must have paid for the house fifty times over since my grandparents moved in just before the First World War, and the company owned streets of them. The lesson of the iniquity of owning other peoples' houses was learned at my father's elbow as he sawed, hammered and painted, repairing the landlord's property. It was an early introduction to the economics of capitalism with its triple-claw grip of rent, interest and profit.

In the thirties, the rent was twelve shillings and sixpence a week (75p), 'Not much if you say it quickly', but more than could be afforded on a carpenter's wages of one and eightpence an hour (9p) with a wife and two children to support. At one time it was three children, but my younger brother died of scarlet fever when he was two years old. The five or six shillings a week the family of lodgers paid helped towards the family budget, especially during times of unemployment.

Our last lodgers, Jim and Sarah Blackshaw were a wonderful cockney couple who came to us in 1936 for a couple of weeks and stayed for seven years. When Sarah, who came from Bow Common, told her family that she was moving to Stratford, they thought it 'very posh' and that she had really done well for herself. I suppose she had, for the house she came from was smaller than ours and was shared by two families: four adults and fourteen children! Jim and Sarah shared our outside lavatory and the scullery and the difficulties of intimate living with strangers can be imagined. Yet it worked. Aunt Sarah and Uncle Jim, and later, 'little Jimmy', became part of our extended family. Jim, a lorry driver, had relatives living next door and in three other houses in the street and we were all part of a close community. Most children started married life by living in one or two rooms with their parents and the whole street seemed interrelated, a community of Aunt Mays, Aunt Flos, Uncle Alberts, Uncle Alfs and the rest. My Uncle Tom and Aunt Kit lived on the other side of the road, so did my Auntie Winnie and Uncle Bob. Families had lived in the street for years, and life, if precarious, appeared stable. The rent collector, a rotund music hall figure with a bowler hat and a leather Gladstone bag, went from door to door, collecting the rent in cash each week, but he was never robbed. Today, it must be doubtful if he would make it half-way down the street. Nearly every house had a latch key hanging on a piece of string behind the letter box, but no one intruded. Perhaps there was nothing worth taking, but burglary in the street was unknown, though at least one householder was known to have rifled his own gasmeter of its hoarded coppers in a time of need.

There was common cause. If someone was ill, a neighbour would cook and take in dinners, children would be cared for and washing done. A death in the street would see nearly all the blinds in the front windows drawn for a week and a street collection taken for a wreath. My mother and Sarah often acted as collectors, and after the funeral, a handwritten letter of thanks from the nearest relative of the deceased would be displayed in our window. Behind drawn blinds on the day of the funeral, there would be refreshments for the mourners, not on the scale of an Irish wake, but beer and sandwiches. Sarah remarked after one such occasion, 'It was a lovely funeral; 'am and port'. It was always ham. With two cemeteries at the top of the street, death was part of life. Regular processions of black horses, plumes waving, drawing a hearse with cut glass sides and silver carriage lamps would be led by an undertaker's mute, bearing death's victims to a Co-operative conclusion to life. If there were funeral directors other than the Co-op in our neighbourhood, I cannot recall them. As a funeral passed, we stood still and raised our hats in respect. When Aunt Flo died, all the regulars from the Traveller's Friend, a pub in Cemetery Road, stood outside and raised their glasses in silent tribute

Apart from the noise of the steam trains – and two thousand a day passed through Stratford – which clanked, rattled and whistled day and night, the street was quiet. There was hardly any traffic and not a single car owner in the entire street during the 1930s. Most tradesmen and services, the coalman, dustman, rag and bone man, greengrocer and ginger-beer man made their rounds with horse-drawn vehicles. Others, like the baker and milkman, pulled or pushed handcarts. When starting on their rounds with the cart fully loaded, it must have been a back-breaking weight to pull. The baker's roundsman had a useful dodge. To pull the cart, he had to stand between the shafts like a horse, so he fixed a leather strap across the shafts, against his stomach to give him more pulling power. On Sunday afternoons a coster would push his barrow, spread with a white cloth, down the centre of the street, crying in a long, loud unmusical voice, 'Cockles, winkles, whe-lll-ks'. They provided the basis for a traditional East End Sunday tea, but not for us; bread and marge spread with salmon and shrimp paste followed by tinned fruit, usually pineapple chunks, and a piece of homemade cake was the rule.

We were a fixed and respectable community of working class families, the men mostly with a trade; bricklayers, railwaymen, engineers, a PLA docker and an electrician among them. Strangers in the street would be instantly spotted. As children we would confront others of our age, demanding, 'What are you doing in our street?' Threatening, we sometimes forced them to go on their way by another route. Despite the unspoken bonding, it was not all harmony. Children fought and women quarrelled over the children who fought. Some men got drunk and one man caused unexplained antagonism by keeping pigeons in a loft in his backyard. An unmarried woman wore a gold coloured chain around her ankle and was considered 'fast', regarded by the other women as 'no better than she should be.' A railway worker who sought to better himself by doing a window cleaning round between shifts and voting Tory was regarded with disdain. There was a street culture of conservatism and conformity with the respected local Labour Party secretary, Mr Williamson, playing the role of a patriarch.

The men worked long hours for low wages and married women 'didn't go out to work'. They simply cleaned, cooked, carried and raised children in an endless cycle of domestic life. Women were the quartermasters and servants to an army of labour, an unpaid back-up to help feed the insatiable maw of industrial capitalism. As a boy, I saw them only as mums and sisters, grannies and wives. It took a lifetime to see them as workers.

Our kitchen range, the altar of family life, was blackleaded and polished daily, the hearth whitened and the lino-covered floors scrubbed on hands and knees. Beds were made, children washed, food carried for miles in shopping baskets and meals prepared and cooked. There was no vacuum cleaner, refrigerator or any electrical appliance. In fact, we did not have electricity in the house until shortly before the Second World War, and then only for the lower floor. Housework was manual and relentless, all mops and Mansion polish. There was little comfort. In our kitchen, we had one armchair covered in leathercloth and four upright bentwood chairs, set around a scrubbed deal table. The table had a little drawer at the end where the cutlery was kept, a miscellaneous collection of yellowish bone-handled knives, blunt and round tipped, plain forks and spoons, a wooden handled bread knife and a tin-opener. A Sunday best set of apostle tea spoons were kept in their cardboard box. Next to the kitchen range were two small cupboards, one held an assortment of crockery, the other was our larder, with just two small shelves. Coal for the fire was kept in a cupboard under the stairs and every shovelful was carried from the passage to the kitchen, invariably depositing a fine sprinkling of coal dust, ready for tomorrow's cleaning.

The first twenty-four years of my life were spent in a street bounded by the church where I was christened, the school where I was taught and the cemetery in which I expected to be buried. It was a narrow world, but it was a life filled with love and hope, enriched by the people who lived in the houses in between.

CHAPTER 2

Squirt Me Mister

Ginger, you're barmy,
Went to join the army,
Got knocked out with a bottle of stout,
Ginger, you're barmy

I had never heard the rhyme until I went to school, but with my flaming red hair, it was a taunt song that was to haunt me for a decade. 'Coppernob', 'blood-nut', and 'carrots' were ready nicknames, but it was 'That ginger Gorman' who was too often remembered for mischief while the 'mousies' escaped identification.

My first school was St James, the Church of England elementary school that stood at the end of our street, a few hundred yards from home. Each morning the school bell would ring from the rooftop and the day came when it tolled for me. I was four years of age. I went unwillingly. In fact, I was dragged, clutching the cast iron railings that stood as sentinels with spears in front of every house. As my mother prised my fingers free I grabbed the next railing with my other hand. It was my first public protest against authority. Hot, dishevelled and with hands blackened with the accumulated smoke from steam trains and the soot from thousands of chimneys that encrusted the railings, I arrived, late.

I was handed over to a diminutive, elderly teacher of infants, Miss Forbes, the kindest and most gentle of teachers, with a natural love of children; qualities I was to find hard to discern in many of the teachers that followed. Miss Forbes washed my hands at a brass-tapped sink in the children's cloakroom and led me into the classroom.

Our street had much of the character of a village, and St James was an urban village school, small and homely, a natural

17

continuation of the houses. It stood taller than the houses, but was single storied, constructed of similar yellow bricks and roofed with grey slate. The classrooms were lit by gaslight and heated by coal fires, just like our homes, and high amid the chimney pots was the bell of blackened brass. The school was shielded from the distractions of street life by a high brick wall, broken by two narrow entrances. These had green painted wooden doors and were surmounted by grey stone lintels, chiselled deep with the inscriptions, 'BOYS' and 'GIRLS'. The doors opened onto two very small asphalted playgrounds, each with an open fronted shed for shelter in bad weather. All children to the age of seven entered by the girls entrance and shared the same playground. I bridled at being forced to use the girls doorway for three years, considering it 'sissy', and could not wait to 'pass up' into the 'big boys'. The infants' classrooms were in one large hall, divided by moveable partitions of wood and glass. It had a lofty vaulted roof with dark wooden beams and appeared to be the size of a cathedral. The apparent vastness was an illusion created by my relative size. Years later, when I booked the hall for a Tenants' Association meeting I was astonished to find that it could barely hold fifty people and the chairs were Wendy House size.

The surnames of a good number of the children were already familiar to Miss Forbes for she taught successive generations. Fathers, mothers, older sisters, brothers, aunts and uncles of the new arrivals had been earlier pupils. I was one of the exceptions. My mother went to school in South Shields, and my father was not enrolled at St James, because it cost a penny a week in 1913. Instead, he was sent to another school close by, Odessa Road Board School. The Board Schools had been established after the 1870 Education Act to 'provide schools for the children of the labouring poor', and generations later Odessa Road Board school was still fixed in our minds as a school for poor children. St James had been built in 1874 by the Rev William Bolton to offer a Church of England education, in competition with the undenominational status of the Board School.

We called the kids who went to Odessa, the 'O Dees.' 'Other denominations' or just an abbreviation? Either way, we regarded the O Dees as the enemy. Winter snowball fights with them were ferocious, with barrages of frozen missiles as hard as cricket balls, aimed with stinging accuracy.

In contrast to St James, Odessa was a two-storied forbidding barracks, altogether rougher and more bleak. It provided free school dinners for necessitous children and also free boots, confirming it as a 'poor school'. St James had no kitchen facilities and needy children would be sent to Odessa Road school for their mid-day meal, the distributed tickets the stigma of poverty. Only a few qualified for school dinners, and I suspect that they must have been children of the long-time unemployed.

As infants, we sat in mixed pairs at double oak desks, arranged in rows, drawing patterns in sand-filled shallow tin trays with pointed sticks. The walls were pinned with animal-illustrated alphabet letters and biblical scenes. The dominant colour memory of the classrooms is brown, the gaslight a dull yellow. On rainy days our coats were hung in turn on the fireguard to dry, the fire stoked at intervals by a cantankerous caretaker. Mornings started with a hymn bright and beautiful, 'The rich man at his castle, the poor man at his gate', and finished with a prayer, recited standing, hands together, eyes closed as I tried to conjure a vision of God. In the afternoons we slept for the first hour on low camp beds stretched with camel-coloured canvas. Miss Forbes taught us to read and write, chalking large printed letters on her blackboard which stood on a pegged easel, 'The cat sat on the mat', and we copied them in pencil on sheets of coarse paper. When she wanted our undivided attention, we sat on our hands, if we chattered we had to clasp them on our heads.

We had scripture every day and learned that Jesus was good and we were bad, but we would all go to heaven if we learned our scripture and tried to be good. God was everywhere and saw everything that we did, even when teacher was not looking. On holy days we were marched in a crocodile to the Church at the far end of the street for services we did not understand, peering over the polished pews at the vicar who wore a white frock and read from a huge bible supported on the outspread wings of a golden, eagle-topped lectern. We sang Ancient and Modern and looked forward to Palm Sundays, when we were given palm leaves made into the shape of a cross; we saw them as swords and after church would sword-fence our way home like little Christian soldiers.

In our second or third year we were taught by Miss Kim, another kindly teacher who taught us our first multiplication tables. We learned them by chanting in sing-song unison, the sound rising to the rafters in a mathematical hosanna, 'Six fours are twenty-four, seven fours are twenty-eight', feeding a musical programme of calculation into permanent memory. Miss Kim also showed us how to make pictures by cutting shiny coloured papers with blunt-ended scissors and pasting the shapes onto blue sugar paper, an introduction to art.

Our parents were asked to send us to school on the first Thursday of each month with a penny for 'Coral League'. It must have been an Anglican overseas mission, for we were told that our pennies and our pictures would be sent to 'native children'. I formed a picture in my mind of black children, in straw huts admiring our brightly coloured collages while a benevolent vicar distributed large copper pennies bearing the head of the King. Were our pictures despatched to some colonial outpost and given to local children? It would seem improbable, but no more unlikely than the wringing of pennies from the poor of East London to spread the white man's religion on a distant coral reefed island. At the end of each year, the vicar would come to the school to test us on scripture, creed and catechism. I do not recall it as a hardship, the questions were simple and every child received a certificate adorned with ornate lettering and an illustration of children listening to Jesus. I treasured mine as testament to my scriptural knowledge; they were to prove to be the only educational certificates I ever attained.

We were well behaved, partly because authority was never questioned, but mostly because of the kind, wise and skilful way in which Miss Forbes and Miss Kim fulfilled their vocations. The only infant escapade I can remember that could remotely be considered naughty was connected with the roofless urinal in the playground. We used to compete to see who could pee the highest up the slate slabs that lined the wall above the trough. One day, the tallest boy succeeded by dint of an extra flick whilst in full stream in clearing the top of the wall, a fine spray showering on some girls leaning against the other side of the wall. Miss Forbes administered a strong rebuke, the nearest she came to chastisement.

Our daily routine was broken on a cold January day in 1936 when we were told with great solemnity that the King had died and we must all feel sad. As I ran home I tried hard to feel unhappy, but it was no good, I never knew him and felt no sense of loss, sadness was not in my heart. However, the subsequent shemozzle surrounding the heir to the throne, the Prince of Wales and his lover, Mrs Simpson, did directly affect me. With the natural lore that thrives among schoolchildren to spread, by word of mouth with wit and rhyme, social comment on events of the moment, I had picked up a topical piece of verse, which was sung to a popular tune of the day:

> Who's this coming down the street?
> It's Mrs Simpson, sweaty feet.

Now, the Simpson brothers were tough and the one with thick matted curly hair, 'Wiggy Simpson', was the toughest. Singing my newly learned couplet in the playground, I was grabbed by Wiggy, 'What's that you're singing about my mum?', he yelled. Before I could explain he gave me a hard kick on the shin which for speed and accuracy would have pleased Stanley Matthews. As Wiggy was wearing stout lace-up boots, the toecap left a purple bruise that became the subject of close questioning by my mother. Dreading the thought of her storming into school demanding retribution, I lied. Football seemed a plausible explanation, though I have scarcely kicked a football in my life.

Miss Forbes and Miss Kim wished all of us well when the time came to pass up into the junior school and although the Boys' entrance spelt initiation into a kind of manhood, the parting was sad. We had all learned to read simple stories and write printed letters, taught with love. Ahead lay the world of joined-up writing; and the cane.

Childhood, the secure innocence of childhood, ended abruptly and violently, the excitement of the move up to the big boys tempered with the sight of the cane and the threat of having your name entered in the 'black book'. Miss Jude, Eton-cropped and serious, demanded 'Silence in class' while she was teaching and enforced her law with stinging cuts of the cane to the palms of tiny hands. The whippy natural cane hung from a hook by the blackboard, a visible threat. 'Getting the stick', as we called it, became as familiar as prayers. The pain caused by the swishing strokes could be alleviated by pressing hot and tingling fingers to the cold iron framework of your desk, but the hurt caused within by the assault in front of the class smouldered on to light the fires of resentment and resistance. Teachers were no longer friends, but enemies. It was class war.

The cane could be administered, not only for mischief, such as talking in class, but for failure. The inability to answer a question on a lesson just taught could result in the stick, the slow to learn suffering a double humiliation. Miss Jude – we never knew the Christian names of our teachers – was sparing with her use of the cane. The terror of the school, a teacher of nine year olds, was

'Tipsy' Hughes. He was a sharp dresser; tightly knotted tie, waistcoat and suit, handkerchief in top pocket, Brylcreemed-hair brushed flat and a neat moustache. His nickname derived from two sources, his nicotine stained fingertips and his practice of caning the extreme tips of the fingers. He ignored Shaw's advice on the beating of children – that they should be struck only in anger, never in cold blood – by thrashing his pupils in a single concentrated session. His method was simple. Any misdemeanour or slowness of learning could bring the snapped remark, 'Two o'clock!' At that time every day, a line of victims would form at his desk to receive two strokes. Systematically, with unerring aim, the cane would be brought down with force on the tips of outstretched fingers. To be the recipient of a 'Two o'clock!' during the afternoon, allowed time for a sleepless night and a fearful morning in cold contemplation of the physical attack to come. He had a selection of canes which he tested with fearsome swishes, prolonging the ordeal so that the waiting caused as much agony as the actual injury. An attempt by one boy to avoid punishment by hiding the canes in the boys' lavatory during the dinner break, brought a threat that the entire class would be caned with a new and deadlier cane unless the culprit owned up. A twenty-four hour deadline, calculated to give time for pressure from classmates, worked, and we watched as the cane descended from high above Tipsy's head, six times on the lad's bottom. Girls could be caned, but it was rare, although one master had been known to put a girl across his knees and smack her bottom.

There were no other forms of punishment, no rapped knuckles, no boxed ears, no lines and we were never 'kept in.' The only other suffering inflicted, was verbal, the lash of a sarcastic tongue, used to ridicule and humiliate. We were defenceless against a superior vocabulary and unanswerable power. A friend of mine by the name of Christopher Curtis, the undernourished inoffensive son of an unemployed bricklayer, was the daily butt of such taunting for his slowness at learning. 'Alright, Christopher Columbus, tell the class what you have learned today about King Harold.' Chris, with the fairest of hair and the palest of skins, reddened and squirmed, his silence taken as evidence of his stupidity. I felt for him, wincing inwardly as the ordeal continued. 'Come out to the front.' His bird-like legs emerged from the wide bottoms of short cut-down trousers, the waist at chest height, the shapeless garment held by tight braces as he stood shamefaced before us. 'Who can tell Columbus the date of the battle of

Hastings?' A dozen hands shot up, waving for attention. Point proven, the boy was a dunce. At home, there were bare boards throughout his house, not a scrap of lino, no shades to cover the gas-mantles, peeling wallpaper and a mixture of rickety chairs and a kitchen table. I wondered if knowing the date had any relevance to our lives.

Lessons were a relentless cycle of desk-tied learning. We were taught 'real writing', classic copperplate, inscribed with thin and thick rise and fall strokes made with a steel nibbed pen dipped in black ink. Ink dripped onto the oak desks to create an acid smell forever to be associated with school. To blot your copybook risked the cane, but blots, splatters and inky fingers were plentiful as we strove to master the calligraphic art, with ascenders and descenders kissing the upper and lower lines of our triple ruled exercise books. Writing had the virtue of being a creative activity, but 'sums', spelling, geography and history taxed the mind rather than the hand. There were few art lessons that I can recall, no handicrafts and no talking in class unless it was to answer up or read aloud. Light relief came with singing, a daily lesson led by 'Miss' who attempted to teach us the tonic solfa, tuning fork in hand, and who led us in the trilling of folk songs which we sang without comprehension, 'We may the keel row, the keel row, the keel row.' What did it mean? History was a concatenation of the reigns of kings, queens and battle dates. Geography was a global journey of countries coloured pink, fading red on a linen map unfurled on the blackboard. On Empire Day, a half holiday, we were told that 'Children all over the empire are thinking of England today.' That night, when my father came home from work, wearing his bib and brace overalls and smelling of sweat and sawdust I told him what my teacher had said. He suggested that perhaps I should ask the teacher what it was they were thinking!

Playtime came as an explosion of released energy, fifteen minutes of shouting, running and horseplay, gender separated now that we were in the big boys, although our classes remained co-educational. We 'bussed-up' in pairs, hands crossed and gripping our partners hands behind our backs as heads down we galloped around barging into each other. It was a game that presumably originated from the time when omnibuses were drawn by pairs of horses. In the midst of playtime fun and laughter stands a cameo memory of unwitting cruelty. In every class there is a tough boy. Ours was Doddington, not a bully, but thin, tall and granite hard with the bite of poverty in his hollow cheeks. His shaven head was a sign of recent infestation, his collarless shirt and elder brother's trousers the mark of penury. On this day, he came to school wearing his sister's shoes, black, round-toed, each held with a single strap and a domed button. Seizing the chance for ridicule, one boy pointed to Doddington's feet and shouted 'Doddington's got girls' shoes'. Doddington stood immobile and without glancing down, faced the foolhardy boy, eye to eye. 'No they're not.' he said fiercely, his tone and look daring rebuttal. 'Yes they are, my sister's got shoes just like those,' the boy replied confidently. Doddington stood his ground but his response lacked his usual strength. 'They're not girls' shoes, they're just old shoes, my others are being mended.' By now, we began to gather round to watch the inevitable fight, but another voice was raised, 'They are girls' shoes, they've got round toes.' Doddington's failure to attack missed the moment when he could have regained control. 'Girls shoes. Girls shoes,' other voices chimed as they sensed the weakness of the victim. The little group grew to a widening circle and began to rotate around Doddington. I joined in as the gyrating circle became a skipping dance, fingers pointing down in mockery and accusation. 'Doddington's got girls' shoes, Doddington's got girls' shoes, Doddington's got girls' shoes,' we sang in nursery unison. The dance of derision became faster the chant louder as we circled the lone figure. Doddington's eyes lowered, his head bent as he stared abjectly at his wretched feet. He burst into tears and our chorus rose as a hymn of victory, the giant had fallen in humiliation – and the shame of it is with me still.

There were a few interludes in my schooling at St James, provided by the usual illnesses that afflicted children, measles, whooping cough and chicken-pox. Measles left me with weakened eyesight and a pair of round lensed glasses, long before they were made unpopular by the National Health Service and fashionable by John Lennon. Visits from the doctor, a gruff Irishman with a permanent stethoscope, were rare, for although we were 'on the panel', a call-out cost half a crown (12.5p)

The high spot of any bed-confining illness was the lighting of a fire in the bedroom. Indeed, a fire in a bedroom was a sure sign of severe illness, for it was never lit at any other time, no matter how cold it may have been. A fire was kept burning in my parent's bedroom as my younger brother, Michael, lay dying of scarlet fever and I linked the carrying of coals upstairs with impending death. Fortunately I came through the various childhood diseases and even survived a minor operation, a tonsillectomy, which is remarkable given the circumstances. I was taken to Queen Mary's Hospital in West Ham Lane by my mother and was terrified by the sight of white coats and the smell of disinfectant. A disinfectant soaked blanket had been hung over the door of the bedroom when my brother had been dying and the association was the smell of death. Without time to contemplate my fate I was wheeled into the operating theatre and a red rubber mask in the shape of a bowl was placed over my nose and mouth, the suffocating smell of the rubber soon drowned by a sickly anaesthetic. I awakened to spit blood into a kidney shaped enamel dish. That same afternoon, my father came straight from work to collect me, wrapped me in a blanket and carried me to the nearest tram and then walked the last half-mile home with me in his arms. Still spitting blood, I was consoled with the unexpected luxury of an ice cream. Next week I was back at school.

I did reasonably well at my lessons and got good marks in 'tests', but we were not given positions in class, a laudable policy that spared the slow learners. I got the stick less than some, though I was never one of teacher's favourites. They were rewarded by being made monitors and allowed to help with the classroom chores, filling inkwells, giving out books and ringing the handbell for the end of the lesson. The most coveted prize for merit, and the only privilege I envied, was being allowed to come to school early and pull the rope that rang the rooftop bell. That was never to be, for soon, in 1939, the bell was to be silenced for six years.

Outside of school hours we played in the street, most of our games being played in the road itself, the tar-blocked road being virtually free of motor traffic. Commercial vehicles were invariably horse drawn, Carter Paterson, the United Dairies and Charrington's Coal company maintaining fleets of horses and carts, all stabled a mile or so from our street. Smaller goods were transported by hand cart, and neither horses nor carts posed a serious threat to our safety. Horse-drawn vehicles did however provide the opportunity and challenge of stealing a free ride, especially the open flat carts of the type used by the coalmen. It was easy to run behind a slow-moving cart and clamber on, unobserved behind the sacks of coal. The only danger came when your mates, for a laugh, would call out to the driver, 'Whip behind guv'nerr', and his whip would flick backwards, high over the cart, cracking like a rifle shot above your head. The more adventurous would avoid the hazard by hanging onto the back of the cart by finger-tips, curling their legs under the cart to seek a foothold above the back axle.

The corner shop provided another opportunity for a game spiced with the risk of incurring adult wrath. The high brick wall which formed the side of the shop, lay in Alfred Road, and bore a concise message of inspired brevity, painted in dull cream letters on a dark wooden board. It read, 'Commit no nuisance'. Even the customary 'By order' was omitted, the anonymity strangely giving added authority. The wall on which the warning was displayed was dotted with vitreous enamel signs for Palm Toffee, Bird's Custard Powder, Camp Coffee, Zebra Blacklead and lesser known proprietary brands unrecorded by memory, about ten in all. This gallery of advertising art formed the basis of a favourite game, to which the shopkeeper added threat to our ritual. A few of us, boys and girls, would gather at the kerb, facing the signs, and take turns to throw a bald tennis ball at each sign in turn, catching the ball on the rebound. The object was to hit every sign without missing, or dropping the ball. Each time the ball struck the centre of a sign, which was only screwed at the corners, a metallic doy-oy-ong echoed from the billowing metal. Not unreasonably, the staccato succession of doy-oy-ongs which some children achieved, wore the nerves of the shopkeeper to a frazzle. He would hurtle from the corner doorway, arms flaying, shouting promise of murder as he attempted to grab the nearest culprit. The danger was not diminished when the shop was closed, which was not often, for he might shoot from the side door that led to his living accommodation, his appearance quicker and more unexpected than if he came from the shop doorway. There were more threats than cuffs, for a clipped ear might lead to a visit from an irate mum, accompanied by an avowal to never shop there again. Despite, or because of the associated risk, we played the game for years, until we surrendered the kerb to a new and younger generation.

The essence of all our games was that they cost nothing, or at the most, a few coppers. Cricket was played with a homemade bat, and a lamp-post for a wicket. Hockey was played using upturned walking sticks purloined from aged relations. For tennis, a line would be chalked across the road, and the open palm of the hand used as a racquet. Many of our playthings were homemade. Scooters were built from two short lengths of plank, two screw-eyes, a six-inch nail and a couple of old roller skate wheels. A team of eight-year olds, scooting along the pavement in formation, made a glorious whirring roar and posed a formidable threat to pedestrians. Boxcarts were another wheeled pastime. A wooden grocer's box, a piece of floorboard, four old pram wheels, some nails and a piece of string would be transformed by communal effort into a racing box on wheels with a turning circle that a London taxi driver would have envied. Momentum on the flat was gathered by a racing push to gain speed, followed by a reckless leap onto the box. On a pavement they were fast enough to terrorise pedestrians, on a downward slope they were potentially lethal, for although they could be steered, there were no brakes.

Lamp-posts were our natural place of congregation in the street, especially during the winter months. Evenly spaced on both sides of the road at fifty-yard intervals, they were gas-lit, and we would meet beneath the yellow light, drawn like winged insects to the flame. The lamp-posts provided a useful pivot for recreation, a rope tied above the ladder bar making an easy maypole as we swung round and round, feet flying at gathering speed, until the rope coiled downwards around the post and threatened to jam the fingers. The bar on which the lamp-lighter rested his ladder to change mantles, offered further opportunity for sport, holding competitions to see how many of us could dangle from a bar at the same time. This led in turn, to us pulling ourselves up and down on the bar in unison until it sagged under our weight, an enterprise at which we proved remarkably successful, most of the lamp-post bars in our street being bent to some degree as evidence of our ability.

The lamp-lighter made his rounds on a bicycle, steering with one hand while carrying a long pole on his shoulder. He would stop at every lamp-post and reach upwards with his pole to turn on the light. It was said that one boy had followed the lamp-lighter on his round, climbing the lamp-posts and putting out every mantle after he had lit it, but this may be children's folk-lore rather than fact. The lamp-posts on foggy November evenings were certainly an irresistible focal point of our street life. As winter came, we would gather to twirl our 'winter warmers', cocoa tins stuffed with paraffin soaked rags, the tins pierced with nail holes, the rags lit and the tin swung on a piece of string in a whistling circle until the rush of air fuelled the smouldering rags. Sparks issued forth from the holes and the tin glowed red in the winter darkness, providing more spectacle than warmth. If the

27

string burned through, the tin soared into the night like a comet.

Our street life followed the seasons and festivals. November saw Guy Fawkes' Night celebrated in every back-yard, little bonfires turning the East London sky to a fiery red, rockets launched from milk bottles adding man-made stars to the heavens, the smell of woodsmoke and gunpowder wafting through the narrow streets. We raised the pennies to buy our fireworks, on sale at every sweetshop, by making guys from the most ragged of discarded clothes stuffed with newspaper, the head finished with a ha'penny pink papier-mâché mask, secured with a band of elastic. As we carried the effigy to the street corner to beg for money, we would chant:

> Guy, Guy, stick him in the eye
> Hang him on a lamp-post,
> And leave him there to die.

We started our evening vigils for funds, weeks before the event, forcing homecoming workmen to run a competing gauntlet of 'Penny for the guy, please mister'. Somehow we scraped enough together to buy a few jumping crackers, thunderbolt bangers, Catherine wheels and skyrockets. We saw no danger. When a boy got a live jumping cracker stuck down his Wellington boot, we roared with laughter as he leaped with every ignited crack. The streets rang with the bells of fire engines as firemen answered hundreds of calls to extinguish bonfires that flamed beyond control in tiny back gardens. 1938 was our last year of fireworks; by the following year darkness shrouded the streets, the lamp-posts unlit, bonfires banned by the blackout of war. The next fireworks we were to see would be anti-aircraft rockets, parachute flares, 'flaming onions', and tracer bullets. The East London sky would glow red again, from a thousand fires started by incendiary bombs.

When Guy Fawkes night had passed, we began to think of Christmas and fund-raising by carol singing. Traditionally, the rounds started two weeks before the holiday, but once we tried a pre-emptive strike, making our first sortie in November, only to be collared by a copper for disturbing the peace, each of us escorted home in the firm grip of the law. Our efforts resumed nearer the festive date, we worked both sides of the street rendering a few bars of 'Good King Wenceslas', followed by fewer bars of 'While shepherds watched their flocks by night'. To relieve the monotony, we sometimes changed the words to 'While shepherds washed their socks by night'. With greater enthusiasm we would rattle a cocoa tin and sing a ditty requesting a penny, a ha'penny or a farthing.

In the spring, we joined in the boat race fever that seized the nation, obliged to declare our support for Oxford or Cambridge. We wore favours to declare our allegiance, the boys with dark blue or light blue celluloid favours in their button-holes, the girls with miniature celluloid dolls in appropriate colours pinned to their frocks. Ever the coward, I would defer wearing my favour until the last moment, joining the majority to avoid minority confrontation when asked by roaming gangs, 'Whose side are you on?' Support would be voiced by chanting:

> Cambridge are upstairs,
> Doing up their braces,
> While Oxford are downstairs,
> Winning all the races.

The university could be changed to suit the majority opinion. On the day of the race, we joined millions in listening to the commentary on the wireless, the result awaited with eagerness, the outcome as important as the football cup final at Wembley. Why should this have been? I did not know of anyone who had been to any university, unless it was our doctor. Oxford and Cambridge as seats of learning were as remote to us as Eton and Harrow.

Roller skating was a thirties craze, and some of us were fortunate enough to own a pair of skates. I was one of the lucky ones. The rink at Forest Gate, where Sammy Samuels, the roller skating champion trained, charged for admission, but we knew which roads were tarmacadam smooth, and used them for our skating games. We shared our skates with those who had none, each strapping on a single skate and propelling ourselves by pushing with the skateless foot. Our skating was relentless, in the summer holidays it was not unusual to spend a whole day on skates, ranging the neighbourhood, clacking over paving stones, hobbling over cobbles, in search of the perfect stretch of road. West Ham Park was laced with smooth paths, snaking grey through the clipped green grass. They were ideal for skating, but skating in the park was forbidden. We were undeterred. Being chased by a raging 'parkie' was all part of the fun. With the park-keeper in pursuit, our gang would separate as the paths divided, leaving the sweating and uniformed park-keeper to decide who to pursue. When safety was reached, beyond the park gates, we would regroup and sally forth into the park once again to tease and torment the now puffing parkie. The skates we used bore little resemblance to the integral booted, nylon wheeled skates of today. They were all metal, adjustable to fit any size feet, and were strapped and clipped to our normal shoes or boots. The straps and buckles chafed the ankles and the toe clips bit into the soles, parting the layers of leather. We skated until the wheels had 'windows', holes appearing in the metal wheels, exposing the cross-bars of the inner construction. They were used until they literally fell apart.

We played games that came with the natural seasons, from winter snowballs – gang fights between rival schools involving scores of children in ferocious battles – to autumn conkers. The latter we marinaded in vinegar and baked in the oven in an accepted gamesmanship to strive for a coveted 'hundreder'. Summer brought cricket. With access to a saw, I became the bat-maker, cutting the shape from odd pieces of floorboards that seemed to litter every backyard, and binding the handles with string. The ball we used was a smooth tennis ball, that met the homemade bat with a satisfying smack. Sorbo balls had too much bounce and a leather cricket ball was impractical. Someone did acquire a cork ball once, as we called a genuine cricket ball, and we decided to give it a try. The first ball I played stung my hands with the power of an electric shock, revealing the reason for sprung handles in true bats. The second delivery split the long grained plank right down the middle. After that I used to bind the bats with insulating tape and reverted to the use of tennis balls. I carefully bound my own precious plank until, in my imagination, it resembled 'Clicky-ba', the big battered bat, heavily bound with brass wire, bloodstained and chipped, that was used by Chung, a character from a serial in the *Wizard*. The story was called 'The Wolf of Kabul', and Chung, a simple Himalayan, used his Clicky-ba, (for being a dark-skinned foreigner he was unable to pronounce 'cricket bat') as a club, smashing skulls in the loyal service of his white master in the Indian Secret Service. His master, Bill Samson, usually disguised as an Indian snake-charmer, had, according to the story, done more than any other man to uphold the prestige of the Raj. So he may have done, but it was Chung who was my hero, wielding the imperial bat, splitting skulls as easily as cracking eggs in defence of British rule. 'Shall I crack his skull, Lord?' Crunch! As I strode to the lamp-post wicket, I would swing my bat, alternatively despatching rebellious natives and belting balls to the boundary.

Played without an umpire, appeals for lbw were invariably the subject of acrimonious dispute, so we had our own law for settling a contentious 'howzat'. It was 'three matchsticks'. To resolve the inevitable argument that followed every appeal, the batsman would face three balls, holding the bat upside down, by the blade, with only the thin handle to defend his wicket. Survival was not impossible, for the bowling was rarely accurate, though a slow straight ball aimed at the batsman's toes usually penetrated the awkward defence. If the batsman missed and the ball struck his leg yet again, the result was pandemonium, the batsman claiming his right to another three matchsticks, while the bowler and fielders demanded that the batsman should stand aside and allow the bowler three balls at an undefended wicket. Such was the fury and passion engendered, that a luckless bowler might hurl or lob without success, the triumphant batsman remaining at the lamp-post, convinced that justice had been done.

There were other seasons, an unwritten calendar of whip and top, hoops, cap-bangers, water pistols and marbles, each yielding to the other in a succession of fads. Girls skipped with fiercesome skill, the rope a blur, smacking the ground with a rhythmic slap, slap, slap, their toes dancing as lightly as their kisses, 'Shirley oneple, Shirley twople . . . Shirley Temple.' They chalked the pavements with hopscotch squares and sometimes we joined in the game, throwing a stone, hopping and balancing on one foot. For devilment, we played 'knock down ginger', banging the heavy cast iron knocker of a street door and running to hide, while a perplexed neighbour answered the door to an invisible caller. More daring, was to tie a piece of string to a knocker, take it around the brickwork to the house next door and tie the end to a second knocker. A tug on the string rapped both doors simultaneously, and we would stand and laugh as both parties tugged to open their doors. If spotted through a window, recognition was instant, especially for that Johnny Gorman with the ginger hair.

There was a street culture, with spontaneous team games of tin can topper, release, kerb and wall, hi-Jimmy knacker, five-stones – known as 'gobs' – and marbles played in the gutters. Summer evenings saw the street filled with children in constant activity, ended only by the abrupt parental call of 'bedtime', from scores of windows and doorways. Bedtime was early, most of us tucked up by eight or nine. In an era before television, homes sparsely furnished with hard upright chairs, the cost of coal and gas to be counted, and dawn rising for manual work six days a week, the nine o' clock news on the wireless was soon followed by watery cocoa and bed for all the family.

Our pursuits, if boisterous and a nuisance, were harmless, and we were not streetwise in the sense in which the word is used today. We never passed a telephone box without going in and pressing 'Button B', the returned coin button on the large black coin box, in the hope of retrieving a forgotten tuppence, but that was closer to a game of chance than illegality. Our pilfering was usually limited to lifting a few sweets from the open topped counters of Woolworth's, the high street chain that traded under the slogan, 'Nothing over sixpence'. That did not stop them from selling a pair of shoes for a shilling, charging sixpence for each shoe! There were boys who would ask our corner shopkeeper for sweets that stood in jars on the highest shelves, to give time while he mounted his steps, back turned, to reach across the counter to steal the nearest sweets to hand, but that was an exception. I considered that unfair, for the shopkeeper was really one of us.

The one entertainment for which we paid, was going to 'the pictures', pronounced, 'pichers'. Our nearest cinema was the Splendid, a flea ridden, single storey building which stood opposite Forest Gate railway station: it resembled a converted factory. On Saturday afternoons at two o' clock, we queued for our weekly treat, the 'Tuppenny Rush'. When the portly commissionaire in his faded blue and gold uniform finally opened the doors, a great cheer would roar from hundreds of ragged children who stampeded to the tiny box office, pushing and shoving. Inside, the mêlée continued as we fought for our favourite seats, all priced tuppence and first come best served. The wooden tip-up seats were unpadded, but were covered with maroon coloured velvet nailed to the seats with continuous lines of upholstery nails, the bronze rounded heads just kissing each other. Such seating was hardly comfortable, but was superior to the Electric in Barking where the cheap seats at the front were merely wooden benches. While we waited amid pandemonium for the first flickering feature, an attendant would walk up and down the centre aisle carrying a shiny tin spray gun. It had a wooden handle with a pump action, the kind of cheap object sold in oil shops for dispensing fly-killer. Filled with a pungent and lethal insecticide for killing the various bugs which made the Splendid their home and gave the cinema its popular name, 'The Bug Hutch', the Flit-gun would be directed over the heads of the audience in an hygienic attempt to subdue the latest invasion of fleas and lice, freely transported by some of the verminous patrons. 'Squirt me mister', we would shout, and if lucky, the attendant would aim a couple of quick pumped squirts to your body to the envious cheers of your mates.

The general uproar, a cacophony of whistling, shouting and bellowed conversation would give way to a stadium-like roar as the lights went down and the little silver screen flickered to life. Just what the magic screen was made of was a source of constant speculation. One boy fired his catapult at it with the conviction that it would shatter like glass. He was disappointed, but claimed that a small hole in the top right hand corner of the screen was the result of his experiment. The quality of the screening was often dismal, the picture dark and at times it seemed as if rain was pouring down the screen. The films frequently broke down and a chorus of groans would be directed back to the hapless projectionist while he frantically grappled with yards of snaking split film. The longer the break, the greater the uproar, with jeers and whistling, until the unfortunate manager was forced to appear on the stage to appeal for patience and order. The booing which greeted him was frightening.

Cowboy films were the most popular, and we shared the action, calling out warnings to our heroes as badmen crept up on them. 'Look out, look out behind', we would yell to Ken Maynard or Hopalong Cassidy, and happily they usually heard our warnings. Every week, in addition to the main feature, there would be a serial lasting about twenty minutes; Flash Gordon in *King of the Underworld*, or some similar cliff-hanger. I must have started my cinema going at episode twenty-something, for I never did grasp the Flash Gordon plot. In my confused mind it seemed as if some Roman centurions had invented the tank and were lost in subterranean caves, destined to clank around forever in pursuit of, or pursued by, some unknown evil.

When we came out of the Splendid after a couple of hours of cheering the goodies and booing the baddies, we would refresh ourselves from an ornate monumental drinking fountain that had thick iron cups secured on anchor-like lengths of chain. My parents warned against putting my lips to the communal cups, for

'You never know who has used them and you will get sores.' I would fill one of the cups and fastidiously drink from the middle, carefully avoiding all contact with the iron rim, to avoid contagion, Our thirsts quenched, we would then re-enact scenes from the film we had just seen as we walked home. If it had been Tarzan, adults must have wondered at our gibberish as we spoke to stray dogs in mumbo jumbo, in the manner of Tarzan talking to his chimpanzee.

Within a few years, the Splendid was to be removed from the cinema circuit forever, blown away by a Nazi bomb. As children we were unaware of the political events leading to war, but we were inextricably involved in the excitement of the preparations. A bonus for our street games came with ARP (Air Raid Precautions), which included the placing of two sandbags and a bucket of water for fighting incendiary bombs at every front door in our street. The filled buckets provided ready ammunition for our water pistols, running battles being fought along the street with a refill at every doorway. The house-proud, like my mother, changed the water daily, while the slovenly allowed their buckets to become little stagnant pools, bobbing with dead flies.

One portent of the coming slaughter does stand out in my childhood memory. Walking with my father, I saw a van parked at the top of Sebert Road, not far from the Splendid. It had a hole cut in the roof, from which the head of a man protruded, covered by a wire cage. The van was surrounded by men in black shirts, standing with their backs to the van, arms folded, eyeing a small audience. The head was shouting, and I asked my father what it was about. 'They are fascists,' he replied. 'They mean trouble.' Within a few months my father was with the British Expeditionary Force in France, and all our lives were changed.

CHAPTER 3
Could Do Better

The preparations for war came as an excitement. Suddenly, the routine of daily life was altered to a higher key, a frenetic level of bustling activity against a background of continuous animated talk. As children, we shared the disruption with a sense of adventure but with little comprehension of the horrors to come.

Our street rang with the sounds of clanking metal as Anderson shelters were delivered to every household. The whole street turned out to see the convoy of carts arrive, conversation at crescendo, curiosity and nervous excitement hiding the real fear. The curved corrugated sheets of steel were piled on the pavement outside the house, then lugged through the front door, down the narrow passage, through living room and scullery, scraping walls and chipping paintwork, out into the backyard. Assembly became a group activity, the men leading a shock assault on digging holes into brick-hard earth with pick and shovel, while women and children bucketed the soil into pyramid piles. Instruction sheets were argued over as the foundation angle irons were bolted, Meccano-like, into place and the corrugated sections lowered into the ground. Then it was all hands to cover the construction with earth taken from the hole, patting it into a protective layer and filling sandbags to build a blastwall in front of the entrance. My father made some wooden steps, with two treads, leading down into the damp hole that was to be our bedroom for so many nights. Some of our neighbours, with an ambition towards gardening, sprinkled grass and flower seeds on the earthen layer as a finishing touch, but ours was left to nature to plant whatever blew on the wind.

With a sense of togetherness, the wooden fence that separated our yard from that of our neighbour, Mrs Giles, was torn down so that we could share our shelters if necessary. Talk of Air Raid Precautions dominated daily gossip over endless cups of tea while windows were criss-crossed with gummed tape as a precaution against flying glass from bomb blasts. Local traders did a roaring trade in selling thousands of yards of plain black cloth to be sewn into blackout curtains and hardware shops enjoyed a boom in selling buckets, to be kept filled with water in readiness for coping with incendiary bombs.

The feeling of urgency and anticipation of the unknown was heightened by the arrival of troops to dig a series of trenches on Wanstead Flats, leaving the excavated earth in a series of parallel ridges. My imagination coloured with stories of trench warfare in the First World War, I thought that it was the preparation of a battlefield, but wiser heads said that it was to prevent German planes from landing. The promise of war and attack from the air was confirmed when a unit of the RAF arrived at Wanstead Flats to establish a barrage balloon site as part of London's air defences. At weekends, people went to stare as the silver monsters were inflated to resemble air-ships, and we watched them bob serenely into the sky, held by long cables, as they joined the floating defence ring around London.

The outward signs of the coming conflict intruded into everyday life. Pillar boxes were painted on top with a khaki shade of detector paint that would change colour in the event of a gas attack, though nobody seemed clear as to what the changed colour would be, the Town Hall was piled with sandbags and an ARP post established in the rag and bone yard opposite our school. Children were evacuated, air raid wardens recruited, and the reservists called up. Initial exhilaration turned to tears when in the July of 1939 my father was called up to join his artillery regiment. He had enlisted in the army in the 1920s for seven years, as an escape from unemployment and hunger, and as a reservist, was among the first to be mobilised. We were left with a terrible loneliness, my mother facing not only separation, but survival on a soldier's pay of thirty-five shillings a week (£1.75). For the next six years we were to become in effect, a single parent family, with my mother as housewife, factory worker, lone decision taker and protector of her children.

We queued for hours at an emergency government office for

the issue of our ration books and identity cards. We were advised to memorise our personal identity numbers and CBIT 93/2 became imprinted in the memory bank of my mind. I was proud of the suffix, for with my father already in the army, my mother was allocated number one, and I assumed that number two signified that I was now second-in-command of the household. I lorded my new found authority over my five-year-old sister Dorothy, who was number three. The issue of gas masks was no doubt traumatic for my mother, but proved a source of wonder and adventure to myself. Trying on the mask, the smell of rubber was overpowering, the plastic window misted up and the apparatus rasped a rude noise as I breathed out. The gas masks were issued with a stout cardboard box and a long loop of string for carrying at all times. 'Carry your gas mask' became the watchword of the day and schoolteachers checked that we all had our masks before the start of each lesson. For the stylish, outer cases in Rexine or fancy coloured materials were sold by stores anxious to promote a new line in fashion accessories. Of necessity, we remained loyal to government issue and I soon discovered that a gas mask case made a useful weapon for street fighting when swung around the head by the string, like a flail. As the war years passed, the boxes disintegrated and some of the masks carried by children were battered beyond practical use.

Fearful of impending war and the threat of aerial bombardment, my mother decided that we should leave London, and made arrangements for us to go and live with Auntie Elsie, her friend in Iver, Buckinghamshire.

Our evacuation from London was unofficial, a sort of extended country holiday. We escaped the unfortunate experiences of many who were caught up in the chaos of trying to billet millions of city dwellers at short notice in areas of safety. My future wife was sent as a ten-year-old girl from Ramsgate to Stafford, packed into a crowded third class railway carriage with a luggage label tied to the buttonhole of her coat. At the end of a stressful and tedious journey which took all day, she was driven from house to house as the billeting officer asked, 'Do you want an evacuee?' 'What is it?' was the usual response. 'A girl.' Some refused. Then, 'How much do you pay?' 'Ten shillings a week.' 'Alright, we'll have her.'

Iver was a *Country Life* village when we arrived by bus in the hot summer of 1939, the trees in full leaf as we heaved our brown Woolworth's suitcases onto the pavement outside the Swan, a medieval pub. The village was surrounded by fields and woods, an idyllic refuge of fresh air and farms. My first impression remains. It was green, not grey. There was space, it was country clean, free from smoke and smuts, the houses built without uniformity, varying in style. Beyond the village was the secluded aristocratic splendour of 'Coppins', the home of the Duke and Duchess of Kent.

Elsie had been in service together with my mother in South Shields, when they were fourteen years' old, and they had kept in touch after they had both married and moved south. Her home was a semi-detached bungalow with gardens at the front and back, the front garden opening onto Love Lane and facing the fields of a local dairy farmer by the name of Sparrow. The lane was well named, for Elsie must have had love in her nature to open her little home to my mother, myself, my sister Dorothy, our lodger, Sarah, and her baby. With Elsie's husband Jim, a foreman engineer, and their son, Brian, there were eight of us in all, facing a future beyond prediction. Dorothy and myself were awed by our new home, considering it posh. It had a bathroom, with a white enamelled bath and a chromium-plated rack for the soap, which was scented. Hot water came from a tap! The dining room was furnished with a table and chairs of dark stained and polished wood, the bulbous legs carved, the seats covered with Rexine. There was no black iron kitchen range, but a fireplace with an oatmeal-coloured tile surround, framed with dark polished wood surmounted with an ornamental mantelpiece. Against one wall stood a sideboard, and on it, an emblem of middle class respectability and comparative affluence, an oak biscuit barrel with a silver shield on its side. At mealtimes, the table was spread with a white cloth and laid with cork table mats. One wall had two bay windows and a door that opened onto the garden, the light streaming in to make the polished furniture gleam like glass. The garden was flanked by sharply trimmed hedges and carpeted with mown grass edged with flowers in guardsmen ranks. We had moved more than twenty miles out of London, we had moved upwards within society.

For a couple of months there was no schooling and I was free to explore, to wander the village and lanes, discover secret ponds, peer into Sparrow's farmyard with its steamy and unfamiliar smell of straw, horses and cows, and absorb the tenor and pattern of country life. I felt free, but I was lonely away from my mates, and my adventures, unshared, began to pall. I stopped my solitary roaming and passed sunny days indoors, voraciously reading books from the travelling library, growing introverted and isolated. Soon, I began to look forward to joining a new school at the start of the winter term and making friends.

By the end of the summer, more evacuees had arrived, a pale-faced contingent of waifs from East London. They were billeted mainly with the working people of the village. Were any billeted at the Coppins? If there were, I never met them. For some unexplained and extraordinary reason, the authorities decided to send the evacuees to a school of their own, creating a division between town and country in the community. With each group being made to feel different it nurtured suspicion and led to hostility between the village children and the intruders from the smoke. While the local children went to their newly built modern school, we were allocated the old disused village school next to the churchyard. It was smaller than St James, having just two rooms and an office, but it was cosy and being able to see the slanting tombstones from the classroom window I had a sense of the familiar. There was no playground, but we had the use of the adjacent village hall which had a railed space in front, and we used that. We had some lessons in the hall and also 'drill', the regimented exercises designed to keep us fit.

There could not have been more than thirty of us, boys and girls, mostly from Bow and Hackney, together with three teachers, two men and a woman. Strangely, their names are forgotten but their kindness is remembered with affection. There was no punishment of any kind that I can recall, certainly no corporal punishment. Perhaps it was because most of the evacuees were separated from their parents, but the teachers cared for us and filled our lives with learning and interest. We were taken on nature walks, introduced to poetry, rehearsed for a school play and encouraged to read for pleasure. The boys were taught technical drawing and geometry, a combined lesson that sowed the seed of my future career. We were shown how to sharpen a pencil to pin point fineness, to use a ruler, set square and protractor and I fell in love with the precision of plotting shapes on graph paper. School was no longer a sentence to be served but a pleasurable series of activities. Teachers were restored to me as mentors and friends.

By now, we were a country at war. We had huddled around the fretwork-cased wireless set to hear the fateful crackling broadcast on that sunny September morning and I had watched the tears trickle down my mother's cheeks. I could not appreciate the awful import of the news. A few minutes later, the first air raid sirens of the war sounded and we watched from the window as an ARP warden wearing a tin hat, and encumbered with a pick-axe and spade strapped to his back, pedalled down Love Lane blowing a whistle and waving his arm urging people to clear the lane. The warning turned out to be a false alarm, and in retrospect the whole episode was sadly naive and somewhat comic, a misleading prelude to the terror to come. The excitement soon over, tranquillity returned to the village and manifestations of the war were few. A tree was felled, its branches lopped and a wagon wheel fitted to one end of the trunk so that it could be wheeled across the lane to block it in the event of invasion. The village street was lined with strange contraptions for creating a smoke screen to protect a local airfield. They were like dustbins fitted with vertical chimneys and stood on both sides of the road at regular intervals. It was said that they were filled with oil and would be lit to provide a blackening cloud if a local airfield came under attack.

While the village awaited the attack that never came, I joined my new mates in exploring the countryside in winter; running the gauntlet of snowballs from the village boys, climbing trees, damming swollen streams and getting stuck in the mud of a ploughed field, losing one Wellington boot and hopping home with a frozen mud-caked sock stuck to my foot. Most daring of all, we invaded the grounds of Coppins, picking up spent cartridges in the woods and taking a surreptitious and wonderous peep at the big house.

The local boys were hostile, but their sisters were not. Introduced to them by evacuee girls billeted in their homes, we fraternised after school as winter yielded to spring and we discovered the awakening pleasure that was dormant within our bodies. A lonely path to a hidden field became a playing field of truth or dare, truth soon abandoned for daring without pretence. It was innocent enough, but the joy of Dora Hazelgrowth or Gwendolen Tarrent pressed into a hedge for full lip kisses, unresisted, again and again brought anticipation with every twilight. Dora, small, dark wavy hair, brown eyed and loveable, Gwendolen, tall, to be kissed on tiptoes, straight combed hair and always wearing her Wellington boots. Sex was an unspoken word, but there was sensual pleasure without knowledge. An older girl, twelve or thirteen perhaps, came to tease with a dark question,

'You don't know what MP means, do you?' 'Yes I do, it stands for Military Policeman'. 'No it doesn't, you don't know what it stands for, do you?' 'Member of Parliament?' 'No it's not,' and she smiled and giggled. Each evening as she joined us, uninvited, she repeated her teasing question, asked with a knowing smile and upturned chin. Eventually her secret was betrayed by her brother, 'It stands for monthly period.' We were no wiser and never enlightened.

'Never cast a clout until May is out', was a favourite maxim of my mother and no matter how the temperature rose, I sweltered in flannelette vest and pullover beneath my jacket until the first of June. The may-blossom flowering in the hedgerows was not only beautiful, it was a revelation. 'Never cast a clout until *the* may is out'. My mother could be forgiven for her misunderstanding, for there was scarcely a hawthorn sprig of may-blossom to be seen in South Shields or Stratford. The spring of 1940 brought my first awareness that the seasons were marked by more than a change in the children's calendar from snowballs to street cricket. The school acquired an allotment and we were taught to grow vegetables and to eat carrots instead of sweets. I learned to love nature, the splendour of lichen-covered trees, to observe birds other than sparrows or pigeons – even if I did not know their species – to watch for newts and frogs and to spend hours building camps from branches, deep in the woods. I found peace in war and London was another life in a distant world. Evacuation created an abiding love of village and country living. Then, as abruptly as we had left Stratford, we returned. The capital was unscathed and our evacuation was without purpose. As school closed for summer term I said goodbye to my friends, promised to find them again after the war and kissed Dora Hazelgrowth and Gwendolen Tarrent for the last time. I parted too from my teachers, with regret, for they were also friends who had broadened my vision of life.

We were part of a mass migration. Government pleas for evacuees to remain in dispersed safety failed to persuade tens of thousands of uprooted Londoners. The strain of maintaining distant homes, the heartbreak of divided families, homesickness and the months of 'Phoney War' combined to convince many that war was a distant battle to be fought in other lands. With an optimism encouraged by spring, parents and children drifted back to the capital to resume their normal lives, their arrival fortuitously timed to coincide with the advent of the hottest of summers, the retreat of the British Expeditionary Force from France and the final fulfilment of the long predicted war from the air.

I have no recollection of anxiety during those sunny days, but vividly recall the weeping with joy and the relief of my mother as she picked up a seaside postcard from Margate as it fell onto the doormat. The message, scrawled in blunt pencil was succinct. 'Back in England, by the grace of God. Jack.' My father had survived the escape by sea from Dunkirk.

I was at the pictures, in the Rio in Woodgrange Road, when the sirens sounded on that sunny Saturday afternoon in September 1940 when the first bombs began to fall on the London docks. An ARP-conscious management led us down into the boiler room under the cinema, where we stood huddled beneath enormous sacking-lagged pipes. The atmosphere was charged with that excited nervousness generated when a group of people are faced with a common danger, strangers talking to strangers, the hubbub hiding fear. In an act of unknown generosity, or to help allay any possible panic, the management distributed free ice cream. Free ice cream! Surely our end was nigh. About five o'clock, during a lull in the gunfire and bombing we were allowed to go home. Running along-side the railway, I could see a huge pall of black smoke in the direction of the Thames. It came from fires started by bombs that had fallen like spilled matches upon the London docks. I hurtled indoors full of the story of the free ice cream to be greeted by my mother as if I had returned from the dead. She had spent the afternoon crouching in our Anderson shelter with my six-year-old sister, terrorised by the noise of the attack. That night the bombers returned to stoke the fires with incendiary bombs.

Next week, all the cinemas were closed as the authorities faced the problem of protecting the civilian population from the German raiders. A week or so later, they re-opened, but a parental ban was not so easily rescinded and for months I was forbidden to leave the street. Familiarity with the pattern of the raids that followed and the switch to night bombing saw audiences return to those cinemas that remained undamaged, but they were few. Of the thirty-five cinemas operating in West Ham at the start of the war, only two remained open immediately after the winter of the London blitz, although most were patched up and re-opened as the frequency of the raids diminished. Perhaps the first back to 'business as usual', was the Kinema in West Ham Lane which re-opened at the end of 1940, extravagantly engaging the cockney comedian and film star, Tommy Trinder, to perform the ceremony. His popular catch-phrase was 'You lucky people', if Trinder was invited to stay and watch the performance he may have had second thoughts about his laugh line, for he would have been introduced to the unique quality of the seats. Well used and worn since the cinema opened in the twenties as the Empire Kinema, the seat covering had lost its nap and become as smooth as silk. That in itself may not have mattered too much, but the metal supports had worn over the years so that the seats sloped forwards. The two defects combined to cause the sitter to slide slowly but steadily forward in the direction of the floor. It was a constant struggle to remain on the seat.

At first, when the daylight raids on London started, we would run to the shelter at the sound of the sirens and remain there until the 'all clear', but familiarity soon led us to carry on as usual until we could actually hear the sound of approaching planes. It was like a game, the planes were high and the anti-aircraft guns distant, most of the bombs dropping in the south of the borough, on the docks, at Custom House, Silvertown and Canning Town. Soon however, the bombing was to become indiscriminate, the German bombers scattering their bomb loads anywhere over the densely populated streets of the capital. A small bomb fell in our street, demolishing the off-licence and a couple of houses, including the home of my friend, Chrissy Curtis, but luckily no one was killed, and the ruins provided a new playground as we clambered over the debris and scavenged through the rubble. We found a new hobby, collecting shrapnel from the remains of anti-aircraft shells, the larger shining pieces of jagged metal changing hands as swaps for comics, cigarette cards and army badges.

There were moments of light relief. Sarah's brother, Harry, came to our house one day for a bath. The tin bath was brought in from the yard and put in the scullery, close to the copper where the water was heated, the door to the kitchen shut. I was sitting in the kitchen – our living room – with my mother, sister, Sarah and Harry's girlfriend Ann, film star glamorous, hair piled high and skirt short, when the siren sounded the alert. Gunfire banged overhead and the throb of bomber engines could be heard. It was an age of modesty, even prudery, but all decency was thrust aside as Sarah threw open the door and led the charge from kitchen to shelter, Harry sitting naked and blushing in a few inches of water as a succession of women and children rushed past him into the yard and down the shelter. It was a story recounted many times during the war years. 'They didn't even close the doors after them,' he would say with a chuckle.

We soon learned the popular songs of the war. The First World War had bequeathed us *Tipperary* and *Pack up your Troubles*, our war quickly gave us *Bless 'em All*, *Kiss me Goodnight Sergeant-major* and somewhat prematurely, *We're going to hang out the washing on the Siegfried Line*. The Nazi leaders were lampooned in cartoons, songs, jokes and war posters as preposterous comic idiots instead of the evil power-seeking psychopaths they really were. Popular among schoolchildren was a naughty verse which we sang to the tune of *Colonel Bogey*, ridiculing the enemy leaders and their monorchid Führer:

> Hitler, has only got one ball,
> Goering, has two but very small,
> Himmler, has something sim'lar,
> But poor old Go-balls
> Has no balls, at all.

The full terror of the blitz came with the switch to night bombing. Every evening we would take our bedding down to the Anderson shelter – which was too damp for the bedding to be left there – and my mother, sister, Sarah and sometimes our neighbour, May Giles, would bed down together on a mattress laid on the floor, the only light a solitary flickering night light which stood in a saucer of water. A sack hung over the entrance to stop any chink of light from showing, lest it might serve as a beacon to guide the German planes. After some weeks of bombing, a Bofors gun, mounted on a lorry was positioned about thirty yards from our house, in the next street, and would crack out a resounding bang at regular intervals. We were reassured by the retaliation as the waves of heavy bombers with their distinctive throb-throb drone flew slowly overhead. It was not until after the war that I learned that the mobile Bofors guns were sent into the East End to boost morale, and that their effectiveness against the high flying planes at night, was negligible.

Sometimes when everyone was asleep, I would pull aside the sack and watch the battle, searchlights sweeping the night sky, parachute flares dropped by enemy aircraft hanging like chandeliers to light the target, white streams of tracer bullets making dotted lines in the semi-darkness, and the bright flashes of heavy gunfire exploding in clusters. Bombs fell in the distance with a dull crump and a rumble, and close by with a shattering explosive bang, the blast shaking the ground and breaking windows. The night sky glowed red from fires as buildings burned and it was a scene that I always wanted to paint, to capture the multi-coloured night sky seen from the dark surround of the shelter, but to my constant regret, I never did. In any case, I could never have captured the sounds of gunfire and exploding bombs or the smell of smoke, cordite and damp earth.

In the light of morning, we emerged like a family of troglodytes to count the cost of the night's mayhem. We were fortunate, shattered windows, fallen ceilings and toppled chimneys was the extent of the damage to our house, but the first casualties among friends was suffered, one school mate losing his mother, brother and sister in one of those early raids.

The resumption of schooling was delayed, the blitz, if it did not bring panic, brought chaos. Schools were closed and there were scattered attempts to hold classes with children split into small groups in the front rooms of the houses of willing parents. The effort failed, and as the pattern of bombing settled to night raids, the schools re-opened and I went back to a changed St James, with discipline relaxed and survival paramount.

To my astonishment, I passed 'the scholarship,' winning a special place, which I imagined was an academic distinction. In reality, it was a scrape-through bolstered with age marks, my August birthday placing me among the youngest entrants. I had qualified for a place at West Ham Municipal Secondary School which provided a grammar school education, my social status to be publicly proclaimed by the wearing of an embroidered badge complete with Latin tag. *Deo Confidimus* was proudly stitched to a brand new brass buttoned blazer and with a second hand leather satchel handed down from an uncle, I was equipped for the last five years of my formal education.

After years at the tiny schools of St James and Iver, I was overwhelmed by the massive scale of my new scholastic environment. Built on four sides around an asphalted quadrangle reached through a narrow iron-gated entrance, the two storied edifice with its ornate gables, rows of symmetrical windows, long corridors and countless identical rooms enveloped me in a way that was strange and impersonal, to be evoked when I read Kafka. It was built at the turn of the last century, an embellished barrack block designed for more than five hundred pupils. The quad, or the playground as it was more usually called, was divided into two by an impenetrable fence, a chastity barrier to separate the sexes. I entered the boys' playground, where the sixth form boys were the size of men, and I was shaken by the force of the noise and the violence of the juvenile battles for ascendancy. A feeling of being isolated in a foreign crowd, like a package tourist who has wandered into a native souk, became absolute fear as I was grabbed by a raging group of giants and propelled towards a flight of stone stairs. I was about to be 'Monkey-Holed'.

The 'Sec', as we called the school until the 1944 Education Act bestowed the grander title of Stratford Grammar, aspired to some of the practices and customs of a minor public school. The most reprehensible of these was an unofficial tradition, unseen by the blind eye of authority, of the initiation of new boys. Inspired by tales of the 'Black Hole of Calcutta', the chosen method was to incarcerate the whole of the new intake into a cavity beneath a stone staircase. Into the 'Monkey-Hole' we were forced, arms and legs interlocked in suffocating darkness until the last boy was crammed in, escape prevented by the brawny backs of upper form Flashmans. When our pleas, yells and groans ceased and asphyxiation was close, we were released, extricated and disentangled like a box of paper clips. My precious blazer, an emblem of educational superiority, was minus one brass button and its woven armorial bearing hung by the last thread stitched with love by the hands of my proud mother. To a small, nervous, uncertain boy on unknown territory the experience was traumatic. For the upper forms, it was all jolly good fun.

We were allocated Houses; Gurney, Lister, Fry and Langthorne. I knew them as local street names, but nobody explained that the first three were distinguished Quaker citizens connected with the borough, and the last the site of a medieval Cistercian monastery in Stratford. In retrospect, Joseph Lister and Elizabeth Fry were worthy choices for their respective pioneering work on antiseptic surgery and prison reform. But what of Gurney, the house to which I was assigned? Samuel Gurney was known as a philanthropic landowner and banker, surely a contradiction in terms to match Military Intelligence. It was the grounds of his ancient mansion, Ham House, that were purchased in 1874 by the City Corporation to form West Ham Park, but I was never clear as to who it was that had taken the land from the people in the first place.

The school was deprived of young male teachers for they were all in the forces, with the exception of a lone conscientious objector, and we were taught by women of assorted ages and men considered too old for military service. Some of the men affected the wearing of mortar and gown and they scurried along the corridors like black beetles. They were authoritative, intimidating and middle class. One of them on his first day at the school asked our class who would volunteer to collect the 'lunch money.' Lunch! Surely that was our mid-morning break when we drank our free milk by a straw, that really was straw, from a bottle that held one third of a pint. He meant dinner money. Fourpence (less than 2p) for a school dinner served by dinner ladies, a meal of wet mash, sploshy cabbage and some kind of meat which would vary from rissoles to a wafer thin slice of mutton followed by afters, too often a soggy dollop of bread and butter pudding or stodgy tapioca. In due time, I discovered that fourpence would buy a dinner of pie, mash and liquor – a vivid green gravy – from Cooke's pie and eel shop in West Ham Lane. Midway through eating, your plate might be lifted by a sudden thumb and finger from over your shoulder and a greasy cloth swished across the marble topped table in a gesture of cleanliness, but the meal was a banquet compared to school dinners in war-time West Ham.

Obsequious attempts to lift us above our cultural station and ape the middle class sometimes took peculiar forms. One teacher of English, the aptly named Miss Bray, saw herself as a female Professor Higgins and introduced elocution lessons to her class in an effort to rid us of our local accent. Twenty-five cockney children forcing aitches, reciting 'How now brown cow' and 'The rain in Spain' was one of the more comic examples. We endured a term of phonetic torment before the attempt to induce BBC standard southern was abandoned as a failure. Despite minor genuflections to the public school model, the general approach to our education was progressive. Officially, there was no corporal punishment by the staff, that ultimate means of control residing with the headmaster alone. In five years I knew of only one boy who was caned, a Polish refugee by the name of Konopinski who recklessly threw a jar of red ink over the headmaster. The principal, his countenance rubescent with ink and rage, was witnessed by half the school as he fled across the quad to the sanctuary of his study. The announcement of retaliation, 'six of the best', was publicly proclaimed to assembly the next morning, though the punishment was carried out in the privacy of the headmaster's study.

All forms gathered for assembly at the start of each day, the lower forms at the front, under the direct gaze of the headmaster, and then in ascending order to the senior forms and trusted prefects at the back of the hall. A short prayer and announcements were followed by a concluding hymn, accompanied on the piano by the music master. Our hymnal, a narrow green-covered booklet was a source of revolutionary inspiration. There was no place for 'God made them high and lowly and ordered their estate', instead, there were stirring chants, some to be found in *The Socialist Sunday School Tune Book, Songs of Freedom* and Edward Carpenter's *Chants of Labour*. Lustily we sang *'The People's Anthem*,

> When wilt thou save the people,
> Oh God of mercy when,
> The people Lord! the people,
> Not crowns and thrones but men.

My favourite however was *Jerusalem*, Blake's splendid vision beloved of Women's Institutes and the Labour Party Conference. Lansbury's Christian socialism was within easy recall in East London in the 1940s and the building of a new Jerusalem an attainable dream. The compiler of that hymnal remains anonymous to me, but the selection places him, or her, close to the religion of socialism.

Morning assembly brought us together as a school. It was also an easy start to the day's learning, a relaxation before the trauma of maths or physics. Occasionally, the headmaster used assembly as a platform for mass admonishment. The Konopinski judgement had been accompanied by a moralising lecture and the affair of the Churchill letter was a saga that continued for days. The school had responded to an appeal from Mrs Churchill to support her 'Aid to Russia Fund', a cause we endorsed with an enthusiasm stimulated by newsreels showing fur-hatted Soviet troops knocking hell out of frozen Nazis, inspired by a genial smiling 'Uncle Joe'. Mrs Churchill duly wrote to the school, thanking us for the money collected, signing the letter with a suitable flourish. The letter was pinned on the school notice board where an enterprising collector of autographs promptly snipped off the signature. The headmaster began the week with a plea for restoration, followed the next day with a stern admonition, He issued a further ultimatum, threatening collective punishment unless the culprit owned up, but finally at the end of the week conceded defeat.

Assembly holds another significant memory for me. I was a 'Bursary Boy'. Our family income was considered to be at poverty level and I qualified for a monthly grant of thirty shillings (£1.50) to enable my parents to keep me at school until I was sixteen, the national school-leaving age being fourteen. Once a month, at the end of assembly, a handful of bursary pupils would be called to the platform in alphabetical order to receive an envelope containing the money. It was an insensitive method of distribution, though I had no feeling of humiliation, for it was a right, and I was pleased to be able to take the money home to my mother. My only resentment was reserved for the audible remarks that sometimes came from the headmaster, 'Do you think that you have earned that money, Gorman?' There was no answer.

Although corporal punishment was officially banned, unofficial physical punishment from a minority of masters bordered on the sadistic. A smarmy, geography teacher with greased blonde hair like flattened straw, delighted in approaching boys at their desks from behind, peering over your shoulder at your written work. Heinous mistakes observed, he would grasp the short hairs at the base of the neck, tug his victim upwards until on tip-toes and then deliver a sharp smack to the side of the head with his free hand. I have forgotten the content of his endless lectures on the Gulf Stream and trade winds, but his spiteful brutality is lodged in my mind forever. Dr Smolden was another iron man who ruled by terror. Although his lectures on astronomy were fascinating, he once hurled a boy down the steps of the lecture theatre for a trivial misdemeanour. Nemesis came to another head-smacking teacher, the tall, gaunt and black-gowned Dr Rigby, when a nimble boy ducked his aimed blow and the master's hand crashed through a pane of glass in an adjacent partition, ripping his arm on the jagged splinters. The sight of him stalking the corridors with his bandaged arm in the week that followed was a source of concealed amusement to all who had suffered from his 'right handers'.

Three times a week we were subjected to a peculiar form of torture called PT. For many, the strong and agile, physical training was an escape from learning and a pleasurable activity. For myself, a small, thin, bespectacled individual, lacking in muscle, it was sheer misery. In a well equipped gymnasium – how

I loathe that word – the wall bars were racks of torment, the vaulting horse an insurmountable monster and the medicine ball a missile to be avoided like a cannon ball. While the athletic contrived to hang from the bars by their toes, I clung to the top bar afraid to let go. They somersaulted over the horse with an easy flip, while I struggled to spring onto the four-legged lump of leather, remaining astride but immobile. I became a figure of fun as I shied from the medicine ball, hands outstretched, not to catch but to protect. Even more painful and humiliating were the organised games held in conjunction with other classes from the same year. They took place in the playground as our playing fields had been commandeered for the duration of the war as an anti-aircraft site. Consequently we were confined to netball, volley ball, or football, especially fiercesome when played on asphalt. The PT instructor would select two captains, one of whom was always a handsome dark-haired athlete by the name of Ron Pickering, later to achieve fame as a British Olympic coach and sports commentator. The captains chosen, they would survey the assembled classes and select their teams, each captain picking a boy in turn, 'I'll have him, sir,' the first captain would say, choosing the tallest and strongest. 'And I will have him, sir,' the other captain would respond, pointing to the boy considered to be the second strongest, and so on, until only two unlikely little prospects were left. Not only did I suffer the regular crushing debasement of being left until last, but on one occasion, Pickering with unconcealed disgust, protested to the instructor, 'But sir, I had him last week!'

The only joy I derived from organised games at school was from hockey, watching the girls play. The love of my life when I was in the Upper Fifth, was Barbara Griffiths, a robust Fourth Form captain known to all as 'Bubbles'. In her white blouse and navy blue knickers, I ogled as she bullied off to the roaring support of her many admirers. Four or five of us were regular supporters of the girls' hockey team, referring to our diversion as the study of 'legonomics'. I did not throw away her 'With love' signed Polyfoto – one of a sheet of forty-eight miniature black and white photographs – until I got married. I think she had written the same message on the other forty-seven and distributed all of them!

As a scholar, I was a failure. During my first year, which was oddly designated as the 'Second Form', I tried hard enough but never matched the learning capacity of my fellows. The uncompromising end-of-year exam results placed me twenty-seventh in a form of twenty-eight and my form master's comment on my annual report read, 'Could do better.' I could hardly have done worse. The unfortunate boy who had the distinction of coming bottom of the class was a fee paying pupil. It was still possible to buy a state secondary education until the 1944 Education Act ended the privilege. Despite the advantage of being better off, the fee-payers seldom rivalled the academic ability of the scholarship pupils, though on this occasion it was close run.

The effect on my self esteem was devastating and I was left depressed and humiliated. As I attempted to evaluate my future, I was crushed by the news that together with others, 'Who had not done too well', I was to be placed in a special form: 3E. Forms for any year ran from A to D, depending on the number of pupils and it was generally accepted that the brightest pupils went into the A form and the others in descending order to D. There had never been an E form. To compound the indignity, it was decided that we would drop French as a subject and switch to Spanish, considered an easier language to learn. While my friends in the other forms moved on to a second foreign language, German or Latin, I was relegated to the study of a language that seemed of little possible use, unless I was to become a bull-fighter.

I was overwhelmed by failure and bedtimes became sobbing times as the start of the new term neared. I pleaded for a transfer to West Ham Municipal Technical College, for a fresh start and the opportunity to pursue my already formed ambition to work at a drawing board in some capacity, as a draughtsman or commercial artist (the term graphic designer had yet to be coined), but my mother and the authorities remained obdurate. They knew what was best for me. I was consigned to four years of potential misery, and in my frustration I lost heart. I gave up on the subjects I found difficult, maths, physics, geography and history, and sought refuge from inability by adopting the role of a clown, a constant funny boy, playing the class for laughs. Seeking to undermine authority with wit, I challenged resulting sanctions with evasion and indifference. One of my few moments of unbounded joy came when I rounded the corner to the school one morning to find that a land mine had shattered the top half of one wing, and classes were reduced to mornings or afternoons only while the building was made rehabitable. It was a brief respite from purgatory.

CHAPTER 4
Wide Games

After a year of determined mischief I was rewarded by being upgraded to form 4A. No explanation was offered, but assignment to an A form restored my confidence and I warmed to teachers who had the measure of me. A seminal influence was a teacher of English, Mr Hewitt, a young man invalided from the army with a wounded leg. He wore a tweed jacket with leather patches on the sleeves, corduroy trousers, smoked a pipe and had no intention of forcing us to learn poetry by rote. He was as casual as the clothes he wore and won my admiration during his first lesson. 'Look here Gorman, I know that you are not interested in clause analysis, but *try* to look interested in case the headmaster should look in.' It was an appeal that obliged co-operation. For the first time I was encouraged to write freely, and the resulting essays were critically discussed for their social and political content, my left wing views already taking form. The Steadman-like ink splatters resulting from the hairy and absorbent wartime exercise paper were ignored, it was the substance that mattered. At last I felt that I had something to contribute.

My reform was not total, and in lessons that bored me I joined with others in diverting the true course of the subject being taught. The wider interests of teachers were craftily perceived, so that a maths lesson might be steered towards astronomy, Spanish grammar shunted to an account of the Spanish Civil War. In chemistry, a class taught by an engaging Welshman with an acid stained suit, the learning of formulae would be forgotten if 'Sir' could be engaged in discussing how to make incendiary bombs.

53

This almost ended in disaster when one boy stole some phosphorous from the laboratory, put it in his pocket and caught fire whilst sitting on the bus on his way home. Another opportunity for non-scholastic activity came when we changed classes at the end of a lesson. The long corridors of our school had been broken up by the building of a succession of blast walls at right angles to the main walls. The purpose was to stop a bomb blast from sweeping along the passages. This made the corridors dark, and the gloomy recesses presented the circumstance for snatched kisses with girl friends. Fulfilment was infrequent and innocent enough, but in defiance of the rules.

I played truant only once, but bent the siren rule to miss the lessons I hated. The instruction was that if the air raid siren sounded during the journey to school, the fail-safe principal applied; if you were more than half way to school, you continued as fast as possible; if you were less than half way, you returned home. I had a walk of about one and a half miles to school, but though the siren might sound with the school in sight, I would turn and run home, risking detection if it was a false alarm, the 'all clear' wailing its monotone a few minutes later.

Out of school hours, the cinema remained a popular diversion. Between the shabby Splendid and the plush luxury of the major cinema chains, we frequented a variety of independent cinemas with bizarre un-English sounding names, the Rialto, Rio, Troxy, Astoria and Kinema, each superior to the Splendid, but with individual eccentricities stemming from near insolvency. The Astoria kept cats to catch the mice which scurried in the darkness, and boring love scenes could be enlivened by trying to grab the mangy cats as they brushed past your legs. Crawling under the seats in search of a moggy was not unknown during the more tedious moments of a tearful Hollywood romance. Excitement was added to our visits by 'bunking-in', the practice of gaining entry without payment. Ever impecunious, we would band together and contribute halfpennies and pennies to raise the necessary fourpence (less than 2p) for one of us to pay for admission. Within seconds of being shown to a seat, he would leave for the toilet. The emergency exit with its crash-bar doors was close by and the doors could be opened from the inside, at a touch, as the law demanded. One push and in we streamed, sometimes accompanied by a few extra gatecrashers. Ushers were aware of the ruse, and timing the dash from the curtain that screened the exit to a seat in the front of the stalls was crucial.

Emergence was synchronised with the disappearance of the usher's flashing torch towards the rear of the auditorium, one at a time making the risky run. It was rather like a prison escape in reverse. Darkness offered safety, but the interval between programmes was a danger point because an observant usher might ask an unrecognised group of schoolboys for their tickets. The trick was to pick up a discarded ticket from the floor, for although they may have been colour coded for the day, it was impossible to identify the time of admission.

As the war went on we progressed to the major cinemas, but always in the cheapest seats. Legitimate entry by unaccompanied juveniles was restricted to programmes showing 'U' films, rated for universal showing. To see an 'A' film, the designation for adult, it was necessary to be accompanied by a grown-up. With fathers away in the forces and mothers on war work, there was not much chance of being taken by a parent. The answer was to join the group of boys and girls aged from about ten to fourteen waiting outside the cinema and ask total strangers, 'Take me in please, mister.' Young men acquired instant families as three or four children thrust their sixpences into an obliging hand under the blind eye of the commissionaire. Compliance with the law observed, we usually separated from our new found parent once inside the cinema. Nevertheless, it was a paedophile's charter as innocent children were led into closeting darkness by chance lone men. I was fortunate to have survived the years of adolescent picture-going unmolested.

The ultimate in forbidden films were those given an 'H' certificate, indicating 'Horror', forbidding admission to persons under eighteen years of age. Older brothers of my mates recounted chilling stories of the Frankenstein monster, created from dead bodies and brought to life by electricity, his head secured to his body by a large bolt. The very name of Boris Karloff was synonymous with horror. We could only stare at the gruesome illustrations on the posters outside the cinemas and wish our lives forward to the time when we would qualify for our weekly experience of terror. At last, when fifteen, wearing long trousers and cigarette in mouth I nonchalantly asked for a ninepenny ticket at a local flea-pit to see the *Return of Frankenstein*, the biggest shock was being allowed in without a second glance. The film was an anti-climax to years of anticipation, but by then I had lived through the London blitz and had seen the government film on the liberation of Belsen, where the living dead were a reality and beyond the imagination of Mary Shelley.

Picture-going throughout the forties was as popular and compulsive as television viewing is today, with the additional attraction of physical transportation to a world of instant luxury, if you could afford the major circuit. For a few hours we left behind our homes with lino-covered floors, hard chairs and thin curtains, to enter marble palaces decorated with gilt, velvet drapes, plush carpeting, soft lighting and even softer seats. The Odeon, Forest Gate, had a three piece lounge suite covered in uncut moquette in the upper foyer when there was scarcely a decent suite in the whole of our street. Certainly not one to match the grandeur of the two armchairs and settee that reposed in the Odeon. The very names of many of the better houses were calculated to lift us into a richer world, Majestic, Queen's, Imperial, Grand, Regal and Rex. The connotations with royalty and empire were blatant. Cinema managers wore dinner jackets, bow ties, starched white dress shirts and stood in the front of house with all the command and superior authority of Victorian stationmasters. Commissionaires were large, rotund, and wore magnificent uniforms with gold braid epaulettes, patent leather Sam Browne belts and guardsman caps. They controlled the patient snaking queues with sergeant-major-like commands. 'Two two and threes and four one and nines' they might bark, and two fortunate couples and a couple of singles would exchange the hard pavement for cosseted fantasy. Smartly uniformed usherettes, lipsticked and permed, glamorous as Hollywood film stars, torch-lit your way to three hours of escapism. The words of Cecil Day Lewis from his poem *Newsreel* are wonderfully apt:

> Enter the dream-house, brothers and sisters, leaving
> Your debts asleep, your history at the door;
> This is the home for heroes, and this loving
> Darkness a fur you can afford.

Performances were continuous, and seeing the 'big film', the main attraction, through twice, was commonplace. The three major chains changed their programmes mid-week and again on Sundays, enabling the dedicated and affluent to go to the pictures every day. Some adults did. As youngsters we could only afford the cheaper cinemas or the lower priced matinee performances. Occasionally Nanny Gorman would take my sister and myself to an afternoon show at the Odeon. Admission before four in the afternoon cost only fourpence and we had to rush from school on the stroke of three-thirty to beat the clock. She would meet us equipped with Thermos flask and sandwiches for our tea and we would eat and drink our way through the first film. If that seems socially unacceptable, it should be remembered that some of the larger theatres boasted a cafe, and that apart from the worst of the war years, usherettes walked the aisles with trays of ice creams, peanuts and cigarettes. Before the war, the Queen's at Forest Gate had served cups of tea in the intervals, passing them along the rows and collecting the cups before the lights were dimmed. A Jewish friend from Cable Street, Stepney, claims that her mother used to bring bowls of chicken soup to her children when they went to the Cable! During the war years when sweets were rationed, one family we knew used to take a jar of cod liver oil and malt to eat from the jar with a spoon, each one licking in turn. It was their uncle Len who worked at the Granada, East Ham, and had his living room covered with a thick pile carpet, bearing a repeat pattern of the diamond-shaped logo of Gaumont British.

Cinemas competed for their audiences, extending their programmes of main feature and 'B' film by adding short films, music and variety. The Broadway Super in Tramway Avenue, Stratford, would follow the Pathé News with a ten minute cartoon, the trailers for forthcoming films and a news documentary, *The March of Time*. We hated those diversions from the main attraction and as the transatlantic voice dramatically boomed, 'The March of Time', we would respond, mimicking the accent and calling out, 'The Waste of Time!' Even more annoying were the attempts of some cinemas to pad out the programme with amateur talent competitions. For half an hour we would be subjected to a succession of aspiring, perspiring, tap-dancing Shirley Temples, hoping for 'discovery'. Between programmes, to allow time for the massive influx of patrons, we would be entertained by the playing of popular tunes on the cinema organ. A massive spot-lit instrument, it rose from hidden depths in front of the screen, played by a musician with the ability to perform with his head reversed and a permanent grin on his face. For me, the organ, even when churning out popular and patriotic melodies like *Shine on Victory Moon*, was too reminiscent of church. During the First World War, music halls were used as recruiting platforms, actresses, jingoistic trade union leaders and public figures, like the charlatan Horatio Bottomley, stomping the boards for recruits. In the Second World War, the government used cinemas in a similar but more subtle way, filling the spot between features to appeal for support for 'Spitfire Week,' Navy Week' and the like. In support of an 'Army Week' we were once subjected at the Odeon to an 'additional attraction' of thirty minutes of entertainment by the 4th Battalion Grenadier Guards Harmonica and Accordion Band.

Despite patriotic diversions and the imposition of talent shows, silly cartoons, slow motion football and The Waste of Time, the cinema was the high spot of our social life. We endured long queues as a necessary prelude to pleasure and revelled in the secret darkness where we could share in an adult world, smoking Woodbines without fear of reproof. We sat in the cheapest seats, ankle deep in peanut shells, heads strained upwards at black and white adventure. Frequently, we awaited the opportunity to make a crouching unseen run, back to the dearer seats, made twice as comfortable at half the price.

When the Luftwaffe carried out daylight bombing raids, cinemas would flash an 'Alert' notice on the screens as the sirens sounded and continue with the film. Few left. The real world was outside. In the latter part of the war, during the flying-bomb attacks, roof-top spotters would communicate the approach of a doodle-bug and the disconcerting message would appear on the screen, 'Enemy aircraft approaching'. If a flying bomb was overhead, it was possible to hear the distinctive rasping sound of the engine inside the cinema. Concentration on the film would then be lost as we listened for the cutting of the engine and endured the peculiar eerie silence that followed as the guided missile plunged to earth. Silence was the signal for an undignified scramble beneath seats, and then, if all was well, an attempt to pick up the plot of the film once again.

My taste in films moved with the drama of war, towards British documentaries like *Target for Tonight, Western Approaches, One of our Aircraft is Missing*, and the semi propaganda films, *The Way Ahead*, and *The Next of Kin*, among the more memorable. Apart from the contrast with Hollywood heroics, they offered a scenario with which we could identify and raised the expectation of ultimate victory. Newsreels reinforced the message with images of cheerful Woodbine-smoking British Tommies and the ever advancing Red Army, red-starred and fur-hatted, carrying sub-machine guns that were replicas of the type used by film star gangsters. When Monty or Churchill appeared on the screen the audience would cheer and clap, though the historian Gwyn

Williams has told me that in the Rhondda, Churchill would be booed as the man who had sent troops to quell the striking miners of Tonypandy.

Despite the war, film romances reached out to audiences lost in shadows and dreams. Cinemas were ideal for courting and countless marriages grew from an evening at the pictures. The Kinema at Wanstead had double seats in the back row, a favourite choice for lovers as their embraces could not be overlooked by people seated behind them. The first time that I asked a girl to go out with me was to take her to the pictures. I was fourteen, and pride demanded something better than the cheapest seats in the front rows. The rear seats of the stalls were the 'two and threes' (11p), well beyond my pocket. My target was the 'One and nines'(9p), but the total of three and sixpence was more than I possessed. I raised the money by selling my Conway Stewart fountain pen, jeopardising my schoolwork for a few hours of sensual pleasure. We went to the Rex in Stratford High Street, one of the smarter picture houses and she wore her school blazer, but also lipstick and perfume. I knew from observation that men sat with an arm around their girlfriends and I readily conformed, slipping my left arm around her shoulders. What next? I put my right arm across her body, pressing her slight schoolgirl bosom as I clasped my hands in embrace. What then? Nothing. I was too scared. Heady with the smell of her Woolworth's scent, I sat with my head at right angles to the screen, gazing into her left ear. I did not dare to move; to take my arms away having made the commitment might have implied some dissatisfaction. Throughout both films, the forthcoming attractions and the news, I sat locked in an unbroken clinch as both arms developed pins and needles and my left arm went completely dead, her lips unkissed and bosom untouched.

Soon after I had started my secondary education, at the age of eleven, I joined the scouts. The vicar of St James had departed dutifully for the hostilities, fortuitously leaving his flock in the charge of a young curate with a sense of mission. He formed the 3rd West Ham North scout troop, giving us a chance to parade in uniform, and the promise of a summer camp. Most of the boys in our street had joined, including my closest friend, Fred Green. Scouting was also to introduce me to John McCormick, an Odessa Road schoolboy, destined to become another life-long friend. Scouting was a joy. I joined a nation in uniform, proudly donning wide-legged khaki shorts and short-sleeved shirt. The trousers were held by a black-buckled leather belt, complete with a dangling jack-knife that had a spike for getting stones out of horses' hooves. Around my neck I wore a green scarf entwined with a lanyard, held in place with a woggle of plaited cord. Socks were held up by garters with flapping green drill tabs, and the outfit was topped with the famous broad brimmed pointed scout hat with four dents in the crown. Scouting was about an outdoor life of self sufficiency, of camping and 'wide games', played across the countryside. The problem was, that just as we had no lame horses from whose hooves we could extract stones with the implement on our jack-knives, we had no direct access to the countryside. Our scoutmaster, the Reverend Albany, always referred to as 'Skipper', allowed us the use of the vicarage garden. There we learned to light wood fires with a single matchstick, to boil tea in a billy can and build bridges over imaginary streams with our scout staves. For wide games we would hike in file to Wanstead Flats.

Acquiring the necessary uniform was not easy, for clothes were rationed, and required precious clothing coupons, and more importantly, cash. Mine was bought a piece at a time, over many weeks, until I was fully kitted. The church provided us with a den, a basement at the back of the church, below the boiler house, a dark, dank hole which was a sanctuary and a second home to keep us from mischief on the streets. We were divided into four patrols, called after animals, Bulldogs, Tigers, Lions and Swifts and each allocated a corner of the den. I was a Bulldog.

Soon we had activities for every evening of the week, working to acquire badges for proficiency in first-aid, cooking, pathfinding, woodcraft and various other skills. We learned to tie reef-knots, clove-hitches, sheet-bends and sheepshanks, to make square and diagonal lashings and how to whip a rope, all useful for survival in the backwoods, if not in the streets of East London. Bonded in an international brotherhood of sorts, we learned the secrets signs of greeting, shaking hands with the left hand and saluting with three fingers. Perhaps Baden-Powell was a Freemason? Throughout the year, we saved sixpence a week to accumulate twenty-five shillings (£1.25) each for a two week summer camp. Some boys could not raise sixpence every week, and Skipper came to the rescue by raiding the church funds to make up the difference. Or did he dip into his own pocket? Anyway, he was determined that no boy should miss the camp for lack of money.

The year-long anticipated departure for summer camp came,

and we loaded our tents, trek-cart, and an odd assortment of dixies, billy-cans, food, kitbags and tools into the back of a battered furniture van. We crammed ourselves in on top of the conglomeration of equipment and with a great cheer from us, and tearful waving from the assembled mums, the open backed van set off for Paddington Station. Shepherded by a harassed Skipper, we loaded the jumble of gear into the guard's van and piled ourselves into the third class carriages and steamed off to the Oxfordshire countryside.

Camping was idyllic. Weeks before, we had prepared the ageing bell tents by camouflaging them with Grangers' solution – a green and brown waterproof paint – to hide us from enemy air attack. Now we pitched them, hammering the wooden tent-pegs into the ground with a giant mallet and boyish enthusiasm.

We roved for miles through the fields and woods, built ricketty bridges over real streams, scrumped unripe apples and attempted to ride the farmer's horse, bareback, a venture not appreciated by the horse. A boy whose father was a coster, professed knowledge of horses, because his father owned a nag. He made a halter and reins from rope, clambered onto the horse and successfully circumnavigated the field. The next boy was less certain and the horse took exception to a crowd of noisy boys, shouting advice and pushing and lifting the lad onto his back. Hardly mounted, the horse bolted, galloping across the field, the little scout clinging with his arms around the horse's neck and yelling for help. His awkward fall as he slithered sideways to the ground ended the escapade, for we were too afraid to go near the horse who was tossing his head in an effort to remove the loosened rope.

Best of all were the evenings, when at the end of a long day in the open air, we gathered around the camp fire, drinking cocoa and eating 'doorsteps' of bread and cheese. We sat on logs, formed into a circle, and sang songs made famous by Ralph Reader's 'Gang Show' – *Green Grow the Rushes O, Ten Green Bottles* and *The Crest of the Wave*, interspersed with African chants bequeathed to us by Baden-Powell. We acted one minute sketches and laughed and revelled in a comradeship of fun and freedom. The war was far away.

On the second week at camp, we were joined by an Oxford troop. Our camping equipment was meagre, we slept on rubber ground-sheets, covering ourselves in a single army blanket, folded to make several layers, held with blanket pins. Our cooking utensils were a hotch potch of assorted dented billy-cans and ex-army dixies. Some of our boys had towels that betrayed their origin, embroidered with the names of hospitals, and knives and forks stamped with the initials of railway companies. Nothing we had matched: there was a miscellany of chipped enamel plates, odd cups, battered buckets and ancient water-bottles, we were a ragamuffin army with second-hand gear. The Oxford boys arrived, bristling with equipment. They had complete sets of shining, matching dixies, that nested one into the other. Their knives, forks and spoons were purpose made for camping, clipped in neat order, their personal possessions carried in framed rucksacks. Skipper was the only one in our troop with a framed rucksack. Their tents were ridged, green and pristine and they slept in quilted sleeping-bags. Their trek-cart was painted with the arrow-head scout insignia, their troop number lettered in gold. They came with a mountain of food, and we stared in wonder. Could there be such wealth? Awe gave way to scouting friendship as they shared their food at the camp fire, let us use their horn-handled sheath knives and joined in our games. We did not envy them, but remained incredulous.

'A scout's honour is to be trusted' is the first scout law. Returning to London, I became part of an escapade that was to break and dishonour the trust that was central to the scout creed. It began when a few of us visited the Scout Imperial Headquarters in Victoria, a holiday outing with the best of motives. Attired in our uniforms, which were now bedecked with a growing number of badges, we descended on Headquarters for a fraternal visit. We browsed in the library, gazed at the portraits of BP and skylarked in a reading room which had a tiger skin rug. That was innocent enough, but after we had left the building, one of the party produced a copy of *Scouting for Boys*, the manual and bible of the scout movement, written by Baden-Powell. 'Where did you get that?' I asked. 'From the shop on the ground floor', he answered. I was surprised, because we seldom had money to spare. Books were usually presents, received for birthdays or Christmas. 'I didn't buy it, I arf inched it,' he said casually. 'It was easy,' he continued, explaining where the books were and how he had simply walked out of the shop with it in his hand. 'Hold on, I'm going to get one,' I said, and within minutes had returned to Headquarters, lifted the book and rejoined my mates. It was too easy.

I could not take the book home, but then I had not taken the book for myself, but for my patrol. The scout shop sold not only books, but charts which graphically illustrated first aid, semaphore and knots. Our collective imagination was stirred by the thought of our patrol corner adorned with the charts and we resolved upon a return visit of plunder. The following week we swooped, pilfering charts and books to order, in an organised and effortless hit and run raid. It was an isolated aberration, not for personal gain, never repeated and never discussed, but the guilt remained. Skipper must have wondered at the sudden appearance of books and charts, but as far as I can recollect, he never asked how we came by them.

I read the books avidly, absorbing the ethos and craft of scouting, but was puzzled by Baden-Powell's claim that he came from a family that was 'none too well off'. His family lived at 1 *and* 2, Hyde Park Gate, and the young Baden-Powell was sent to be educated at Charterhouse. He subsequently took a commission in the calvary, bypassed officer training and was made an honorary colonel! In adult life I travelled to Kenya and visited Outspan, the luxury home near Treetops where Baden-Powell spent his last years during the Second World War. I thought back to our scouting days in Stratford and reflected that 'none too well off' was a relative term.

His class background was reflected in his book, *Scouting for Boys*, the second scout law urging that we should not only be loyal to king and country, but also to our employers. He exhorted us to be patriotic in defence of the empire and warned against the 'discontent stirred by agitators'. Much thriftlessness and poverty he attributed to drink and there was an implied assumption that being poor signified moral failure. Nevertheless, he promoted the ethic that 'A scout is a friend to all, and a brother to every other scout, no matter to what country, class or creed the other may belong.' We were taught the concept of chivalry, to 'do a good turn' every day, to be self reliant and kind to animals, the latter oddly conflicting with Baden-Powell's own reputation as a champion pig-sticker. His often eccentric ideas, that sexual desires could be aroused by eating too much rich food, and that they could be 'cured' by bathing in cold water or by exercising the upper parts of the body by boxing, taxed our credulity. We gave weightier consideration to his claim that cigarette smoking weakened the eyesight, though many a Woodbine was puffed in secret. I found my own way to sexual fulfilment, shunned cold baths, abjured boxing and took to smoking a pipe, but all in all, gained from the fellowship and adventure provided by scouting.

We remained as scouts for about four years, winning the Gilwell Camping Trophy in competition with the other East London troops, and taking ourselves off on unsupervised camping holidays as often as possible. As we grew to puberty, Skipper resisted our optimistic pleas for a joint camp with the Girl Guides and gradually our interest in scouting began to wane. We never decided to leave, but just drifted away as our cultural activities widened. Soon, Fred, John and myself, discovered a new interest, equally as absorbing, English, imperialist and eccentric as scouting – cricket.

CHAPTER 5

Bombs at Random

From the time of my enrolment at West Ham Secondary School, I had walked to and from school each day with my friend, Fred Green, another of the scholarship boys from our street. After the blitz, we made our journey through streets that were as a ghost town, passing rows of deserted houses. Some were botched with hasty repairs, tarpaulins on roofs and tar-paper covering holes where window frames had been blown inwards. Others gaped open to the elements, houses vivisected, their entrails exposed, a wardrobe perilously balanced on the remains of a bedroom floor, the bed hanging precariously as if on a cliff edge, peeling wallpaper revealed. The broken remains of personal possessions protruded from debris. A house was blown to smithereens, but a tin bath still clung tenaciously to a nail on a leaning garden fence. After a night of heavy bombing, we would pick our way over broken glass, skirting the rubble that spilled into the roads. Whole sections of the route became a trek through a wasteland of heaped and broken bricks and splintered timbers.

After school, the empty and shattered buildings became a vast adventure playground as we rampaged through the shattered homes. Exploration was irresistible. We careered as a small gang from one ruined house to another, climbing over fences as we moved on to enter from the backs of the bomb-damaged houses, unobserved from the street. There was mutual shock when we burst in through the back door of one apparently empty house to find a woman laying the table for tea, a shared moment of disbelief, then instant flight. In a big house in Earlham Grove, we found a walk-in pantry filled with mouldering food and engaged

65

in a rollicking battle as we threw handfuls of rice and barley at each other. From a bombed undertakers in Romford Road, I carried away the top half of a polished oak coffin, quick to recognise the quality of the wood. I took it home, planning to make it into a shoe box to stand by the hearth, but my mother was horrified, convinced that it would bring death, and ordered me to take it back from where it had came. When we heard that the Trebor sweet factory in Forest Gate had been bombed, we made a bee-line for the spoils of war. We were a day too late, the scattered sweets had already been foraged, and the site displayed ominous government posters warning that 'looters would be shot.' Another time, we spent hours in a bombed-out chemist's shop, opening and examining the contents of hundreds of glass bottles, arguing over the meanings of the Latin names on the labels, wondering if the blue-coloured bottles contained poisons and searched in vain for chloroform. We would have tried it first on the cat. Our most gruesome find was a headless dog, which we discovered floating in a water tank on a bomb site. The circular metal tanks were erected for fire fighting purposes and had EWS – Emergency Water Supply – painted on the side in giant letters. The dog was bloated and covered in green slime and prompted endless speculation as to how he became decapitated.

Through shelter life and the constant playing in bombed houses, I caught impetigo, a scabby skin disease which shamed my mother, for it was considered to be an affliction of the dirty. It could not be concealed, for it took hold on my right ear and had to be treated with sulphur ointment, the evening ritual of the nit-comb followed by the generous application of yellow paste to my ear. I was really quite proud of the contagion, for I considered it to be a war wound. Sometime in 1941, Beckton gasworks was bombed, and for two weeks we were without gas, our usual fuel for cooking. On the first day we queued at a British Restaurant in Water Lane for a sixpenny dinner, an inauspicious introduction to dining out. The following day, our old kitchen range came into its own, saucepans simmering on the hob and the tiny oven used for baking. Soon after, bombing cut off the electricity supply, but that caused little problem, for we had no electrical appliances apart from the wireless set. Lighting was hardly necessary as we spent our evenings in the shelter which was lit by 'night lights', stubby candles which stood in saucers of water. Bombed water mains left us queueing with buckets and bowls at an emergency water tanker which toured the streets once a day. I played the patriotic card and volunteered to give up washing, but my mother was not deceived. Being without main services added to the feeling of adventure and cemented the blitz spirit – which is no post-war myth – as neighbours made a joke of the difficulties and shared the hardships.

Throughout the destruction, joking and laughter buffered the reality of constant danger. A story spread one morning that Beck's balls had been blown off and found floating in the horse trough in Stratford High Street. So they had. Beck was a pawnbroker and his triple brass-balled sign had been blasted off to land yards away in the granite trough. The nine o'clock news on the BBC was compulsive listening for the nation, and enemy air activity was usually reported with the vague phrase that 'bombs were dropped at random.' Having heard that for the umpteenth time, Sarah said innocently and with seriousness, 'Oh, that poor place has copped it again.' 'What place?' 'Random.'

Despite the protective humour, there were times when the awful reality of war intruded and tears were shed unchecked. Our milk was delivered by a Co-op milkman known to all as 'old whooper', a nickname given because of his whooping street cry as he left the milk on the doorstep. He called on us towards mid-day and would come into the house to sit at our kitchen table for a while, to take a break and have his dinner, a bottle of Guinness and a sandwich. My mother supplied him with a glass and he would sit and chat to my mum and Sarah for ten minutes or so. He was a short, strong, jovial man with a weather-worn craggy face. He wore a blue striped apron with his shirt sleeves rolled tight above the elbows and carried a leather cash satchel, suspended from a strap which crossed his stocky body. One day, as he poured his beer, he began to cry, huge tears rolling down his creased face. His son, an eighteen-year-old sailor had just been reported killed in action. He showed us a photograph of a smiling smooth faced boy in naval uniform, and I can hear old whooper's words now, between the sobs, 'The bastards, the bastards', and at every house he called his tears were shared.

Night raids were relentless, the pattern broken only when bad weather made flying conditions hazardous. We used to crane up at the sky as evening came to look for the 'bombers' moon', knowing the sirens would soon sound if the sky was clear. In May, 1941, the Luftwaffe came in force to rain fire, causing the biggest conflagration since December. The city blazed and night became as day, the capital lit by a thousand fires. Morning dawned like dusk, smoke blotting the rising sun, grey ash blowing as dust in a desert storm. The heritage of generations burned in the city as medieval buildings succumbed to the flames and treasures melted in the heat. I was not aware of it then, but the British Museum lost a quarter of a million books to the fire. Tucked into a book by Margaret Cole, on my bookshelves, is a letter to her from Beatrice Webb telling how she and her husband Sidney lost their private collection of seven thousand books in that December fire-raid. The loss of the books was a tragedy, but the greater crime was the incineration of human beings, almost fifteen hundred people were killed that May night and even more were injured. Thousands of working people were left homeless, their few possessions destroyed, leaving them with nothing more than the clothes they wore.

Incendiary bombs showered in and around our street and were fought by wardens and neighbours with stirrup pumps and sandbags. Few caused serious damage, a good number dropping into the grounds of the Sick Home and the Jewish cemetery, but I learned an early lesson about demand, supply and value. The small metal fins of the fire bombs, jealously sought by us to be polished and treasured as souvenirs, lost their trading worth as scores of them littered the streets.

The blitz created a tremendous hatred of the Germans. Civilians called for retaliation raids and soldiers on leave swore vengeance for what they had seen. The fierce, irrational, but understandable hatred towards the entire German race was reflected unwittingly by a schoolmistress in a class attended by my future wife. To a pupil who was misbehaving the woman teacher reprimanded him with the injunction, 'Stop behaving like a little German boy.' During a daylight raid, we saw a parachutist descending and knew that he must be German, for there had been no British fighter planes in sight, only the sound of anti-aircraft gunfire. He was directly above, suspended in space, and it seemed as if he would drop slowly and helplessly to land in our street. Women stood, watched and told each other what they would do to him if they could get their hands on the bastard. There would be no more little Germans made by him. They were boastful threats, for they would probably have offered him a cup of tea, but in their anger and sorrow they longed for retribution. In the event, he drifted away on the wind and came to earth well past Romford.

After the great fire, the raids eased and we returned to sleeping in the house, but moved the beds to the ground floor for greater safety, sharing the front room of the house with Sarah and her son Jimmy as a communal bedroom. We became hardened to war, ignoring the sirens during daylight raids and seeking shelter only when we heard the sound of German engines. We could identify the whine of Spitfires and Hurricanes, and 'it's alright, it's one of ours' became a catch-phrase. We settled to a war of calm resignation, turning to hope as the years passed. I followed the war news avidly, reading the newspapers to check the daily advances on the Russian front, the thrusting arrows on the maps biting deeper into Nazi held territory. Admiration for the Red Army was unbounded as they relentlessly hacked at frozen divisions of once arrogant fascists, reducing them to savaged remnants. Even the American band leader, Glenn Miller, broadcasting on the Forces Network joined in the tributes to the Red Army, announcing a 'zoot salute to our Russian Allies' and playing a swing version of *Cossack Patrol*. I tracked the progress of the Eighth Army led by the egocentric General Montgomery with vested pride because my father was with them. He seemed so far away and I would look at the photograph of him that he had sent from North Africa, wearing an open necked khaki drill shirt, white sergeant's stripes on his sleeves. I never confided my fears, but I would gaze at his gentle eyes and wonder if he would ever return.

When victory seemed in sight, the war returned to us, savagely and unexpectedly, after D Day, when allied forces were pushing into France from the west and the Russians were relentlessly advancing into Poland from the east. It was delivered to us by pilotless planes, guided bombs that rasped and flamed through the sky, to stop abruptly and drop silently, two thousand pounds of high explosive falling to earth and demolishing rows of houses at a single blow.

The first flying bomb to be aimed at Britain fell on Bethnal Green, a measure of accuracy, for it is within a few miles of the centre of the city. It came unrecognised for what it was and exploded as just another bomb. A couple of nights later, we saw our first buzz bomb, or doodle-bug, as they came to be commonly called. It appeared as a red flame in the night sky and we all but cheered, thinking it to be a German bomber in flames, and the explosion when it landed, its bomb load detonating. The pilotless planes were launched at the rate of one hundred a day, and within a week the government announced that London was under attack from the V1, a Nazi secret vengeance weapon. It was just like a story from the *Hotspur*.

In daylight, the little planes with short stub wings looked like black crosses in the sky, hurtling at four hundred miles an hour with a sound like a motor-bike with an exhaust flutter. When the engine cut, it fell steeply and you could hear the silence as you awaited the impact. If it cut overhead, we threw ourselves to the ground or dived for cover, regardless of the indignity. Just as some children go train-spotting, I kept a tally of flying bombs spotted, and the number rose daily, passing fifty and on to almost eighty before the attacks ended. Stratford was heavily hit by the flying bombs and our immediate neighbourhood sustained more damage than it had done during the blitz.

When a flying bomb fell in nearby streets, we ran with childish curiosity to the scene of the incident, guided by a pall of black smoke and dust, to gawk at the damage. In one of the worst incidents, a flying bomb fell on a packed trolley-bus near Wanstead Flats, and wardens cordoned off the area, stopping us from getting near to the carnage. We learned what had happened a few hours later, when a docker who lived a few doors from us returned from rescue work, the front of his shirt saturated with blood. He was a huge man, of enormous strength, but he stood and wept as he told neighbours of the horror he had seen. The next day, a few of us children went again to the scene. The street had been cleared, and there was nothing to see but the usual heaps of rubble, twisted metal and shattered buildings. In the midst of the tragedy, humour surfaced in a macabre resilience to death. A nearby pub, the Holly Tree, severely damaged by the blast, was open with a 'business as usual' sign, and a chalked notice, 'The Holly Tree, nearly uprooted.'

Familiar and friendly landmarks in our lives disappeared as the flying bombs fell, day after day. Close to us, our local newsagent's was demolished, as was the barber's shop. The barber was Jarvis, and his shop was no more than the front room of a small house, sparsely furnished with two barber's chairs and a motley collection of odd cane chairs for waiting customers. When cutting the hair of small children – for tuppence (less than 1p) – he would place a board across the arms of a chair, to raise the infant up to working height. I had sat on the small plank, many times, and had graduated long ago to sitting in the chair itself. Shortly after the bomb had fallen, old Mr Jarvis was led past our house, supported between two women. We knew him well, as did everyone in our street, and my mother offered a few words of comfort, 'Don't worry Mr Jarvis, you'll start up again when all this is finished.' He was a small, slight man, with flat grey hair, and he seemed to have aged and shrunk even smaller since my last haircut. He was trembling and crying. 'It's no good, I've lost all my scissors.' It was so pathetic, he never had much, and the little he had was gone. I felt angry, not only at the Germans, but for the helplessness of a poor man, beaten by war and poverty. What would a few chairs, clippers and scissors cost? Whatever it was, he saw no way of starting again. Whatever glamour the war may have held, the uniforms, patriotism and the togetherness of sticking it out was gone in that moment.

One Sunday, when I went to church, a regular practice since joining the scouts, the vicar, home on leave in the uniform of an officer, preached a sermon reminding us that God was on our side. He recalled how God had calmed the seas at Dunkirk, to enable the rescue of our troops, how God had again calmed the channel for the D Day landings (in fact it was quite choppy) and how, despite the present difficulties, the Allied troops with the help of God would soon drive on to victory. I looked at the military flags by the altar and thought of German priests preaching similar sermons of national salvation. I remembered an account of the Nazi troops who after a thousand miles of mass murder had decorated Christmas trees at the threshold of Moscow and sung hymns of praise in the Russian snow. The sanctimonious and partisan claim that God was on our side, active in his support for the Allied cause, struck me as such demonstrable nonsense. If it was true that an omnipotent God was on our side, then he indeed appeared to move in a mysterious way to resolve the conflict.

I gave up going to church, but perhaps my religious faith had never sprung from conviction. My father had some belief in God as a life force greater than ourselves, but my mother never expressed an opinion. They went to church for weddings, christenings and funerals, and encouraged us to say our prayers when we were very young, but that was the convention in the area where we lived.

Two of my mates, the Barrett brothers, did not conform, and they attended the little spiritualist church made of corrugated iron in a turning off our street. When I was about eight or nine, I had joined them. It was a move of unprincipled opportunism, for it had transpired that once a month the spiritualists took the children on an outing to Epping Forest, transporting them by an ancient coach to Fairlop, Chingford Mount or Loughton, for a day of adventure, lemonade and buns. The temptation was irresistible, and a group of us enrolled *en masse* to qualify for the monthly treat. There was no objection from home, possibly because my father used to read a column in the *Daily Herald* by Hannen Swaffer, the well known long-haired Fleet Street journalist and socialist, who was also a spiritualist. Seances at the little church were strictly for adults, but we submitted to a weekly talk and a session of callisthenics, graceful exercises performed with Indian clubs. Exactly what this had to do with spiritualism was not revealed, but the material reward on offer every fourth Sunday seemed heavenly. When joining the scouts, in 1941, I had returned to the Christian faith, but by 1944, I had reached the age of scepticism.

In the summer of 1944, I watched a black flying bomb stop directly overhead, dashed from the street through our open front door and threw myself flat in the passage as it fell, feeling the shock waves of the explosion. The front windows crashed in with the force of the blast and a piece of metal landed on the doorstep. I went to pick it up, but it was too hot to hold and the street was clouded with brick dust. The flying bomb had fallen a couple of turnings away, in Odessa Road, where my friend John lived. I called for Fred and the pair of us ran to see where the bomb had dropped, to find that John's home had disappeared, along with a dozen others. It was impossible to get near, but we learned that the family had been in their shelter and had survived and that they had been taken to a rest centre. Nobody was able to tell us to which centre they had been taken, and John, an inseparable part of our trio of friendship, had vanished from our lives.

Towards the end of the school summer holiday, my mother decided that we should travel north to spend a couple of weeks with her parents in South Shields. It was to be a holiday that would also remove us from the daily danger and stress of the flying bombs. The journey by steam train from Kings Cross to South Shields was made at night, at a crawling pace with long periods of stopping as the passenger train gave way to military rail traffic moving to the south coast. We sat upright in a third class carriage, blinds drawn in total blackout, our heads resting on hired pillows, but there was little sleep and we arrived tired and fractious.

Shields was a mining and seafaring community and my grandparents' house was within walking distance of the sea and close to a pit, where long lines of trucks loaded with coal clanked and snaked in slow procession. Entering the house where my mother grew up was like stepping into the past, entering a Victorian time capsule with brass bedsteads, lace curtains, heavy furniture and a horsehair-stuffed sofa. My grandfather, a former miner, had not worked since the 1930s, when unemployment stretched into his old age and retirement. He had been the treasurer of his union lodge and was a figure of respectability with a watch and albert in his waistcoat. At home his word was law and he appeared to me as the epitome of a Victorian patriarch, stern and uncompromising, his character moulded by the harshness of pit life. He would stand for no talking by children at the meal table, 'wisht' he would say firmly, demanding silence. At first I was rather afraid of him, and it took time to learn of his underlying kindness. My grandmother complemented him perfectly, a solid figure of Victorian motherhood, always dressed in ankle length black and given to wearing a broad-brimmed high-domed hat. She seemed to spend all her life baking at the vast black-leaded kitchen range that dominated the living room, or toiling amid steam in the brick built wash-house that was in the backyard. The rows of terraced houses were not back-to-backs, but were separated at the rear by narrow back lanes where children played, the washing hung and where concessionary coal was dumped at intervals to be shovelled into the coal house that stood in the backyard, next to the lavatory.

Like all mining communities, the people were close and friendly. The front doors of their homes were never locked during the day and my aunts and uncles who lived in the same street as my grandparents came and went into each others homes without invitation. The pattern was familiar, but it was the voices of the people that first struck me as the greatest difference between Shields and Stratford. The lilting Geordie accent rang strangely in my ears as my sister and myself were referred to as 'bairns', or 'hinnie' if we were spoken to directly. Although my mother had lived in London for twenty years, she slipped back into broad Geordie within minutes of our arrival. It was odd, for she looked like my mother but spoke with an alien voice.

My uncle Jimmy was a miner – though it was said that he spent more time in the pub than at the coal face – and my uncle Osborne a surface worker at Westoe colliery. It was from them and my aunts and grandparents that I heard the stories of pre-war poverty in Shields and Jarrow. They were matter of fact accounts of bitter struggles against the coal owners and lives of daily desperation that made my life appear easy and prosperous by comparison. Their commitment to 'the union' was passionate, their loyalty to Labour as solid as Marsden Rock, a local landmark. Forty years later, during the 1984 miners' strike, a local council official visiting my aged mother made a disparaging remark about the miners. In an instant, she blazed in reply, 'don't you say anything against the miners, my father was a miner', her pride and loyalty to the colliers undiminished by the years.

My first few days in Shields were packed with interest, absorbing new sights and sounds, accompanying my grandfather to the Miners' Welfare where the men played bowls, visiting the bleak beach where the cold North Sea lapped an unguarded shore and sampling the local chips which were cooked in fat and tasted better than London chips. The family lavished affection but I was a child among adults and I missed my mates. Strangely, I also missed the excitement of the flying bombs and felt cut off from the war that had been part of my life for the past five years. When my mother said that we were going to extend our stay to remain safe from the bombing I was cast into the melancholy of loneliness.

I wandered the streets with little purpose, browsed in bookshops where I could not afford to buy and drifted into a daily routine of bored idleness. My despair was suddenly broken by one of those coincidences that Arthur Koestler found so questionable. I was making a solitary walk along the beach near Marsden when I saw another lone figure sitting on the deserted sands. I stared at a boy of my own age. It was John McCormick, my missing friend from Odessa Road. There was a moment of mutual disbelief and then, as we asked simultaneously, 'what are you doing here?', a flow of exchanged questions. John and his family had been swiftly moved from the rest centre following the destruction of their home to temporary accommodation in South Shields. They were given a few rooms in a large bleak house in the town and supplied with the barest of essentials, for they had arrived with no more than the clothes in which they stood. A table, chairs, beds, a basic set of cutlery and crockery and blankets were their only possessions. The rooms were bare-boarded and totally lacking in any sort of comfort, but John and his family were safe and unharmed.

My gloom vanished immediately as we shared days of youthful friendship and freedom together. We learned to play bowls at the Miners' Welfare, talked to the local girls and walked for miles, talking continuously. As the end of the school holiday drew near

I regretted having to return to London. The chance meeting on the beach was indeed an astonishing coincidence. That we should both have been sent to South Shields without choice was a singular chance, but that our paths should have intersected at a given moment on a lonely beach was extraordinary. Fate, providence? We shall never know.

We had returned from evacuation to Iver in time for the blitz on London, and we now returned from South Shields with immaculate timing for the start of the rocket attack upon the capital. The V2s, the second of Hitler's vengeance weapons came without warning of any kind. Attributed at first to exploding gas mains, a myth soon exploded as five or six a day fell, the rockets travelled faster than the speed of sound, their rumbling approach being heard *after* the explosion and subsequent devastation. It was impossible to take shelter as they came literally like a bolt from the blue. They were more effective in damaging civilian morale than all the attacks by the Luftwaffe and the flying bombs because there was no means of defence and death and destruction could, and did, come at any second of the day or night. The effect on the nerves was shattering.

It was mid-day, and my mother, sister and myself were sitting at our kitchen table having dinner, when there was a knock at the door. The table was directly in front of a window where my mother sat facing the glass with my sister and myself at either side. As mum moved away from the table to answer the door, there was the biggest bang I have ever heard, a gigantic sharp explosion that pressured the eardrums followed by total darkness. A rocket had fallen next to the railway line at Hamfrith Road bridge, about two hundred yards from our house. The darkness was caused by the falling of every plaster ceiling in the house, creating a blinding wall of dust. The entire window frame with both sashes had been blown across the room to become embedded in the wall opposite. Had the rocket fallen a split second earlier, my mother would have been sliced to shreds. We staggered out, choking, into the back yard but could see little through the pall of dust and smoke that filled the backyards, while at the front of the house, a very shaken baker was reeling in the porch, unaware that his knock had saved my mother's life. Our house had lost most of its roof, but that was nothing compared to the scene of carnage at Hamfrith Road. The crater caused by the rocket could easily have held a double decker bus, a dozen houses and shops had vanished and there were over one hundred and sixty casualties. Our post office, greengrocer's, general store and cobbler's shop were all destroyed, the unfortunate cobbler losing both his legs.

I was witness to a sad sequel to the rocket attack, when a few days later, a friend of my mother called at our house. She told how she had come home from work at mid-day on that terrible day, to find Forest Lane roped off by the rescue services. She explained that she lived on the corner of Hamfrith Road, and they let her pass. As she approached the bridge, dreading lest her home should be damaged, she turned cold as she clambered over the rubble and saw that her home was virtually flattened. Where was her son? Fourteen years old, he had just left school and was due to start work the next day. She rushed to the ruins of her home, just as a warden found the body of her boy, on top of the lavatory cistern in the backyard. She choked on every word as she slowly recounted the horror and then wept in huge uncontrollable sobs. There was no way of comforting her.

Years later, after the war, I was enjoying a holiday with my wife in a comfortable hotel at Chagford, in Devon. On the first evening of our holiday, we were seated in deep armchairs in front of a great log fire, enjoying after dinner coffee and a night cap, along with the other guests and the owners. A 'common room evening' as my wife amusingly likes to call the after dinner gatherings in English country-house hotels. The other guests included some American diplomats, and they were listening to a radio commentator describe the re-entry to earth of an American rocket carrying two astronauts. It was early in the U S space programme and everyone was gripped by the drama. As the mission was successfully concluded, one of the Americans began to praise the work of Werner von Braun, the German rocket scientist working for the Americans. I remained silent, until, noticing that I had not contributed to the general acclamations of praise, the most loquacious of the Americans, fortified by several brandies, pressed the point, looking directly at me and saying, 'Werner von Braun really is some guy, isn't he?' I was unable to avoid his question. With the memory of the Hamfrith Road rocket resounding in my head, I replied, 'I have been on the receiving end of Herr Braun's rockets. He's a Nazi bastard and should have been hanged as a war criminal.' There was a hush to match the silence of Dartmoor at night, filled with unspoken embarrassment. Then, a defence of von Braun. He wasn't really a Nazi, he was 'just a scientist doing his job'. I pointed out that he had held a Nazi party card since 1933, then bade everyone goodnight,' and went to bed. Next morning at breakfast, Mrs Douglas, the joint proprietor, wife of Major Douglas, ex-Indian army from the days of the Raj, said, 'You were very naughty last night Mr Gorman', as though she were a teacher admonishing a naughty child. Naughty? What about that Nazi and his rockets?

In the months leading to the end of the war, a prisoner of war camp was established on Wanstead Flats, and on Sunday afternoons people paraded the periphery to stare through the barbed wire, curious to see the enemy. Young girls incurred the wrath of older women by throwing cigarettes over the wire to the handsome blond prisoners in grey uniforms, the Germans encouraging the girls in schoolboy English. Words of hatred poured from the tough, war hardened women as they unleashed verbal abuse, directed at the girls and Germans alike. The prisoners had lost little of their trained arrogance and incensed the curious watchers by citing the Geneva Convention in demanding to be removed from the danger of rocket attacks to a place of safety. It was a plea treated by most of us with scorn, and we fervently hoped that the next rocket to fall would drop smack in the middle of the camp as an act of chance but just retribution. When the British army liberated the inmates of Buchenwald and Belsen, the first pictures released of the shaven headed, emaciated dead and dying, were seen as an horrific confirmation of the innate evil of the enemy. The revelations from the concentration camps cemented a loathing within me for the Germans, not just the soldiers, the camp guards, the brutal wardresses, and the SS, but the whole German race. It was an unreasoning hatred, nurtured by the effect of six years of war and propaganda on a formative mind. I knew nothing of the German trade unionists, Communists and pacifists who had been incarcerated in the concentration camps along with the Jews, Gypsies and Jehovah's Witnesses.

My schooldays were ending. Politics dominated school activities in the period before the 1945 General Election and the political opinions of the staff were scarcely disguised. We had a new weekly lesson, social studies, and the teacher, a woman with a Lancashire accent, described how she had been thrown down the steps of the Manchester Free Trade Hall in 1936 by Mosley's Blackshirts for heckling his tirade against the 'Reds and the Jews'. Her message for Labour was unequivocal. Our teacher of Spanish, a gentle older woman, never without a cardigan, tweed skirt and lisle stockings, related her experiences as an ambulance worker in the

International Brigades. She was filled with sadness, feeling that her generation had failed us by allowing fascism to triumph in Spain. She explained that we now had the opportunity to build a new and peaceful world. To that end, the teachers helped us to organise a mock election, with pupils standing as candidates and running lively and highly vocal campaigns. At first we treated it lightly, one boy forming a party that was a parody of the Socialist Party of Great Britain, grabbing at unfettered democracy to found a Sexualist Party of Great Britain and standing on a platform of free love. He painted a banner of Durex yellow with the motto, 'Penis Erectus', and called for a march to the women's shelter in the recreation ground to proclaim his manifesto. It took the form of ten commandants of unbridled licence and neatly put our new lessons on free speech and parliamentary democracy to the test. The venture was outrageous and our headmaster was not amused, but the young politician adroitly suggested that the banning of the party would be undemocratic.

On our election day, a few weeks before the real thing, Labour swept to a massive victory, the Liberal and Communist candidates well behind and the Conservative absolutely crushed. The mock election mirrored the spirit of the times and anticipated Labour's coming triumph in July. In assembly we clasped our radical hymnals and fervently cantillated:

> These things shall be –
> Nation with nation, land with land,
> Unarm'd shall live as comrades free,
> In every heart and brain shall throb,
> The pulse of one fraternity.

During the campaign, it was my assessment that five of the teachers supported the Communist candidate.

My final year at Stratford Grammar School, as it was called by then, was the happiest, partly because release from schooling was near, but mostly because we were treated more like adults. If I had not learned as much as I should, I had learned about learning. During those last years, the public library in Water Lane became an alternative school where I could explore a wider knowledge. Although my reading followed no charted course, it was a journey of constant wonder as I discovered, Aldous Huxley, Shaw, Wells, Robert Lynd, Oscar Wilde and the books of the Left Book Club. I would lose myself in a silent world without sunlight, touching the books with the anticipation of a lover. The pediments of the great bookcases in the reference library were carved with inscriptions, my favourite, 'No furniture as charming as books'. At home, books were beyond my pocket-money purse, but in the library, all the books were mine. Perhaps I read the wrong books, for I failed matriculation spectacularly, passing only in English, art and woodwork.

Although the end of the war in Europe was anticipated, the final news of the unconditional surrender of the German Supreme Command came as an abrupt end to a nightmare. Could it really be over? A spontaneous eruption of joy all around me dispelled any doubts. Car horns sounded a cacophony of victory morse, dot, dot, dash – V for victory – train whistles blew, flags and bunting were produced to festoon the streets in a blaze of red, white and blue, the ships in the docks sounded their fog horns, people sang, wept and danced, hoarded bottles of spirits were opened and shared as strangers embraced, kissed and simply yelled with joy, the famous British reserve cast off in tumultuous celebration. Two bricklayers working on repairs to a bomb damaged house in Forest Lane left a permanent reminder of that historic day, working two V signs into the brickwork, one above each of the two bedroom windows that faced the street.

As darkness came, bonfires were lit in the streets and blackout curtains were ceremoniously burned as the windows of the houses shone with forgotten light. The ruins of bombed houses made for a ready supply of fuel, floorboards, joists and doors heaped into the flames. Men, women and children of all ages circled the fire in the middle of our street in a frenzied knees-up that was repeated again and again, interspersed with the community singing of every popular song that could be recalled. A snaking conga of humanity threaded its way in and out of the houses in an uninvited triumphant procession. The fires blazed into the early hours and the insatiable demand for fuel reached absurd and desperate proportions as we became deliriously irresponsible. The heavy wooden gates to some waste ground adjoining the church were lifted from their hinges and were only saved from being added to the flames by a lone voice of sanity crying that to burn the church gates would be an act of sacrilege. The chimney sweep's barrow was discovered outside his house and trundled towards the fire only to be saved at the last moment. The ruddy sky over East London recreated the illumination caused by the great fires of 1940 and 1941 as smoke and sparks were sucked heavenwards into the vacuum caused by the heat. Next morning, the fires still smouldered, and the borough engineer was left bewildered by the extent of the damage to the roads, ruminating on the cost of the repairs.

The victory celebrations continued for days, and Fred and myself took a bus to the West End to share in the euphoria that gripped the capital. We stood for hours in a light summer drizzle awaiting the appearance of Churchill on a distant balcony, stood among thousands patiently waiting outside Buckingham Palace, but left without a glimpse of the king, and wandered among the milling crowds of servicemen and women still celebrating in Piccadilly and Trafalgar Square. Some weeks later we joined the crowds lining the streets in Whitechapel to see and to cheer General Montgomery, wearing his famous two-badged beret, as he was driven through the East End in an open staff car.

As we settled to a quieter life, John McCormick, who had returned to London, and myself went camping in August, cutting ourselves off from all news of the continuing war in the Far East. On our return journey home, we bought a newspaper to read on the train and learned that the Americans had dropped their secret weapon, an atomic bomb, on Hiroshima, killing one hundred thousand people. We welcomed the news as it was clear that the Second World War was being forced to speedy conclusion. There was little sympathy for the Japanese, who had earned the reputation of being a cruel and remorseless enemy. The atomic bombing of Nagasaki followed, and most of us considered that the dropping of the atomic bombs was justified. It was some time before the moral debate on nuclear weapons became a public issue and I could not have imagined my future role as an activist in the Campaign for Nuclear Disarmament.

After VJ day – victory over Japan – the men and women who had fought the war began to return home, and individual houses were decorated with flags and welcome home signs, as loved ones who were almost strangers came back to civilian life. Eventually, the news came that my father was returning home and we hung flags from the bedroom windows and my mother painted 'welcome home Jack' on a piece of silver card which she fixed on the wall next to our front door. We knew the time of the train on which he was travelling and my mother suggested that I should walk down Forest Lane towards the station to greet him, while she waited indoors with my sister. It was a warm day, and dressed in my best clothes, with my hair smartly brushed into a large quiff, I set off to find the father I had not seen for four years. Recognition was instant as he came towards me, a distant figure in a civilian suit with an army kitbag on his shoulder. He dropped the kitbag, ran towards me and lifted me from the ground, hugging and kissing me like a child, which mixed my feelings of happiness with a sense of embarrassment, for I had been the man in the family since I was fourteen. His breath smelt of tea and tobacco and he seemed wizened, his skin a grained mahogany, coloured and wrinkled by years of the North African and Italian sun. I had never seen a white man so brown. At home, my sister was cuddled and then we watched as he embraced our mother, hugging and kissing with all the passion of years of absent loving to be reclaimed. There were tears of joy that we had all survived, a special tea with supplements to our frugal rations, and then an evening party, crowded with neighbours to share our elation. It was held in Sarah's front room, and the floorboards sprung like diving boards as *Knees Up Mother Brown* reverberated through the house and sounded into the street. Brown ale flowed and our happiness was unbounded.

I wanted stories of the battles, but my father with his Burton-made demob suit and a gratuity of seventy-eight pounds – the most money he had ever had – in his pocket, only wanted to talk of the future. I had hoped for war souvenirs, a German bayonet perhaps, or even a revolver, but my father was an extremely practical man, the spoils of war that emerged from his kitbag were a magnificent German screwdriver and a polished steel hammer, taken from an emplacement in the Gothic Line.

In time, he told two stories of his war experiences, both of which emphasised the old class differences between officers and men. The familiar story of them and us. In North Africa, he was among the troops assembled to hear General Montgomery address them before a battle. Before Monty arrived, the commanding officer briefed the soldiers on procedure. 'When the General has finished speaking,' he told them, 'I will call for three cheers and you will raise your cap with each cheer.' 'And remember', the CO continued with a plummy accent, 'it is not hooray, hooray, hooray, *but*, hoorah, hoorah, hoorah.' His other tale was an even sharper reminder of class difference. Prior to the invasion of Sicily, during a period of special training, a young officer fresh from Sandhurst had the bright idea that all the men should go without food for twenty-four hours so that they would be used to going without rations should the necessity arise. My father refused, saying that he had years of experience of going hungry and that he did not need any practice. He could have been court martialled, but as staff sergeant, a former regular soldier and a veteran of Dunkirk and the desert, already battle hardened, the inexperienced officer decided that it would be prudent to relent.

The war was over and our streets swirled with the brick dust blown from the rubble of countless bombed homes. St James Road had changed little, the cast-iron railings had gone, taken for scrap during the war, the off-licence and a few houses had been destroyed, and all the houses showed signs of bomb damage, but the children still played in a street free from traffic and the school and church bells, silent for six years, pealed again. The real damage was unseen, hidden behind the lace curtains of homes where loved ones would never return. It was a time for rebuilding, lives as well as homes.

CHAPTER 6
Glad Rags

An admiral once came to our street. It was during the war, and he came to make a patriotic speech, winning approval by referring to Hitler as 'a black-nosed bastard'. He came in uniform, but had he strolled down the street in mufti, he would have been equally conspicuous, because clothes and class were inextricably linked, one stamping the other with visual recognition of place in society. Suits were rarely worn by the men in our street, being conserved for weddings and funerals, bought 'off the peg' from the Co-op, the tally-man or the Fifty Shilling Tailor. Made-to-measure might have come from Montague Burton's, but they hardly matched the quality and style of bespoke tailoring from the Army and Navy Stores or Savile Row. Ours was a street without 'officers and gentlemen', where the only suit was saved for the rites of passage and Sunday best.

Working clothes betrayed occupation and I remember only one man who wore a suit on weekdays, an elderly office clerk who lived a few doors away. He left home for work at eight each morning, respectably dressed in black jacket, pin-striped trousers, shoes army polished, stiff fly-away collar and homburg hat set square. Yet, there was a concealed shabbiness that would have precluded him passing for a banker. The men of the London and North Eastern Railway works went to and from work, wearing baggy blue trousers, loose fitting jackets and oil-skin caps – their 'grease-tops' – lunch tins and tea cans in hand. A docker, a few doors along, wore a belt of leather so broad that it might have belonged to a pantomime pirate, around his neck a knotted muffler to soak up the sweat. A bricky's labourer clonked the pavement with dusty hob-nailed boots, his half-mast trousers tied with string below the knees. My father went to work wearing his bib and brace overalls – if he was on outside work – his hessian carpenter's bag slung from a length of sash-cord over his shoulder. For indoor work, his white apron with its wide front pocket would be folded away inside his toolbag. He was a shrewd observer of sartorial order. When a foreman's job was in the offing with its few vital extra shillings a week, he reckoned that it could be won, not solely on merit, but on appearance. He took to putting his overalls in his bag, wearing a jacket, and speculated seven shillings and sixpence (37.5p) on a bowler hat. He got the job and proved his perception of class prejudice well founded. When the building contract was completed and he was back to work as an ordinary 'chippy', the bowler was put in the wardrobe. There it remained until after the war and eventually finished its life as a stage prop at Unity Theatre. My future father-in-law did not fare as well as my dad. When he turned up for work at Shepherd Neame's brewery in Faversham wearing a trilby hat, he was called to the office and told 'workmen wear caps, foreman wear bowlers, and only managers wear trilbies.' That was in 1945!

Brewer's draymen, who delivered to our local pubs, were massive men with beer-barrelled stomachs covered with long leather aprons. They would drop the coopered barrels with skill from their shire-drawn wagons onto cushions of plaited rope, rolling the casks swiftly towards the pavement flaps of the pub cellar. The flaps open, the sour smell of bitter beer wafted out as they wound the barrels with thick rope, taking the full weight on their muscular arms, lowering the barrels into the cavernous depths. The empties would be heaved onto their leather protected thighs and lifted to the back of the cart. At every call, the landlord would offer a free pint to slake their thirst, and it was fortunate that the horses knew the round as well as the men. Our coalman sought protection when delivering from his horse-drawn cart by wearing a glistening black coal-sack, cowled monk-like on his head, to cover his neck and back. It served to stop the worst of the coal dust pouring down inside his shirt and to soften the spine-rubbing effect of humping one-hundredweight sacks of knobbly coal down the narrow indoor passages to the coal-cupboards. Old Tetsall, the chimney-sweep, who pushed a handcart filled with bags of soot crowned with a profusion of rods and brushes, had given up any hope of protection from his sooty work. He perambulated the streets as a wandering minstrel, the whites of his eyes flickering from a lamp-black body.

The dustmen wore hats with long flaps at the back, legionnaire style, to stop the detritus going down their necks when hoisting the dustbins onto their shoulders. The dustcart, drawn by a single shire, was an open wooden high-sided cart into which the galvanised metal bins were banged and emptied in a cloud of ash. Raked from the grates, the ash helped to soak up the sloppy mess of putrefying vegetable peelings, fish heads and kitchen garbage. In the summer as the dustmen raked the emptied rubbish across the cart to spread the load, the stench could be smelt half way down the street. The cart moved from house to house with its own cloud of flies. The dustmen were covered in a grey ash and it was a filthy lousy job. My wife's grandfather was a dustmen for thirty years, a member of the old National Union of General and Municipal workers. A proud man, he went mad one day when a toffee nosed housewife referred to him by the older name for his trade, as a 'scavenger'.

There was a uniformed class of workers. The postman was dressed in strong blue serge, a bright red vertical stripe running down each trouser leg, the outfit topped by a wide round hat with a stiff shiny peak. He walked the streets with polished boots and long strides, giving a rat-a-tat on every knocker as he delivered the post three times a day. The telegram boy, a silent messenger on a red bicycle and the eternal bearer of bad news in working class districts, was crowned with a pill-box hat. He carried his grim yellow messages in a narrow black pouch with a brass catch, looped to the belt around his waist. Tram drivers, bus conductors, railway porters, ticket collectors, commissionaires, cinema attendants and even the man from the Gas, Light and Coke Company, who came to empty the pennies from the gas-meter, were all attired in livery, a public proclamation of company identity and conformity.

Some, with lesser authority, were only partly uniformed. The baker, a Co-op roundsman, wore a brown knee-length coat, and a Wall's ice cream man, who pedalled the streets in summer, with his 'Stop me and buy one' tricycle, had a blue jacket and peaked cap. In the shops, the chemist, barber and the grocery assistants of the Home and Colonial Stores wore knee-length starched white coats, crisp as morning frost. All were regimented units of the great army of labour. In a way, women at home, housewives, also wore uniform. It was the ubiquitous pinafore, floral of pattern with right hand patch-pocket and tapes at the back. They were worn throughout the day, and pinafored mums could be seen leaning on brooms, grabbing a few moments rest while they chatted to a neighbour over the yard fence or at the front door. Few of the married women in our street went to work prior to 1939, but the war broke the pattern and 'pinnies' were exchanged for loose slacks and headscarves. For safety at work, where there could be moving machinery, long hair was swept up and bound beneath a scarf, wound in the style of a turban. Each morning, the single deck buses that ran down Carpenters Road, stopping at almost every factory, were packed to capacity with the 'turban brigade', as the women factory workers were commonly called. Large 'curlers' could be seen poking from their scarves, hair tightly rolled to force waves, for evenings and weekends of glamour. To be a lone youth on one of those buses was to be the subject of a bawdy ribaldry that caused red-faced embarrassment. 'Look out Doll, keep your hand on your ha'penny . . . '

Mums struggled on a housekeeping pittance to keep their children 'decently' dressed, but children of large families were inevitably clad in hand-me-downs. Fly buttons that reached to the chest, and trouser legs wide enough for several legs, were evidence of a bigger brother. Likewise, coats, with buttons moved inches across, that still hung like a sack, and frayed cuffs that reached to the finger tips. For girls, woolly cardigans might have sleeves turned up to several thicknesses. Dresses were shortened and 'taken-in' but the wide shoulders and shapeless form could not conceal the second-hand. Footwear was an immediate indicator of family poverty. Sloppy gaping uppers, worn down heels and flapping soles were familiar sights. Woollen socks were quickly holed with the constant rubbing of shoes a size too large, half the hole peeping over the backs of the shoes to reveal dirt ingrained flesh. We called the holes 'spuds', probably because they were the shape and size of potatoes. Boots were popular for men and boys, because they were tougher, and promised a longer life. Nevertheless, the leather soles soon wore through and layers of brown paper would be stuffed inside the boots to keep out the wet. Although there was a cobbler's shop in the next turning, repairs were often carried out at home. Ours were repaired by a neighbour, Mr Green, who had a three footed last, a sharp knife and a short handled hammer. He would 'sole and heel' for sixpence, and how the cobbler ever scraped a living is beyond me. In an effort to prolong the life of boots and shoes, we would smother the soles and heels with 'Blakey's', metal studs that came in clover leaf shapes with crescent tips for the heels and toes; they made a wonderful metallic clatter when walking on paving stones or cobbles. Plimsolls, rubber soled gym shoes with glossy black toecaps, were usual summer wear for children, though the sight of children wearing them in the snow and arriving at school with soaking and frozen feet was not uncommon. Conversely, some children spent the entire year in Wellington boots, their feet sweltering in the summer heat.

Children's fashion was unknown to us, our clothes were simply smaller versions of those worn by grown-ups but rather more shapeless. Without central heating in our homes, and travel made on foot or by public transport, our clothes tended to be thicker than those of today. Children would be clad in flannel underwear, often combinations, a one piece article combining vest and pants. I was a 'coms' boy, and in the winter they were worn beneath a shirt, a high necked woollen pullover and a knitted tie with horizontal stripes. On top of them came a thick double breasted jacket. There were no man-made fibres and our clothes were woven from natural materials, wool and cotton, and soon showed the threadbare evidence of daily wear. Patches and clothes went together like needle and thread, the seats of trousers and elbows of jackets sewed with extra fragments of material that rarely matched the original.

Like all the other boys, I wore a cap, which I raised when a funeral or the headmaster passed by. I can't recall raising it at any other time. A schoolboy cap could prove a formidable weapon for close quarter fighting. Folded into three, boomerang shape, and held between thumb and fingers at one end, it could be wielded at arms length to effect, the stiff edge of the peak cutting at exposed knees. Trousers were short, above the knees. They were sensible wear for summer, but winter meant chapped legs where the bottoms of the trouser legs rubbed the skin in the wet and the cold. Grazed knees were perennial, and a bloody handkerchief knotted at the joint an everyday sight. Boys were kept in short trousers until the age of fourteen, no matter how tall they may have grown. My friend, Fred, wore them until he was almost fifteen, and by then he was well on his way to his adult height of over six feet.

Clothes as gender symbols could be the cause of humiliation, witness the episode of poor Doddington wearing girl's shoes. My mother shopped at the Co-op, for the 'divi', rather than from socialist conviction, the dividend being a cash rebate that

87

averaged a shilling (5p) in the pound. 'Divi day' was held in our domestic calendar as a bountiful occasion to rival birthdays, Christmas and Easter. The dividend was used to supplement the buying of clothes, and on one such day I was taken to the London Co-operative Society's main store at Maryland Street to be bought a new pair of school trousers. I was sat at a counter on a high cane chair, and the shop assistant, an elderly and spruce man, asked my mother, 'Can I help you madam?' 'Yes', she replied, 'I would like a pair of school trousers for the boy.' 'Certainly madam, boys' knickers.' Knickers! I blushed and squirmed at the very sound of the word. 'Girls wear knickers,' I thought to myself with some embarrassment. I waited in silent torment until the man returned. Thankfully, the 'boys' knickers' proved to be normal short trousers with fly-buttons. I was relieved that none of my schoolmates had been present to overhear, to deride and to taunt.

I yearned for the day when I would be fourteen and initiated into manhood with a pair of 'longies'. I was fortunate, and received my first long trousered suit just before my fourteenth birthday, but it was only for Sunday best. For one day in seven I became a man, doing up the long buttoned fly and thrusting my hands deep into my trouser pockets, gazing down the vertical creases to 'fourteen inch bottoms' with their deep turn-ups. With the manliness of a real suit, it was obligatory to acquire adult objects to fill the pockets. Endless scheming was devoted to the bartering of juvenile possessions to come by a cigarette case, lighter, wallet and diary, the latter totally useless, for I had no appointments to keep and nobody to pursue for payments on quarter days. Further adornment to Sunday style came with a chromium plated tie-clip, worn at forty-five degrees across my Paisley-patterned Tootal tie. Suits came with waistcoats, and I envied a friend with a pocket watch, but that represented a capital investment beyond my means.

Owning a suit gave confidence and brought a feeling of security. A friend of mine from East Ham, Gordon Gimble, was less fortunate. His father had died while Gordon was still at school and the family subsisted from day-to-day in a permanent state of penury. When the time came for Gordon to leave school at fourteen, he was faced with the humiliating prospect of seeking work in his schoolboy short trousers. There was simply no money to buy the long trousers that were essential for a boy about to become a working man. There was no Social Security and his mother's pride precluded knocking on the Church door for charity. She did the only thing possible, she made him a pair, a venture that was endowed with more love than skill. From somewhere, she obtained sufficient material, a thick, grey length that was more like felt than cloth. She was no seamstress, but in all the circumstances she made a fair job, following his older brother's trousers as a pattern. Sadly, the material was stiff and unmanageable. As a consequence, the legs of the finished trousers stood, self supporting, as two columns, without creases. With his kindly nature, Gordon accepted the trousers with gratitude, but was secretly ashamed of the sight he presented in his pair of grey felt tubes. His first day at work as an apprentice bookbinder, passed without comment on his peculiar garb, for in truth, the men and boys where he worked were poorly paid and also badly dressed. Determined to advance his position, Gordon decided to go to night school to study for a City and Guilds certificate in his chosen craft. Enrolment night came, and as he entered the college hall along with better dressed lads of his own age, he was acutely aware of the odd figure he presented in his home-made trousers. He stood behind the waiting group of boys, at the back of the hall, in a corner shadow, awaiting the formalities. To his horror, the secretary began to call their names in alphabetical order, each boy in turn having to go to the desk at the front of the hall to register. 'G' did not prolong the ordeal of anticipated indignity, and the self-conscious Gimble was soon summoned to the stage in full view of the assembly. The mortifying experience remained a painful memory for the rest of his life. It was a secret that he hid for years, recounted to me in his later life as he sipped champagne on his yacht, moored at Mylor, in Cornwall. He told the story without bitterness, but with an abiding sadness and compassion for his mother, trapped by the helplessness of poverty.

My own experience of sartorial shame wrought by straitened circumstance, came in the form of an overcoat. Early in the war, my mother took a job as a daily cleaner to a Jewish family in Earlham Grove, to supplement the pitiful army allowance on which we existed. The Grove was a better class street in Forest Gate, its pavements lined with brutally pollarded plane trees. The houses were large, solid, with semi-basements that once housed servants, and although the quiet street had known wealthier times it was still occupied by the better-off. The family my mother worked for treated her well, and although the pay was small, her 'lady' often gave her little extras, including the occasional cast-off.

I must have been eleven or twelve, when mum arrived home one day with a boy's overcoat, as good as new, given to her by her employer. It was made of a thick Melton cloth of the finest quality, with a narrow waist, a half belt at the back, and fitted me as if it had been tailor-made. The snag was, that it was bright blue, a startling kingfisher. In an era when boys' and men's clothing was universally drab, all greys and browns, it was a coat of unusually vivid hue. Like all children I wanted to belong, to be the same as other children, and this coat shouted its difference. I protested that I did not like the coat, but in vain. My mother argued, 'It's a lovely coat, nice and warm, just the job for the winter, you will never get another like it.' She was right. I was sent to school, walking the drab streets, as bright as a peacock in a field of partridges. Determined to wear it out as quickly as possible, I rubbed the elbows on a brick wall, climbed, fought and rolled in the coat, my only concern, its rapid destruction. The lady had bought well; the garment withstood my assault for a whole winter, and I was spared a second season only because I outgrew the wretched thing.

At secondary school, the girls wore white ankle socks in the summer, like American 'bobby-soxers'. In the winter, their legs were encased in lisle stockings, thick and sensible. At weekends, after 'Amami night', the Friday hair washing ritual, they longed for the sheerness of silk stockings or the new gossamer-like nylon, to flash their legs at eager boys. Silk stockings were an unobtainable dream, precluded by scarcity and price. Nylons were the largesse distributed by American troops to pretty young women, and the staple commodity of black market spivs. Not for schoolgirls. The solution came in small bottles, labelled 'Lovely-legs', a stocking-coloured liquid with which they painted their legs in an attempt at deception, encouraged by the wartime campaign, 'bare legs for patriotism'. Too often, the result was streaky and cheap. The more skilful achieved an unblemished sheen, giving added realism by drawing imitation seams on the back of their legs with eye liner, a skill requiring a steady hand. It was said that one fifth form girl stood on the kitchen table, while her boy friend, an apprentice signwriter, used his brush to paint the lines with poster colour.

Sometime during 1944, my Uncle Norman arrived to spend a few days with us; he was a merchant seaman and found himself docked in London, with some leave due. He appeared as an adventurous explorer, a man who travelled to the far-off lands that I had only read about in geography books. Before the war, only the rich travelled abroad, sailing in the great passenger liners accompanied by huge cabin trunks smothered with garish labels. The only other traveller I had met was our lodger, Jim Blackshaw, who was a lorry driver. Now, Norman was home with stories to tell to a boy whose experience of travel was limited to a few bus and train rides. He had the weathered salt-sprayed face of a sailor and wore a dark blue roll-necked sweater, as thick as a sheep's coat. His trousers were strange, poor looking, without creases, made from a strong blue material that reminded me of my father's bib and brace overalls. The turn-ups reached an unbelievable four inches, showing the paler blue of the wrong side of the stiff material. They were jeans – the first pair I had ever seen – not the designer-labelled, figure-hugging garments of today, but stiff awkward denim with baggy legs and a sagging bottom. I felt sorry for him, that he could not afford a proper pair of trousers. I must have made some comment about them, for Norman said, 'Everyone in America wears them.' I was incredulous. 'Even when they are not at work?' I asked. 'Yes, weekends, evenings, all the time.' I could not argue, but it was hard to reconcile my Hollywood informed picture of America with the rough working trousers before my eyes. Neither did they match the evidence of the GIs, who roamed the West End of London in uniforms of smooth worsted, comparable to the quality worn by British officers. I remained doubtful.

From the day of my birth, my parents had subscribed to a penny-a-week endowment insurance, that was in effect, a tool fund. The policy matured when the child was fourteen and yielded a sum of fifteen pounds, enough to buy the basic tools for a trade and give a lad a start in life. However, when I reached fourteen, I was still at school and due to remain there for another two years, an unforeseen circumstance to confound the plan. Furthermore, my father was away from home, with the Eighth Army in Italy. With correspondence, it was decided to put the money in a Post Office savings account until I was sixteen and about to leave school. It had originally been expected that I would follow my father into the trade as a woodworker, but by the time my sixteenth birthday arrived, I was already looking to work as a commercial artist. Nevertheless, the money was dutifully handed over to me without condition regarding the tools I would buy. Perhaps, influenced by my father's tale of the bowler hat, I walked out of the house one Saturday afternoon with the fifteen pounds in my pocket and went directly to a local Jewish tailor. There I ordered a made-to-measure, double-breasted suit at a cost of exactly fifteen pounds. There were two fittings, and it was hand stitched, the stitches pulled tight to emphasise that they were not machined. It was an unparalleled extravagance and the first bespoke suit in the family. My parents were stunned by my profligacy, yet it was to serve as my 'glad rags' for years ahead. I wore it on my wedding day, at other people's weddings and for 'high days and holidays', until the trouser bottoms frayed, the elbows wore thin and the seat shone. Eventually, ten years on, it was consigned to the rag and bone man in exchange for a goldfish for my son.

While I was still at secondary school, I envied my friends who had left elementary school at fourteen and were able to buy clothes of their choice, even though they were restricted by clothes rationing and apprentice wages. One of my mates, John, who worked as an apprentice coachbuilder, bought a leather bomber jacket. He would stroll raffishly, the lambswool collar turned up and his hands buried deep in the slanting side pockets. It was aircrew glamour, casual and brave. It was also an assertion of independence, of a freedom of choice that broke the dull conformity of the Co-op, Dunns and Meakers, with their endless tweed jackets. My own ambition was a 'Manhattan coat', modelled after the design of American officers' jackets, but rather more casual. It was made of a soft, brown, blanket-like material, unlike any other coat I had seen. To appear different was all right if the difference was by choice, and obviously expensive. The coat, displayed in the window of a small outfitter, cost four pounds, and it took a year before I accumulated enough money to make the purchase. Once acquired, I joined John on a Saturday afternoon parade as we swanked towards Woolworth's in Stratford Broadway where we spent hours chatting to the Saturday girls, to the point where exasperated supervisors threatened them with the sack.

Clothes, like most commodities, were rationed, and clothing coupons were a ready black market currency, moving inexorably from the poor who did not have the money to spend on their allocation to the better-off who had more money than coupons. When my father was demobbed in 1945, he had been home for only a few days when he was stopped in Stratford High Street by a man hailing from a car. It was his former guv'nor, and they had last seen each other in 1939. The building boss, a man named

Clemens, greeted him after six years of war service with a cheerful and hopeful, 'Hello, do you want to sell your clothing coupons?' The need of my father to retain his pre-war job, strangled the reply he would like to have given, but he was furious. He recounted the episode many times, for it seemed to sum up the fundamental difference between 'us and them'. Money.

On Sunday mornings during those post war years, I used to walk with my friends, Fred and John, to Woodford, crossing the no-man's land of Wanstead Flats into a suburb of tidy semis with rising sun gates and leaded light windows. The objective of our weekly walk was one of the many pubs, all oak and horse brasses, where we could enjoy a pint and an hour of intense political discussion. There, we mingled with 'Woodford man', tweed jacketed with brown brogues, Fairisle pullovers and yellow ties patterned with horses heads. They drank halves from glasses with handles, 'In a jug, please,' and contrived to drop the name of Churchill, their constituency member of parliament, into conversation, as if they knew him personally. We envied their quality shoes, loathed their ties, persuaded my mother to knit us Fairisle pullovers and fiercely debated the merits of nationalisation. In summertime, as we walked home, there was cricket on Woodford Green, the plonk of tennis balls from tree-surrounded courts at Wanstead, and men in plus-fours on their way to Wanstead golf club. What of the women? They were at home, cooking the Sunday roast.

As I moved further to the left in my political beliefs, I discarded my Manhattan coat, an American symbol of western decadent capitalism, and adopted the mode of dress worn by earnest young comrades, baggy corduroy trousers and a red tie as wide as a red flag, a political statement enhanced by a dark coloured shirt. The carried accessories were the *Daily Worker*, the *Manchester Guardian* and the *New Statesman and Nation*. It was the garb of the bookish worker, redolent of a cartoonist's picture of a 1930s subscriber to the Left Book Club. When it was cold, my topcoat was a drab gaberdine double-breasted raincoat. A few years later, in the early fifties, the required outer garb for young socialists became a hooded duffel coat, but I remained faithful to my 'trade union official' raincoat. The total effect was flawed by my habitual wearing of a 'County cap'. Not the greasy flat cloth cap of a worker, but a rather more stylish affair of corduroy, with a tighter peak, the sort of thing favoured for wear at a point-to-point meeting. It betrayed the influence of 'Woodford man' and my love of English county towns. The final touch of bourgeois incongruity came when I bought an umbrella, cane handled and tightly rolled, it was nevertheless extremely practical when it came to long waits at bus stops in the rain.

Clothes rationing was abolished in 1949, ending a decade of coupons and Board of Trade utility fashion. Young women, weary of years of enforced austerity which kept skirts above the knee and restricted frills and pleats, eagerly turned to the calf length skirts and coats of the 'New Look'. Created by Dior, the fashion used yards of material and swept away the military look of a nation at war. Working class women did not shop in Bond Street, but the fashion was copied by thousands of clothing manufacturers and sold by high street stores at affordable prices. My girl friend, Pamela, scraped together the money for a New Look coat, narrow waisted, flared and long, extravagant and feminine. Despite the lifting of restrictions, men's fashions were slower to change. My father continued to wear his demob suit on Sundays and it did not look out of place ten years later. Where men gathered in crowds, at county cricket or football matches, the scene was the old colourless mass of sombre jackets, wide trousers, braces, drab caps and trilbies. Many still wore their pre-war clothes, and ex-army battle dress tops remained popular as work clothing for years after the war had ended.

The erosion, if not the ending, of class difference in dress, the outward symbol of pelf and place, started in the mid 1950s. The long years of shortages, forced first by war and then reconstruction, gave way to a new prosperity built on the economic foundation laid by the 1945 Labour government. In the pre-war days of mass unemployment, young people worked for apprentice wages that were reckoned in shillings, often contributing to a family income where the father was unemployed. They were cheap labour, to be sacked as soon as they were old enough for the rate for the job. Now, in a Britain with full employment, the forty-hour week and higher wages, they had more genuine leisure time and money to spend. Real wages had risen by seventy-five percent between 1948 and 1956, and working class youth gave expression to their new economic power by dressing in a way that distanced themselves from their parents.

The emergence of a separate youth culture led an assault on the traditional distinctions in dress between rich and poor. Teddy boys and Teddy girls, with their exaggerated Edwardian dress, may have been a minority, shocking an older generation by flaunting day-glo socks, velvet collars and winkle-picker shoes, but it was a cutting edge of fashion. Young people, rejecting the traditional British sports jackets, grey flannels and floral printed dresses, were spreading a new culture that was to transcend class barriers.

With money to spend on consumer products like record players, radios and long playing records, the record companies responded to the market by promoting young performers and their music. As the new media of television superseded the cinema as the popular form of visual entertainment, the young entertainers were brought into the living rooms of millions. The pop stars were young and working class, teenage (itself a new word in the English language) idols, their mannerisms, hairstyles and dress aped by their followers, working class, middle class and upper class alike. It became difficult to tell at a glance if the wearers of teenage fashion were rich or poor. The growth of chain stores selling fashion clothes matched economic growth, and city analysts soon realised the purchasing power of the young. The market for long-life clothes fell to the demand for instant fashion as television flashed rapidly changing style to millions, equally, throughout the country. Overnight, the North London Area Boot Supply Company, a local boot and shoe shop, became 'Michelle's', boots for workers giving way to blue suede shoes and stiletto heels.

When I was a boy, the dress of doctors, clergy, schoolteachers, managers and directors, asserted their status. They were well shod, tailored and comfortable. Our clothes were cheap, inferior, shoddy, with shirt collars turned, socks darned and elbows patched. The better-off looked better off, the wealthy looked wealthy. As late as 1946, when I mentioned to my mother that I had the ambition to buy a pair of Veldtschoen shoes, leather walking shoes of good quality costing five pounds, I was told that I had ideas beyond my station. An age of T-shirts, jeans and trainers, traversing social class and gender was unimaginable.

In the Communist Party, which I was to join in 1949, we stuck to our shabby raincoats and cloth caps. A renegade Communist wrote in 1952 of how he was castigated by Harry Pollitt for wearing a colourful patterned tie. 'It was bourgeois, not working class.' The story may be apocryphal, but the essence of the tale is true. As the spending power of young workers increased in a society of full employment and they dressed to demonstrate their independence, we Communists were to remain moulded by the grey and grim thirties, oblivious of the revolution around us.

CHAPTER 7

Another Boundary

The peacetime summer was warm and relaxed, the activities of peace nudging a tired nation towards normality. It was Fred, the lanky scholar of our group, who made the suggestion, 'Let's go to Lord's.' I had no idea where Lord's was, but on a June day, I joined Fred and John, my closest friends, to make the first of a lifetime of pilgrimages to the Mecca of cricket. We descended into the grimy underground station at Bow Road, and emerged into the space and light of Stanley Heap's thirties masterpiece, St John's Wood station, cream tile clean, curved and modern with bronze lamps flanking the escalators. We walked, holding packets of sandwiches, down Acacia Road, past the detached Edwardian villas, to Wellington Place, paid a shilling (5p) each at the turnstiles and stepped into another world.

The tightly mown grass of the Nursery, strung with practice nets, was the largest lawn I had ever seen, until, a moment later, I saw the playing area. It was a field of light and dark green stripes, each blade of grass meticulously ordered into place by the head groundsman. The thousands of white painted slatted seats dazzled the eyes and presented a bewildering choice, any seat available for the cost of our ground admission charge. We moved with argument from seat to seat, from the Nursery Stands to the sweeping Mound Stand, and back past the Nursery Stands to the Grand Stand, as we sought the best vantage point. Oblivious of the finer points of watching cricket, we sat square with the wickets, because the Grand Stand balcony was closest to where the wickets were pitched. Father Time peered down at us, the famous weather vane somnambulant in the still June air.

With one tuppenny scorecard to share between us, we settled down, taking in the unfamiliar surroundings as we waited for the start of play, between the Royal Australian Air Force and the South of England teams. Opposite us was the Tavern, a classic beer house, its open bars entered from the ground, or from St John's Wood Road. Drinkers in the St John's Wood Road bars could catch tantalising glimpses of the cricket, enough to intrigue, but not sufficient to follow the game. To the right of the Tavern were the members' boxes, fronted with heavy cast iron work, ornate Victoriana, and the south clock-tower, ivy clad, the clock face a target for a long on-drive from the nursery end. The pavilion was imposing splendour, terracotta and white, rising to second and third balconies between its twin towers, each crowned with the interlaced ironwork monogram of the MCC.

A few members, dark suited, arms and legs protruding from behind copies of *The Times* or *Daily Telegraph*, sat facing the full leafed trees behind the Nursery end stands. The lazy Tavern cat, black, silky and content, lay curled on the boundary, squinting at the groundstaff as they pulled the heavy roller, manning the shafts designed for a horse. We watched the ritual as the creases were whitened, and the head groundsman carefully poured water from a Tizer bottle into six holes where the stumps were to be placed in the parched ground. The white seats were splattered with drab-clad spectators as the two captains, blazer smart, walked to the wicket to toss for innings. Ten minutes later, a steward leisurely perambulated the boundary, holding a chalked notice in an attempt at mass communication – for there was no public address system – 'South of England won the toss'. The morning silence was broken as the pavilion bell unexpectedly clanged out a five minute warning, and the two umpires, Beet and Fowler, walked slowly to the middle. They wore long white coats, reminiscent of bygone housepainters, and trilby hats, to add authority. The stumps were carefully checked for vertical correctness and the bails placed with mathematical precision. Everything about Lord's was unhurried, ordered and proper.

The Australians jogged onto the field, threatening the tranquillity with youthful vigour. For the South of England, Robertson, upright and graceful, opened with Fishlock, the aggressive Surrey left-hander, and within minutes Australian energy in the field was rewarded with the run out of Robertson for two. I am not sure that the names of the English players meant much to us. Who was the Reverend J R Bridger, batting at first wicket down? I almost expected him to emerge from the pavilion wearing a dog collar. No doubt he was following a pastoral tradition that led to an advertisement in the *Church Times*, which read, 'Curate needed for West of England village parish, slow left-arm bowler preferred.' Squadron Leader Edrich was a familiar name, as was the kerchiefed Lieutenant Colonel E R T Holmes, but Flying Officer A E Wilson, L Thompson and H Taylor were merely printed names on the scorecard.

The Reverend Bridger left his pulpit, the players balcony, and made his way down among the congregation. Despite the presence of eleven thousand people, the ground was as quiet as a cathedral as Bridger faced his first ball. Bridger made a decent thirty-eight, taking unhurried singles, and we munched our sandwiches, all destined to be consumed before lunchtime. The score moved past one hundred, Squadron Leader Edrich, short and powerful, being run out for 43. It was all so civilised; applause was polite and England was at peace, the crowd enjoying the most English of pastimes. Then it happened. Lieutenant Colonel G O Allen had made twenty-two, when he played defensively at a ball from Flight Lieutenant Roper. The ball appeared to hit his pad, or possibly bat and pad, and the ball rolled gently towards the stumps. Allen bent down, picked up the ball before it reached the stumps and tossed it back to the bowler, just as Roper appealed, presumably for lbw. The umpires finger went up, Allen was given out, 'handled the ball.' The lieutenant colonel, Eton and Cambridge, former captain of England, stood immobile in disbelief, his gentlemanly act in a one-day friendly match construed as unfair play. Slowly, without a further word, he left the crease to begin the long walk back to the pavilion. Carmody, the Australian captain, recently liberated from a prisoner of war camp by the Russians, talked to the umpire and the bowler. It was a misunderstanding, 'Call Allen back', but Allen, now halfway to the pavilion would have none of it, and with flushed face continued to walk, as petulant as a chastised schoolboy. Ray Smith, of Essex, came in as the next batsman and prepared to face Roper. There was no respectful silence this time, but an outburst of booing from some of the spectators as Roper, unfairly blamed for the incident, began his run up. Smith walked away from his wicket and made it clear that he would not commence his innings until the barracking of Roper had stopped. More jeers. Was this cricket? Yes it was, a familiar re-enactment of any one of a score of happenings in our street cricket. All could have been resolved and honour preserved if only the umpires had had the authority to ask Allen to play 'three matchsticks'.

We saw three brief overs from a fair-haired flying officer, his hair quite unbecoming an officer, long and tossed back as he turned for his shortish run. The ball was startling-fast, whipping past the bat and smacking into the keepers' gloves while the batsman was still completing his defensive push. It was Miller – K R Miller – to return to England in 1948 with the greatest Australian side ever to visit our shores. In tandem with Lindwall, he was to devastate English batting, while his own batting was played with a verve and obvious joy that was surpassed only by Constantine and Compton,

The South were all out for 208. Craig and Pettiford opened for the Australians, but then we experienced the frustration brought by an English summer, rain and bad light stopped play. We clambered over the railings into the covered upper balcony and shared the stoicism of the other spectators as we waited ninety minutes for play to resume. Miller hit a fast 78 not out in an effort to force victory against the clock, but close of play came with the Australians 25 runs short of their target. The match was drawn, but I was hooked for life. With a sense of history, I waited at the latticed window of the Lord's printing shop to invest twopence in a completed scorecard that included the rare form of dismissal of Allen. I did not know it then, but the last time the law had been invoked in a game at Lord's was in 1857. W G Grace had been wilier when playing against Surrey in 1887. A return throw to the wicket lodged in his shirt and he refused to hand over the ball, lest he should be given out, running three until the ball dislodged.

A few weeks later, we were back at Lord's, wisely provisioned with lemonade to help wash down our dry sandwiches. We arrived early, which was just as well, for by nine o'clock when the gates opened, the waiting queue was pavement-wide around the ground. We sprinted to the Nursery end and sat ourselves in the front row, as near as was possible behind the bowler's arm. The match was billed as an 'unofficial' Victory Test Match, between England and Australia, but the significance of 'unofficial' was lost on a nation anxious to forget the long weary years of war and eager to savour the joys of peace. These were the first of the special post-war years for cricket, from 1945 to 1948, when, such was the interest, the county ground in Glamorgan could attract fifty thousand spectators over three days for a visiting tourist match. The atmosphere of those cricketing days when the latest score was chalked on every news-stand and passed on by word of mouth around offices and factories – for portable radios and television were virtually unknown – lingers as a halcyon memory.

Four or five Saturday visits to Lord's that year gave the chance to see some of the great players from the pre-war years, now nearing the end of their careers. There was the burly Hammond, majestic with the power of his off driving and still eagle-eyed at slip, and Constantine, the West Indian encapsulation of dynamic human energy, whether batting, bowling or fielding. I was to meet him within a few years at the West African Students' Association in Chelsea, where he came to talk on racial prejudice. After the meeting, we took the bus to Victoria together, talking politics and cricket. I paid his tuppenny fare with casual generosity, coppers I could ill afford, but worth more than both pennies for the privilege of his company. Sutcliffe, as solid as Yorkshire, appeared for a Lord's XI, as did Ames, no longer keeping wicket but still lofting the ball with might. Bill Bowes, with his smooth faced complexion, army haircut and round spectacles was still turning his arm over, fast, for Yorkshire, and Bill Voce, another bowler from the 'bodyline' tour, was hurtling down left arm deliveries for Notts. All of them showed glimpses of the greatness that was theirs in the fullness of youth.

The 1946 season brought the first post-war touring team to England, the Indians, the last all India side to tour England, for independence and partition was imminent. Until then, the only Indian I had ever seen was a cold and lone salesmen hawking a cardboard suitcase full of silk ties from door-to-door. Soon however, the strange sounding names of the tourists were to become familiar, as Gul Mahomed, Hazare, Amarnath, Mankad and the Nawab of Pataudi among them captured us with their graceful play. The first match the tourists played in London, was not at my beloved Lord's, but at the Oval, where they came to play Surrey, early in May. This was my introduction to the Oval, both the underground station and the cricket ground. Kennington is not St John's Wood, and the grey and the grime was no escape from my normal environment. Fred and myself arrived at about seven in the morning, for attendances were huge, the grounds packed to capacity, with gates often closed before start of play, even for some county matches. We joined the queue against the curving prison-like wall, and settled for the long wait, nibbling premature lunch sandwiches of mousetrap cheese and beetroot, which contained more beetroot than cheese. To describe the wall of the Oval as prison-like was close to the truth, for the ground had been used during the war as a prisoner of war camp, a very English Stalag. The ground was not derequisitioned until November 1945, and the evidence of war had not then been finally erased.

While we waited, we were entertained by buskers, who also queued in turn to entertain the patient cricket followers. First to perform, although he always waited until the queue was large enough for worthwhile reward, was a thin man in a black suit and a bowler hat. He appeared with a portable harmonium and was known to the regulars as 'old mutton eye', due to a severe cast in one eye. Between snatches of scarcely harmonious music he would keep up a patter of corny jokes, repeated every time he performed, largely to the same Saturday audience. His favourite was that he had 'played before the Prince of Wales, the Duke of Cumberland, the Duke of York – and most of the other pubs in south London.' He would be succeeded by a large cloth-capped man who tore telephone directories in half, and then, perhaps the best of all, an escapologist whose assistant bound and padlocked him before tying him in a sack. Three minutes later, he was free to a round of applause, but little else, for the pennies had gone to 'old mutton eye' and the halfpennies to the strong man.

When we were finally admitted to the ground at nine o' clock, the shock contrast with Lord's was immediate. Instead of thousands of white seats, there were concrete terraces more suited to a football ground. There were no white-tiled toilets, but smelly urinals, no trees as a backdrop, but two gasometers and blocks of flats. This was no Elysian field, no Broadhalfpenny meadow, but a London recreation ground. The 'free seats', surely a misnomer, for we had paid to go in, consisted of a few rows of green painted low bench seats on the gasometer side of the ground. Among the first in, we grabbed our position, in the front row, square with the wicket. To our left, was the only building of distinction, the twin-towered Victorian pavilion, used during the later war years for the storage of furniture from bombed homes. The ground itself had been hit by seven high explosive bombs during the war and numerous incendiaries, but the field of play was again as smooth and flat as it had been when England had passed nine hundred, batting against Australia, in the final test match in 1938. For spectators conditions were more than austere, they were Spartan. It must have been the only cricket ground in the world that hired out waterproof blankets by the day as protection from the elements.

The bleakness of the setting was forgotten as Merchant and Hazare opened for India, Merchant facing the first over from Alf Gover, whose arms pumped like pistons, elbows high as he steamed to the stumps. Gover bowled fast, but it was big Alec Bedser, fast medium, that took the wickets, having Hazare lbw for nought and then clean bowling the square shouldered Modi for a duck. Merchant made a neat 53 and Gul Mahomed 89 as nine wickets went down by mid afternoon, five of them to the promising new young bowler, Bedser. The groundsman, Bert Lock, walked onto the field as the ninth wicket fell at 205, to ask Bennett, the Surrey captain, which roller he would like used at the end of the innings, which was considered imminent. Bennett gave his instructions and tea was delayed while the Indian tail enders, numbers ten and eleven, Sarwate and Banerjee, awaited early dismissal. It was not to be. Resistance continued and tea was taken, late. They resumed, growing in confidence as the score mounted towards respectability. Cricket watchers enjoy runs made by a wagging tail, though to a fielding captain who has watched his bowlers sweep aside the specialist batsmen, there is nothing more frustrating. The partnership grew to fifty and edged singles gave way to middle-of-the bat twos and fours. Sarwate reached fifty to generous applause, and shortly after, a smiling Banerjee held his bat aloft to acknowledge the clapping for his half century. I sensed history in the making and willed the little Sarwate, run by run, towards his century. All loyalty to the home side was abandoned as the two tail enders batted like openers, their scores mounting through the sixties, seventies, eighties, towards improbable centuries. By close of play, my hands stinging with the intensity of clapping, Sarwate was 102 not out, and Banerjee just eleven runs from his hundred. On Monday morning, Banerjee reached his hundred, and by the time that Parker bowled him for 121, the partnership had reached a world record for a last wicket stand of 249. It was the first time in the history of the game that numbers ten and eleven had both scored centuries in the same innings.

Cricket became a euphoric drug. Like addicts, we counted the minutes to our next fixture, living for Saturdays, the sub culture of averages, dominating our lives. Every Saturday, we journeyed to Lord's or the Oval and our knowledge of the grounds, the game and the players grew. Arriving at St John's Wood station, we would run to Lord's, overtaking the middle aged and elderly in our rush for a good seat. We wandered around the ground in the lunch and tea intervals, past the flower beds where the tulips grew in MCC colours and would peer beyond formidable stewards into the dark, cool, polished interior of the pavilion, a sacred shrine where only the rich and great could worship. Positioned at the doorway a couple of hours before start of play, we watched as our heroes, the players, arrived, though sometimes they were difficult to recognise in trilby hats and dark suits. Edrich would saunter into the pavilion as if it belonged to him, while lesser players from visiting counties entered as we might have done ourselves, had the gods allowed, cautiously, even diffidently, with awe. The members themselves appeared old, slow, and straw hatted, wearing garish red and yellow striped ties and carrying polished sticks or umbrellas. During play, while we absorbed every ball, they sat in the best seats in the ground, in the pavilion, behind the bowler's arm, reading their newspapers or dozing after lunch. The obvious inequality, and not a little jealousy, confirmed a developing class awareness of the privileges that accompany wealth. On big match days, we read the printed lists posted to inform the public of the names of the luminaries occupying the members' boxes, Sir This and Colonel That. These were the men described by Sir Pelham Warner as men you would 'meet in the long room, 'Viceroys, Governor-Generals, Prime Ministers, Cabinet Ministers, members of the bench and bar . . . famous bishops and church dignitaries . . . all united in a common bond and love of cricket.' United, I was sure they were, in an inner world of patrician privilege. We saw them sitting aloof and apart, dipping into wicker hampers that contained delicacies other than sandwiches and refreshment with more fizz than R White's lemonade.

Class prejudice apart, we accepted our role on the periphery of the world of cricket, watchers who supported the first class game. We learned to admire line and length, to shake our heads in silent disgust at a loose ball, to say 'shot' at a perfectly executed cover drive, 'well held' at a blinding catch or to groan in unison if a 'sitter' was dropped. We breathed with relief if the dropped catch meant a 'life' for a favourite batsman. We joined in the general laughter when an umpire had to jump sharply to avoid being hit by the ball, and shook with mirth if he were actually hit, and then applauded when he recovered and resumed his role. We did not move from our seats while an over was in progress because it spoilt the enjoyment of others and sat immobile if we were behind the bowler's arm while he was bowling. Those who did move, to the distraction of the batsman, we considered to be ignorant of the finer points of the game. I acquired a cheap cardboard-like attache case for carrying sandwiches and progressed from lemonade to cider. My father made a small folding stool, a necessary seat for the long hours of queuing that preceded almost every match. Queueing from six in the morning was not unusual; even so, I never equalled Denis Compton, who has told me that as a schoolboy he spent all night outside Lord's waiting for admission to the 1934 test against Australia, sleeping on a camp bed. I bought a scorebook, entering the details of every ball with a neatness and accuracy that would have astonished my schoolteachers. Watching cricket had become a passion destined to outlive my youth.

When stumps were drawn on the 1946 season, the outlook was bleak. Food rationing, austerity, the coldest winter on record and a national fuel shortage of coal made Britain a nation under siege. The gloom that prevailed was scarcely relieved by the news from Australia, where England fought a losing battle against the 'old enemy', led by the indomitable Bradman. For those who did not have to leave for work early, a half an hour of partially audible short wave wireless commentary from down under at seven in the morning, hissed doom for England.

On a freezing December lunch time, I left the factory to buy an early edition of an evening paper to check the score in the first test. On the front page, in the large black type usually reserved for national disasters, was the dreadful news, 'Hutton out for 7'. Since making his record test score of 364 at the Oval in 1938, Hutton had become a folk hero, and his early failure on the first post-war tour, added to the winter misery. The special place that Hutton occupied in English life was well illustrated by a story told to me years later by a business associate, Arthur Morgan. He was a German Jewish refugee from fascism, struggling to make a living in post-war England with his little printing company. He had secured an appointment with the print buyer of a large advertising agency and was shown into the buyers' office, full of hope. He was greeted by an unsmiling face and two curt words uttered with a Yorkshire accent, 'Hutton's out.' Nonplussed by the incomprehensible statement, Herr Morgan smiled, and said, 'Good.' It seemed a safe response. 'Get out,' shouted the buyer, and the German and the Yorkshireman never met again.

The 1947 and 1948 seasons run together as a golden memory,

like the long hot summers of remembered childhood, but this time verified by the records of the meteorological office and *Wisden*. They were the vintage summers of Hutton, Bedser, Edrich and Compton, laced with Lindwall, Miller, Barnes and Bradman. The 1947 season, was one of the hottest summers this century, and the numbing arctic winter melted away as every Saturday saw Lord's packed with spectators to marvel at the batting of Edrich and Compton. In my memory it seems that Middlesex were always 350 odd for six by late afternoon, and snatching a couple of wickets before stumps. Edrich was magnificent, a miniature dynamo who drove straight and hard and bowled fast furious slingers, but it was Compton who became the nation's idol. He played with the impish enthusiasm of a schoolboy and the talent of a genius. It was Compton, Brylcreem-glamorous and dashing, running out partners, dropping his bat while running quick singles, charging down the wicket to fast bowlers and then changing his mind to forsake the drive for a delicate late cut, that was a dream fantasy become reality, to enthral millions. It was not just that Compton scored more runs and more centuries in 1947 than any other batsman, before or since, but the carefree way in which he made those runs that is fixed forever in the memory of those who were blessed to see him. The Compton sweep to long leg became the ambition of every schoolboy and the despair of many a cricket coach as their young pupils sought to emulate their hero. 'Compton is batting' sent hundreds scurrying to grounds already crowded, a compelling attraction matched only in the past by Grace, and in my own time by Bradman and Botham. There may have been greater batsmen, like Hobbs, the master, but none with more charisma.

1948 brought the Australians to England and the opportunity to see Bradman. It was said by some critics that he was past his best, though he arrived with an average of 131.2 for his previous season at home. I could make no comparison with his batting of pre-war days, but could only measure his prowess against his contemporaries. It was formidable. I saw him score several centuries, the first of them 146 in under three hours against Surrey, the memory encapsulated by a pull to leg, the bat swinging past his baggy green cap with elbows at shoulder height, the ball sizzling across the grass, bisecting the fielders to reach the seated spectators before anyone had moved.

The final test of the series, at the Oval, followed a week of rain, but did not deter some from queueing all night to ensure a seat for the first day's play. I arrived at six in the morning and waited six hours, for a delayed start at noon. It was worth the wait. In a superlative spell of fast bowling, Ray Lindwall, requiring sawdust for a secure foothold on the sodden turf, varying his pace and bowling with controlled accuracy, hit the stumps of Yardley, Evans, Bedser and Young, and had Hutton and Compton caught. His figures were 6 for 20, and England were all out for 52, only Hutton reaching double figures. Hutton, the first of the England batsmen to face Lindwall, was last out, for 30, the remaining batsmen mustering only sixteen runs from the bat between them. It was the innings of a master, stylish and confident against the torrid pace bowling of Lindwall and Miller, moving the ball late in a humid atmosphere, and coming through at a varying height. Hutton, who finally fell to a great catch by Tallon from a fine leg-glance, demonstrated his position as the greatest bad wicket player in the world, be it wet, sticky, dusty or crumbling.

Australia, with conditions easing in warm sunshine, opened with Morris and Barnes, and progressed to a comfortable 116, before Barnes was caught at the wicket, off Hollies, the Warwickshire leg spinner, for 61. It was the prelude to one of the most poignant, and one of the most unlikely moments in the history of the game. Bradman, the batsman who had exhausted all the superlatives that cricket writers could contrive in describing his run scoring, came to the wicket for his last innings in test cricket, needing just four runs to end his career with a test average of one hundred. Twenty thousand people stood as one, in an ovation that started as he emerged from the pavilion door and lasted as Norman Yardley, the England captain, shook hands with him and called for three cheers. Bradman stood still at the crease, a slight figure, cap in hand, as the caps of the England players were lifted three times in unison to the accompanying cheers. We resumed our seats, Bradman looked around the field, settled in his familiar stance and played the first ball from Hollies with a defensive push. It was six o' clock, and anticipation for a Bradman century on the morrow, was savoured by all who swore to be there to see it. Suddenly, it was a lost dream. Playing forward, Bradman missed Hollies' googly and was bowled, the bails lying on the ground as incontrovertible evidence. His lonely walk back to the pavilion was joined with a standing ovation that would not have been surpassed for a double century. We clapped and sang, 'For he's a jolly good fellow', until mounting the pavilion steps he disappeared with finality, through the centre door and into the darkness. We sat silent, stunned, cursing Hollies for a feat that at any other time would have been greeted with rapture. Some cricket writers have speculated that Bradman's eyes were clouded with emotion as he faced the fatal ball. I think not. He was simply bowled by a good ball. For all who witnessed his parting, they will say, like old soldiers, to their grandchildren. 'I was there.'

My fascination with the art of cricket, and it is an art, of graceful and creative movement, power, beauty and skill, led naturally to reading the literature of cricket, poetry as well as prose. I began with Cardus, which meant that I started with some of the best writing on the game and had to search hard at the shelves of the West Ham Central Library to find his equals. Some would argue that he has no equal, though Arlott at his best runs him hard. R C Robertson-Glasgow, Herbert Farjeon, Hugh de Selincourt and the poet Edmund Blunden were early discoveries. *Wisden Cricketers' Almanack* with its daffodil coloured covers, the herald of each new season, became essential reading and I bought my first copy in 1950. The thick volumes have lengthened along the bookshelves with the passing of the years and I have filled the gaps from the date of my birth in 1930, the objective to reach my century of *Wisdens*, before my innings is closed.

Tucked amid grander books on my cricket shelves are three small paperback cricket annuals published by the *Daily Worker* in 1948, 1949 and 1950, which must now be rare collectors items for cricket lovers and socialists alike, as rare probably as the sight of the *Daily Worker* being read at Lord's, a Saturday habit of mine for many years. The 1949 *Daily Worker* annual includes an exclusive article, totally non-political, by the Kent and England leg spinner, Douglas Wright, on 'Bowling in tests'. There is a story that Bradman once said 'I wish I had Doug on my side,' to which Wright replied, 'I wish I had Don on mine.' The following year the annual featured a piece by Harold Larwood, entitled, with some pertinence, 'Where are our fast bowlers?' Larwood, a former miner, who learned his cricket 'in the streets, on rough park pitches and on the waste ground at the corner of the street' made a plea for cricket facilities for schoolboys in industrial areas whose only wicket is 'a cold hard playground'. Learie Constantine, writing especially for the *Daily Worker* annual at the start of the West Indies tour to England in 1950, was forthright in his condemnation of the colour bar. He wrote of 'the hurt' inflicted on himself and other West Indian tourists in the past, by the 'reticence, coldness and wordlessness' of officials and some players, 'never saying two words where one would do, or one if silence would serve.' Constantine also attacked the colour prejudice that prevailed in West Indian cricket administration, which ludicrously dictated that the team must be led by a white captain. How many who can readily recall the names of Worrell, Weekes, Walcott, Ramadhin and Valentine from that 1950 triumphant test side can remember the name of the captain with the 'right' coloured skin? Although no mean cricketer, John Goddard was openly criticised by Constantine for his timid captaincy, adding that the 'extraordinary policy of white captaincy had been a cricket laughing stock for two generations.' Nevertheless, Constantine was full of hope for the future of West Indian cricket, and with some foresight claimed that, 'sending down the ball with pace and sting would eventually lay low the Goliath of English cricket.' So it has proved, but close as he was to the West Indian game, even Constantine did not foresee that victory for the West Indians that summer would be fashioned not by speed, but by the guile of Ramadhin and the accurate spin of Valentine.

National service inevitably curtailed my cricket following, though I contrived to arrange my leave to coincide with the test match at Lord's, in much the same way that certain bishops arrange their pastoral calendar to leave themselves free of diocesan duties towards the end of June, when the Lord's test is played. I saw the whole of the 1950 test against the West Indies at Lord's, where the Caribbean players finally beat their teachers for the first time in England. It meant more to them than winning a game of cricket, it was an assertion of equality. There were few West Indian immigrants in Britain in 1950, but those who came to see their countrymen vanquish their masters did not conceal their unbounded delight at the conquest. As the last England wicket fell, to give the West Indies victory by 326 runs, a small group of immigrants, wearing drape jackets and peg-bottom trousers, skipped onto the field, one of them with a guitar, singing and dancing to an impromptu calypso, a sight never before witnessed on an English cricket field, let alone at Lord's. The victory caught the public imagination, and the fairy-tale success of the two nineteen-year old West Indian spin bowlers was immortalised in calypso by Lord Beginner, as 'those two pals of mine, Ramadhin and Valentine.'

Cricket was a game of empire, played wherever the British flag was flown. If the colonialists had gone forth with sword and bible to 'civilise' the peoples of distant lands, they also packed their cricket bats. The Empire was ruled by king or queen, and cricket was ruled by the MCC, comfortably ensconced in Imperial Headquarters, at Lord's. At home, the ruling class played as 'gentlemen', class difference epitomised by the continuance of the annual fixture at Lord's, Gentlemen v Players. Monied amateurs appeared on the printed scorecards with their names preceded by their initials – P B H May and F R Brown, for example, opposed by players such as Compton D C S and Washbrook C. The amateurs, like F R Brown, often sported a tied silk kerchief at the neck, a Wooster-like affectation redolent of country house cricket in a byegone age. The fixture, an English anachronism, survived the 1945 social revolution, the retention of the autocracy of the public schools ensuring that a paid player knew his place, which, no matter how good a player he may have been, denied his fitness for leadership. Lord Hawke, the reactionary captain of Yorkshire from 1883-1907, once uttered a public prayer, 'Pray God the day never dawns when a professional captains England.' It was an entreaty to the deity endorsed by the bishops and generals of the MCC until 1954, when, wealth, public school and university education could no longer be sustained as the only valid qualifications for leadership in a changed society. Hutton L, the unassuming hero, was appointed with public acclaim, as the first professional captain to lead England at cricket, and very good he proved to be. The annual fixture of Gentlemen v Players, with claims that all the gentlemen were now players, and all the players, gentlemen, survived the 1950s, though it belonged to a byegone age.

With political awareness and left-wing commitment developing from the age of fourteen or so, it may be asked, what was the appeal of a game so steeped in tradition and dominated at the highest level by the influence of the establishment? Quite simply, it is the best of ball games, a dramatic spectacle involving individual skills, yet dependant upon teamwork, played often in the loveliest of settings. It is a game of intellect, human chess, with the added dimension of being influenced by the vagaries of the weather and the state of the pitch. Cricket is mostly about long days in the sun with ample periods of restfulness for watcher and player alike. A player may sit padded-up for hours as a steady partnership builds a substantial total. Spectators have time to reflect upon the pattern of play while admiring individual feats of immense skill. To watch a batsman in the days of uncovered wickets confront a left arm spin bowler on a rain affected wicket was to observe a battle of minds, as well as skills. The game has movement as graceful as a ballet, the flowing action of a bowler at full pace, the gentle curve of a flighted ball, a delicate late cut to third man, a ball picked up single-handed on a full run and returned to the wicket keeper without a break in the rhythm, all giving pleasure to the eye of the beholder. By contrast – and what game has more contrast of style – see the flashing blade as a ball is cracked past point or hooked high beyond the boundary or a bowler hurling the ball with aggression, digging it in, to rise sharply, challenging split-second reaction from the batsman. It is a game of infinite variety, like life itself.

Cricket is closely linked with my love of the English countryside, open greens nestling at the centre of village life, fresh mown grass, deck-chairs dotted in front of miniature pavilions, with afternoon tea between innings. After the game, beer in the local pub, where the game is played again with all the mistakes avoided – 'if only I had let that ball pass . . . ' The equality of squire and blacksmith on the fields of yesteryear may be a myth, but the game remains a great leveller as the garage mechanic thrashes the wayward bowling of an ambitious executive. Not that all cricket is played on village greens. With nearly twenty thousand clubs taking the field every weekend, factory sports grounds in towns and cities are as important as the village green. The game is imbued with the spirit of fair play, fielders applauding an opposition innings of merit, players standing aside to let a triumphant bowler lead the team from the field, ahead of his captain. When did you see a football team congratulating an opposing striker for scoring a goal? The very term, 'cricket', is synonymous with 'playing the game', its peculiar vocabulary part of our language – 'playing a straight bat', 'keeping your end up' or finding yourself 'on a sticky wicket'. When General Montgomery talked to his troops before the crucial battle of El Alamein, he told them that they were going 'to hit the enemy for six'. They knew exactly what he meant.

Why is it, that being so obsessed with the game, I have never really played? The question is often asked, and I have my excuses. I went to schools that had no cricket fields, growing up in East London during a time of war. It hides the fact that apart from street cricket, when opportunity occasionally occurred, I was singularly useless. Jim Blackshaw, medium fast, who with his family shared our house, played cricket for his firm and had been a member of East Ham Town club since he was fourteen. Every March, our house would be filled with the smell of linseed oil as he prepared his bat for the coming season. Aware of my new found interest in the sport, when I was fifteen, he generously paid half a crown to enrol me for the indoor school where his team practised during the winter months. To call it an indoor school in the present sense of the term, may be too grand, for it was a strip of coconut matting laid on boards, surrounded by nets, at Baalham Street Baths. Nevertheless, it was a chance to give an enthusiastic youngster a few tips and see how he might perform. It was an embarrassing failure. The myopic schoolboy, perhaps overawed in the company of men, bowled wide and groped to put bat to ball. After a few sessions I spared us both further shame and joined the many who would like to have been cricketers. To have played at any level would have been a joy, and maybe I should have persevered, for it is only a game.

Instead of playing, I have watched others play, and shared the game by storing images in the mind. My throwing is abysmal, but I can see Washbrook at cover point, returning the ball to the keeper with the speed and accuracy of a bullet; Compton, football fast on the boundary picking the ball a yard from the ropes and sending it a full fifty yards directly into the keeper's gloves. My bowling is erratic, but in my mind is Laker, left palm facing the heavens, hitting the right spot, over after over to take all ten wickets against the Australians at the Oval. How I prayed after he had captured the first nine, that Lock would not take the tenth. I play, and more often miss than hit with the bat, but in my mind's eye is Hutton and Graveney sweetly driving off the meat of the bat, Worrell, sleeves buttoned at the wrist, leg glancing with delicacy, and Miller, hooking with ease to send the ball to the very back of the Mound Stand at Lord's.

Sometime in April of every year, I see the first ball of the new season, bowled in a chilly wind on a local ground, at Bell Common or Woodford Green, and I watch for a moment and listen to the satisfying sound of a ball clipped away. Soon, the first class season will be underway, with easy runs for county professionals against the universities. Then, once more the beauty of Lord's beckons as the gates open and another *Wisden* is added to my bookshelves.

CHAPTER 8
Daily Bread

You go to work,
To earn the money,
To buy the bread,
To get the strength,
To go to work,
To earn the money . . .

That piece of repetitive doggerel, often recited by my father in a manner that was less than half joking, summed up the position of millions of wage workers. Payment for labour was calculated at a subsistence minimum, barely allowing an hourly paid worker to scrape by from pay-day to pay-day, compelled to repeat the cycle until reaching the age when he or she was too old to work, but not quite ready to die.

The trade union rate for a carpenter in 1939, the rate my father was paid, was one shilling and eightpence an hour (9p) for a forty-four hour week. There was no pay for absence through sickness and holidays with full pay were virtually unknown. Only two bank holidays were paid, Good Friday and Christmas day. The one week annual holiday entitlement was based upon accumulating a weekly contribution stamp throughout the year, but unemployment and short time working caused by wet weather ate into the collecting of sufficient stamps for the full week to be saved. Outdoor work, such as roof building, was impossible during heavy rain or snow and if no indoor work was available the workers would be sent home without pay. The result was that we never went away on holiday.

My father had followed his father into woodworking and the tools of the trade had been in his hands since infancy. Indeed, some of the tools that he used had been handed down to him from my grandfather as his only inheritance. The old tool chest which

113

stood on the landing outside my parents' bedroom was guarded as jealously as a jewel box filled with treasure, and every tool was hammer stamped with his name. The tools were handled with love, honed, oiled and worn to fit the hand with comfort. I used to enjoy just gazing at the deep yellow boxwood handles of the chisels, the rich rosewood and burnished brass of the mortice gauges, the sculptured curves of the spokeshave handles and the shark-sharp teeth of the blue steeled rip saws. The chest had sliding trays filled with a plethora of small tools, square topped nail punches, steel dividers, steel and brass shoe planes, bradawls, marking knives and tiny metal try squares. Wrapped dry, in a green baize roll with a series of pockets, were long twisting bits in ascending sizes, each curving spiral as sharp as a Gillette razor blade. Scattered throughout were stubs of oval shaped pencils and odd shaped tools made for special jobs, created to suit the purpose and the man. At the bottom of the chest were the rebate planes, weirdly shaped for a variety of mouldings and a self-made wooden instrument with moving parts that held a pencil and could describe a perfect oval.

My father started work in 1920, at the age of fourteen, a five-shilling-a-week apprentice to a cabinet maker at Maryland Point, Stratford, who made 'antique' furniture. They faked worm holes, aged chair legs by tapping them with rounded stones to simulate years of wear and applied a patina created with polish, colourings and cunning. When a job was finished, my father had to push the furniture on a hand barrow to a dealer at Bow. After a few years, the business failed and my father was unemployed, my grandfather was also out of work and the family of nine struggled to exist on the dole. It was a time of desperate poverty, and my father told how the younger children were put to bed as soon as they came home from school when there was no food. That was in 1923, and unable to find work of any kind, my father sought to lighten the burden on the family by joining the army, signing on for seven years in the colours and fourteen years on the reserve, a fateful decision that was to see him called up three months before the outbreak of the Second World War. The plus side of his early days in the army were the three square meals a day. When he came out of the army in 1930 he found work as a carpenter with a small local builder, W J Clemens. in Bridge Road, Stratford. It was rougher work than cabinet making, but it was a job, and preferable to the furniture sweat-shops of Shoreditch. He joined the Amalgamated Society of Woodworkers at the end of his first week in the building trade and remained a member for the rest of his life, including the war years.

He kept his everyday work tools in another chest, in the shed that he built in the backyard of our house. It was packed with brass-backed tenon saws, panel saws, hand saws, oil stones, claw hammers, giant jack planes, dark with age and use, smoothing planes of engineered precision, pliers, pincers, mortice chisels with battered and steel-rimmed bands at the top of the handles, and an ancient bow saw tautened with oily sisal and a wooden peg; tools he laconically described as for 'wood butchery.' In the early days of his marriage he could not afford to buy a carpenter's vice and so he made one, from wood, laboriously carving the thread by hand. Each morning he would fill his carpenter's toolbag and walk miles to work, the heavy metal tools stretching his arm muscles and banging his back before he started the 'daily grind', the euphemism he used for his job.

After the Second World War, his wage had risen to 'two and six' an hour, but it was not until the Queen's Coronation Day, a national holiday in 1953 that he finally received a full day's pay for a holiday without saving for it. Perhaps he was lucky. My friend's father, Reg Sprague, who was an engine driver, once drove the royal train. He was obliged to take a day of rest before the royal journey so that he would be fully composed and alert. For that privilege, the Southern Railway Company docked him a day's pay from his wages. When he complained, the directors rewarded him for his 'exemplary service' with a grocery voucher for one pound.

When my sister left school at the age of sixteen in 1950, to start work as a typist, she brought home a wage that was just a few shillings less than that paid to my father. He measured his lifetime of skilled work and the inherited tradition of craftsmanship against the untrained office work of his daughter, and the injustice of a system that despised the worth of craftsmen was obvious.

He worked on and off for thirty years with the builder, the off times being when he was unemployed due to the slump in the thirties and his service during the war. When he was fifty-five, he found the outdoor winter work in the building trade too much for him, and after thirty years with Clemens, he gave in his notice. The governor thanked him for his loyal service and gave him two pounds. He obtained a position at Queen Mary's hospital as a maintenance carpenter, a job which gave him enormous satisfaction, for he was a stalwart supporter of the National

Health Service. When he retired in 1969, he gave me his wage slip for his penultimate week at work, which I have used ever since as a bookmark in my first volume of Marx's *Capital*. It shows a grand total of five pounds, ten shillings, before deductions, a net wage of four pounds, eighteen shillings. (£4.90), the weekly reward for a lifetime of labour.

He measured his purchasing power in terms of his labour. A galvanised metal bucket cost one shilling and ninepence (8.5p) before the war, roughly the equivalent of one hour of his paid work. When he bought a new bucket in 1950, it cost five shillings (25p) and he was quick to observe the increased cost in labour terms, almost two hours work. He never read Marx, but he had an instinctive understanding of the theory of labour value.

His shed in the yard was a workshop, used for making the occasional piece of furniture for our home, repairs to the house and for doing the odd job for neighbours. During times of unemployment he would look for work on his own account, but competition was fierce and prices were savagely squeezed. He made stepladders for Boardman's, the departmental store in Stratford Broadway for one and six a tread, supplying his own materials. He described it as 'daylight robbery.' He would happily repair an old man's crutches or replace a broken window sash for a neighbour without thought of payment, but he never solicited for paid work unless he was unemployed. At the end of a week's work he felt that he had done enough. Some people expected him to make odds and ends for them on the cheap, and he taught me a basic lesson about work, based upon his experience. If you want to help someone, do the job free. Work charged at a cheap rate is never appreciated as such, and you will be expected to perform and deliver as if the buyer was paying the full price. If you are not prepared to do the job for nothing, charge the 'rate for the job.'

Despite the interruption of the war, when he was away from home with the Eighth Army for almost six years, I grew up in a practical world of wood and tools. My first building bricks were offcuts of oak, sandpapered smooth oblongs of even thickness but differing lengths, neatly fitted into a dovetailed jointed box. Bliss was accompanying him on a Saturday afternoon visit to the woodyard to select timber for a job, the tall lengths a sawn forest, the assorted woods offering as many scents as a herb garden. The circular saw buzzed and the sawdust fell, the softwood particles yielding an aroma of pine. In hot weather, the softwoods oozed tears of amber-coloured resin, sticky as glue. He looked at each piece with a true eye, hand picking the close-grained, knot-free straightest lengths with as much care as a sculptor selecting marble.

When he worked the timber, I would watch the shavings curl from the mouth of the plane, coarse as cardboard if he was using the jack-plane, or as sheer and light as paper if he was finishing with the smoothing plane. The woods offered as many colours as scents, from the palest of watery yellows through a spectrum that ran from ochres and umbers to the rich reds of mahogany and the night-blackness of ebony. Only blue was missing. When he used his chisels, as keen as surgeons knives, the sound was a crisp whisper as the steel pared across the grain. The work was quiet and thoughtful, set against the gentle bubble of the glue-pot, its cast iron outer filled with water, the inner with toffee-like slabs of brittle Scotch glue. A cloistering heavy smell blended with the aroma of cut wood as the gas-ring hissed and the slabs melted to a thick treacle.

I watched too, the joy of work with his hands, the way he slip-slapped a plane iron on the palm of his hand, to 'take the dairy off it', he said, as his flesh gave the final edge. He would squint along a piece of wood with an eye that could detect a twist measured in thirty-seconds of an inch, 'as cunning as your eye'. Close-toothed saws for cutting dovetails left sawdust as fine as sharp sand, male marrying to female as a key fits a lock, clicking into place. He made drawers of a cabinet with such precision that as you closed one drawer, the compressed air would force the next drawer open. He loved to experiment and would try his hand at jobs beyond his trade, wiping a joint when plumbing with lead pipes, bricklaying, french polishing and graining. Seized by a 1930s decorating fashion, he bought a red-rubbered stipple brush, stripped the woodwork indoors and stained and stippled half the house in two-toned brown.

Observing his work at the bench, I learned some of the tricks of the trade, and when he was demobbed in 1945 I turned to making small articles for sale, ziggurat art deco styled photo frames, small hardwood boxes, and clothes horses, hinged with webbing. Useful, but not a career, for my father advised against 'taking up the tools', for the work, as he put it, 'was not worth the candle.' In any case, by that time I had set my heart on working at a drawing board. Aspiration to become a draughtsman was shattered by a career's adviser at school who said that mathematics were essential, and reminded me that maths was my weakest subject.

'Could I become a commercial artist?', for art was my strongest subject. It was an occupation he had never considered.

Eventually, as I refused to yield to other suggestions, including training as a pharmacist, an appointment was made for me to attend an interview with a company called Display Craft. It was situated on the south bank of the Thames, next to a tall narrow tower built for the purpose of making lead gun shot for the Crimean War. Clutching a roll of Indian ink drawings, painstakingly penned on the kitchen table, a mixture of technical drawing, sketches and lettering copied from library books, I journeyed to Waterloo. With the hope and uncertainty of youth, I walked past derelict and bombed buildings to a spot where the Festival Hall now stands. Double gates opened into a yard surrounded by ramshackle buildings that could have pre-dated the Crimean War. Dickens would have been quite at home in the office, where I was interviewed by the company secretary, a tall, thin, pin-striped man with a squeaky voice. He looked kindly at my drawings, and if there was condescension, it escaped me. He explained the work of the company but did not show me around. 'Yes,' they did employ artists, and signwriters, making exhibition stands, multiple window displays and even floats for the Lord Mayor's Show. I could not be offered a job as a commercial artist immediately, but I could start as an apprentice silk screen printer, and if I progressed well, would be promoted to the design studio. The wage was sevenpence halfpenny an hour (2.5p) for a forty-four hour week, Monday to Saturday, with one week's holiday pay a year. The sight of a float which stood in the open yard, persuaded me, for there was an artist, brush in hand, painting a huge scene. I accepted immediately and in September 1946, I arrived for my first day as a worker.

I set off at six-thirty in the morning, walked half a mile to the bus stop and took a trolley bus to Bow Road underground station, where I bought a 'workman's return' to Waterloo for sevenpence halfpenny and a copy of the *Daily Herald* for a penny. I arrived at the main line station to a blare of stirring martial music, played over loudspeakers, presumably to awaken bleary eyed travellers. Another walk, to Belvedere Road, past the Lion brewery with the statue of a giant red lion over its entrance, and on to the yard of Display Craft.

I was shown into a small low workshop, catching my breath on the cellulose fumes from an internal spray-booth. There were a couple of wooden printing benches, piles of wooden drying racks, and in the corner, two drawing boards, where white coated men were already at their high stools. One of them, the foreman, showed me how to clock-on and told me to hang up my jacket on a nail and roll up my sleeves. I stuffed the packet of sandwiches I had carried, into a pocket of the jacket and was led to a galvanised metal tank. A job had gone wrong and I could sense the atmosphere of recrimination. Two thousand Bakelite panels, sprayed white and screen printed in three colours, advertising Fridgidaire refrigerators had to be replaced. The scarcity and cost of the materials forced retrieval, and my task was to strip the print and paint, back to the raw brown plastic. The galvanised tank was filled with paint stripper and I realised why I had been told to roll up my sleeves. For the next three weeks I worked at soaking and rubbing, my arms raw to the elbows with the stinging solvent. I came home after that first day disillusioned, tired, dirty, hands sore, arms and back aching, for I had stood all day, back bent over the tank, and collapsed into the solitary armchair. I reflected for some time on my future. So this was work, a life sentence, up at six, clock-in by eight, locked in all day, home at six-thirty, too tired for leisure, five and a half days a week — for we worked on Saturday mornings — fifty one weeks a year for the next fifty years. My father came in shortly after me, and the first words he spoke, still echo. 'Have you joined the union?' I had.

Somehow I endured the cleaning job, sustained by glimpses of work at the drawing board. I began to warm to the lifestyle of industrial work, the manly act of buying my 'workman's' ticket each morning, the camaraderie at tea break, when the eight of us who worked together would sit on the benches among the paint and the racks, talking of work and politics. I wore a boiler-suit, had a union card for the Sign and Display Trades Union, my fingers were paint stained and I felt part of the trade. I took to silk screen printing as easily as my father had taken to woodwork, though I still aspired to be a designer. Silk screen printing was a virtually unheard of process, still in its infancy. It was not printing on screens, but a method of printing by using stencils supported on a mesh of silk, stretched taut on a wooden frame, the paint forced through by pulling a squeegee across the mesh. It was a hand craft process that embraced the use of colour, the handling of paper, the skill of stencil cutting, the disciplined beauty of lettering, the production of artwork, the rudiments of woodwork and the emerging use of photography. There was daily improvisation involved in extending the process and Heath

119

Robinson would have found the workshop a source of inspiration. Nevertheless, it was a creative hand printing process that would surely have appealed to William Morris.

I was fortunate that the foreman, Ernie Girling and his co-worker at the drawing board, George Hipkin, were true craftsmen, combining skill of eye and hand with infinite patience. Girling's father had worked as a wallpaper printer in the Morris & Co. workshops at Merton, and his son had grown to work to the same exacting standards. He would never 'let it go' – pass shoddy workmanship – every step of the process had to be perfect. Just how perfection was to be achieved was not always easy to learn, for he jealously guarded the mysteries of the craft, imparting his knowledge gradually, never hastening to full disclosure. New techniques would be perfected in secret, behind a locked door in the dinner hour or when alone, late in the evening. It was a practice born of anxiety, a memory of pre-war days when unemployment was high and a bright but low paid apprentice a threat to the job security of the full rate craftsman. If you could engineer a position where you were the only one with the ability to handle the especially difficult jobs, your bargaining power was strengthened, your position almost unassailable. It took time to earn his trust, and then came that special relationship that develops between master and pupil. I learned to cut stencils in paper, as intricate as a lace curtain, to match colours, to 'see' the red in a grey or the green in a blue. I spent hours stirring the thick china-clay based paints, for they were not then referred to as inks, blending the shades to a 'spot-on' match to the artwork. The thick oil colours were quick to skin in open tins, forming a solid crust on the surface. No matter how carefully it was removed, flecks of skin were bound to get stirred into the paint causing streaks when printed. To avoid this, we strained the paint through a nylon stocking, pouring in the paint and squeezing it down the length of the leg by hand, the refined colour oozing over the fingers, leaving lumps of skin trapped within the toe.

In the confined space of the workshop, I breathed a daily mixture of the solvents we used, cellulose thinners, turps substitute and methylated spirits, all blended with the vapours of shellac, paints and gum Arabic. A trade cocktail. The printing itself was done by hand and the worth of an operator was measured by speed and accuracy. I was taught how to handle paper without creasing it, to float the paper on air as it was lifted with its wet print from the bench to the racks. There was joy and skill in every move.

Working conditions were primitive. The company employed about sixty people, working in a series of old wooden buildings situated around a large yard, resembling a Hollywood wild west town. One of the timber-framed buildings had been patched up by using old doors to cover the holes where the timber had rotted away. In clearing the knee-deep rubbish from an upper floor for an extension to the print shop, a man came across a door lying on the floor. He lifted the door, placing his hands, palms up, beneath the door, to raise it upwards so that he could carry it away. As he stepped forward beneath the rising door, he dropped through a hole in the floor that had been covered by the door, down into the workshop below, the door slamming flat above him in a slap-stick finale. Fortunately he survived without serious injury. The same building had a pair of double doors at one end of the upper floor and so much rubbish had been simply swept out of the doors over the years that it was possible to leave the upper workshop by running down the slope of compacted debris. Soon, the whole site would be swept away by Labour's re-development of the South Bank, launched with the Festival of Britain in 1951, as a 'tonic to the nation'.

My enthusiasm for screen printing led me to enrol for 'night school' at the London College of Printing, in Bolt Court, just off Fleet Street. I paid my own fees, and twice weekly after work I would walk over Hungerford Bridge, towards The Strand and Fleet Street. There, I studied the latest developments in the industry, involving process photography and the making of photographic stencils. I became familiar with the new smells, the cloying bouquet of collodian and the acrid fumes of fixer. My tutor was Frederick MacKenzie, a balding pioneer of the trade, known to us all as 'the Professor', later to make his fortune as the inventor of Letraset, an instant lettering process produced by screen printing. Fellow students were mainly ex-servicemen and after the classes we would congregate in the Moo Cow Milk Bar in Fleet Street. There, we would drink milky coffee and I would listen to stories of their experiences with the 14th Army, tales of harrowing jungle warfare against the Japanese. Nothing glamorous, just rain, leeches and cruelty.

At dinner times at Display Craft, some of us would take our sandwiches and sit on a moored barge where the yard led down to the Thames. It was a working river and we would watch the lines of cargo laden barges sailing the current, floating as easily as matchsticks carried by water in a gutter. Throughout the day, the sound of commentaries from the loudspeakers of pleasure boats could be heard and I learned the words without trying . . . 'on your left, is Shell-Mex House, its clock is the second largest in the world. The largest is in Times Square, New York. On you right, is the old lead shot tower . . . ' and the words would fade on the wind.

The founder and owner of Display Craft was Ashford Down, a religious man, tall and upright, with a clipped moustache. In the summer of 1947, as Edrich and Compton brought joy to a generation of schoolboys, Ashford Down brought us the Christian Crusaders. The entire staff was assembled in the yard, backs to the Thames, as we soaked up the sun and an hour of evangelism. The lure was an early finish to the day of work, all clocked off by three and paid until five. The words of the preacher competed with the amplified words from the pleasure boats . . . 'all can be saved' . . . 'the second largest clock' . . . 'time is running out' . . . 'in the world' . . . 'I would rather have Jesus than silver or gold.' I looked at the boss and thought, 'how nice to be him and have both.'

Time ran out for the factory, demolition was nigh. At the end of the summer, as work began on clearing the riverside site for the Festival of Britain, the business was moved to a former tram depot in Brixton.

My daily journey to work was extended; a walk to the bus stop, a trolley to Bow Road, buy my morning paper, now the *Daily Worker*, then take a District line underground train to the Bank, change to the Northern line to Clapham South and another long walk to Acre Lane. I thought of finding work nearer home, but I was happy in the company of my fellow workers at Display Craft, and the company was the largest and most progressive in the industry. I decided to stay, rising earlier and arriving home later.

Once a month I attended my union branch meeting, held at the National Trade Union Club, near Leicester Square. A couple of dozen of us from various firms would meet in a small room upstairs, filled with rows of hard chairs, in an atmosphere thick with tobacco smoke. 'Good evening brothers', there were women in the trade but none ever attended the branch. It was a male dominated industry and the union rule book referred to the 'Branch Chairman', the 'Committee men' and rule fourteen, concerning the duties of the President, read, 'He shall take the chair at the Annual Delegate Conference'. The prevailing attitude towards women was harshly demonstrated when I became involved in my only industrial dispute. The owner of Display Craft had introduced his two young nephews into the company, to learn the business. A number of us objected to working with non-union labour and I was informally delegated to raise the matter at the next union branch meeting. The chair was taken that evening by John Torode, the pioneer founder of the union and a veteran Communist. Towards the end of the meeting, under 'any other business', I raised the question of the two non-union nephews. 'What could we do?' 'I could tell you what to do if they were the boss's nieces,' replied Torode, joining in the peals of laughter that followed his innuendo. I had little understanding of the extent of the subjection of women within society, but I was shocked by the frivolous and coarse reply. I pressed the question and it was ruled that as they were related to the owner and were being trained for management, they did not have to join the union. Dissatisfied, I decided to continue to try and force their enrolment, and the following day went to see the factory manager. He could scarcely believe my audacity and made it quite clear that if I pursued the matter, I would be looking for another job. He sent for the shop steward, who had not attended the branch meeting, and told him to bring the affair to a rapid conclusion. A full meeting of members was called at dinner time and it was put to the vote, the steward speaking in support of the management. A large majority voted against my resolution calling for a closed shop and I was censured for raising the matter without being officially delegated.

It was a hard lesson. I believed passionately in the essential need for trade unionism and I felt let down by the union's General Secretary, Johnny Torode, let down by the shop steward who was intimidated by the management and let down by my workmates, most of whom did not support the principle of the closed shop. There was a strange sequel. The works manager called me to his office, sat me down and gave me a fatherly talk. He was not unsympathetic towards the union and explained that I had 'gone it alone', had not assessed the measure of support before raising the issue and had left myself isolated. He shook hands, recommended that I should read the Webbs' *History of Trade Unionism* and told me to get on with my work.

My enthusiasm for screen printing was undiminished by my tussle with the management and I continued to make progress towards becoming a proficient printer. The new factory was vast in comparison with the old workshops at Waterloo, but conditions were bare and cheerless. The former tram depot was about as cosy as an aircraft hangar. The winter of 1947 was bitterly cold and the factory was heated by an ancient system fuelled by a coke-fired boiler stoked by a septuagenarian. Despite his efforts to burn anything combustible, we worked in freezing conditions as fuel supplies broke down all over the country. Work became a test of endurance. To compound our difficulties, materials were in short supply following the years of war and priority was given to essential services, which did not include commercial advertising. Government posters on the hoardings carried the stark message, 'Work or want'. It was a battle for survival. With paper supplies virtually unobtainable, we slit and flattened cement bags, coating them by printing a solid white and trimming the smoothed sheets to use as poster paper. For showcards, the management scrounged for alternatives to white display board, and we printed on metal, Bakelite, plywood and raw strawboard. A wartime spirit of 'making do' prevailed, and we developed a natural stinginess with everything we used. Economy was the rule, nothing was wasted.

At home, I made a small screen of my own, a few wooden drying racks, and set up to print in our back room, now vacated by our lodgers who had moved to a house of their own on the opposite side of the street. Using offcuts of paper, the photographic facilities of the London College of Printing and free sample tins of colour, I soon had the house reeking with the smell of paint and turps as I spent the winter evenings printing a series of Christmas cards. I produced a run of two hundred and fifty each of four designs, which I sold to neighbours at sixpence each. After paying for the envelopes, I made a profit of twenty pounds, the most money I had ever possessed.

As I sold the last card, my call-up papers arrived for National Service. My career was to be interrupted by one and a half wasted years in the service of His Majesty. By the time my Christmas cards were dropping through letter boxes, I was an airman.

CHAPTER 9
Ginger's Back!

'Why do you want to join the Royal Air Force?' The terse question was put by a flight lieutenant with a penetrating eyes and a handlebar moustache. 'Because it is the most distinguished of the three services, sir,' I replied promptly. 'Jolly good', he purred with a satisfied smile and made an entry on an official looking form. I had misled him on two counts. Firstly, I did not want to join the RAF, or any of the other services, but conscription left me with small choice. Secondly, it was a popular belief that life in the air force was easier than that endured by those in the army or navy. Having been dragooned into the armed forces, I was seeking what I supposed was the cushiest option.

National service came as an unwelcome interruption to my career, and I enlisted with reluctance and considerable trepidation. A railway warrant and instructions to report for basic training at RAF Padgate duly came in the post, and on the 7 December, 1948, I caught an early morning train from Kings Cross for a journey into the abyss of military life. Seated opposite me was a lad of my own age with a downcast expression, jet black wavy hair, a wide-shouldered bespoke draped suit and a tie with a broad Windsor knot. We exchanged surreptitious glances and then I asked, 'You going to Padgate?', a question put in the hope of finding a companion to share my doubts and fears. He said that he was and we settled to an avid swapping of information, each of us sketching the background to our lives. He was Lionel Begleiter, from Whitechapel, the youngest of seven children, Jewish, a

125

commercial artist and the son of a tailor. There was an immediate rapport, partly because he was from East London, but also because he had succeeded in winning a scholarship to St Martin's School of Art and subsequently obtaining employment in a West End studio. His employer was Philip Zec, the brilliant cartoonist for the *Daily Mirror*, and Lionel chatted away about artwork and questioned me on my work as a printer. It may not have been an encounter to match that of Mr Rolls and Mr Royce, but it was a moment of fate, for we were destined to become business partners, artist and printer combining to build a flourishing design and print company and a lifelong friendship. Lionel was to go on to achieve world fame as Lionel Bart, the composer and writer of songs and musicals.

Lionel was gentle and sensitive, traits popularly and mistakenly attributed to all artists and was obviously apprehensive of future barrack room life, as I was myself, but he attempted to conceal his doubts and shyness with an outward worldliness. He talked of his father's tailoring business – which I later found was run from a small workshop in the backyard of his home in Stepney Way, his few workers having to pass through the room where the family ate their breakfast to reach their place of work – and I thought that Lionel must be well off. He went on to tell me that part of his own work in the Zec studios occasionally involved helping with the drawing of 'Jane', the famous strip in the *Mirror*, and this added glamour to the imagined wealth.

At Padgate, we joined hundreds of other gawky young men as we went through the induction process of being medically examined, 'cough, bend over, any lumps or bumps? OK.' Then on to be kitted out with rough blue serge uniforms, boots, shirts with detachable collars, shapeless underpants that reached to our knees and a white linen wallet containing needles, thread, spare buttons and a thimble, known collectively as a 'housewife.' Finally, we were given our service pay books and identity cards. From the moment of our arrival, Lionel and I stayed close together, clinging to a tenuous mutual security. As a result we were allocated consecutive service numbers, mine being 2416698 and Lionel's 2416699. They were to become the winning numbers in the lottery of service life as we were posted to various stations together, sharing billets and working in the same sections throughout our time in the RAF, building the relationship that was to shape our future for years to come.

Our first evening in the RAF came as a culture shock as we were billeted with an intake of Scotsmen, their accents from Orkney to Glasgow being almost unintelligible to ears tuned to cockney. At first, unable to distinguish the Celtic brogue, I thought they were Irish. It was not just the accents that were strange, but also the turns of phrase, 'What like is it?', instead of 'what is it like?' 'Ooch gingerrr', I was asked, 'Do you no have a book for reading?' What other kinds of books were there? 'Books for writing', of course. Lionel broke the border barrier and won instant admiration by sketching likenesses of the lads crowded around the coke-burning stove. Whilst most of us had arrived with toothbrush, razor and a change of underwear, Lionel had come equipped with his artist's materials, as if he were on some sort of a holiday.

For the next two months we never had a spare moment, from six in the morning when we were shouted from our beds by loud mouthed drill instructors, to wash and shave in cold water, until lights out at ten, when we collapsed exhausted after a day of square bashing and weapon training. It was a calculated process of breaking the independent spirit to mould us as unthinking automatons. When the DIs said 'jump', there was a Pavlovian response as we jumped like circus animals. The discipline was total and at times absurd. When a corporal instructor entered the billet, we had to spring to attention, but if we happened to be in bed, we were expected to lie to attention! It was a wonder that they did not check to see if our thumbs were in line with the seams of our pyjamas. The DIs were tough, fit and had absolute power. Tin Gods. Surprisingly there was no real brutality, but the will was assaulted with insults, sarcasm and humiliation. Assembled for our first parade, an Irish corporal by the name of Buckley, stood in front of Lionel with eyes burning from beneath the black, curved and shining peak of his drill cap, the peak flattened over his eyes so that he could only see by thrusting his chin upwards in a Mussolini pose. 'You're a spiv, what are you?' he shrieked. Lionel remained silent, as if petrified. 'Where do you come from?' he barked. 'London, corporal.' 'I thought so,' said Buckley, 'You are a fuckin' spiv, I can tell by your tie.' He pronounced it as 'toy', and staring at the broad Windsor knot at Lionel's neck, he proceeded to grab hold of the thin end of the tie while at the same time he pulled downwards on the thick end, drawing the knot tighter and tighter, then sliding it upwards towards the throat, the knot shrinking to the size of a tied bootlace as Lionel's face reddened. Buckley then repeated his rhetorical question. 'You're a fuckin' spiv, what are you?' But Lionel bravely remained silent,

127

a response known in the services as dumb insolence. Back in the billet the tie had to be cut from his neck, for it was impossible to undo the miniature knot.

For eight weeks we ran everywhere, dressing in full battle kit within seconds, polishing the toe-caps of our boots with spit, hot pokers and elbow grease, rubbing candle wax inside the creases of our trousers to retain a razor-like edge, polishing brass buttons and buckles to a mirror finish with Duraglit, lining our back packs with cardboard to keep them square, folding blankets with geometric accuracy and laying out our kit for inspection with a degree of precision that rivalled a Mondrian grid. It was impossible to resist any command, for apart from the threats of court martial and the glass-house, there was a system of control known as 're-flighting'. Basic training, the intensive course undergone by every recruit, lasted for two months and every new weekly intake was known as a flight. Any indiscipline carried the threat of being 're-flighted', that was, being put back to join the new intake and to start training all over again. Re-flighted time we were told, did not count as time served, and in theory, you could be kept in the service indefinitely. Under such a threat, we meekly complied, submitting to every stupid command given by drill instructors chosen for their dedication to producing an unthinking and obedient flock. Drilling to numbers we shouted the timing aloud as we made each move, 'one pause, two pause . . .'

We learned to respond when addressed as 'airman', not an easy reaction, for we had yet to see an aeroplane, to call raw recruits 'sprogs', to 'gen up' on aircraft recognition and get the 'griff' on what we were expected to do the next day. It was an insular male world of blue uniforms, icy parade grounds and bellowed commands. We ploughed over muddy assault courses, peeled potatoes in the cook house, marched in step, fired wildly on the rifle range with ancient Lee Enfields and sat through lectures on the Russian menace. I reflected that if all that stood between capitalist democracy and the Red Army was us, then I did not give much for our chances. This was confirmed by an older friend of mine, Johnny Barrett, from St James Road, who had been conscripted into the army and sent to Germany. Given the job of escorting a train to the British sector of Berlin, the train was stopped by regular Red Army soldiers who had fought from Stalingrad to Berlin. The heavily armed and fiercesome troops with fur hats, long greatcoats and hammer and sickle badges, halted the train at a checkpoint and asked him if they could search the train. Johnny felt that the request was more in the nature of a command, and with a sense of self preservation replied that as far as he was concerned, they could have the bloody train!

The culmination of two months' training was a grand passing-out parade before the gaze of a gaggle of officers and the Air Officer Commanding. As hundreds of airmen marched and countermarched to martial music, we silently sang to ourselves some unofficial words to the ceremonial air:

Stand by your beds,
Here comes the Air Vice Marshall,
He's got lots of rings,
But he's only got
One arsehole.

We left the parade ground with the obscenity still ringing in our heads and celebrated the end of our square-bashing ordeal with an evening of heavy drinking, being allowed out of camp for the first time. I had been a moderate beer drinker since I was fourteen, but this was my introduction to 'serious drinking', the pace being set by the Glaswegians who seemed blessed with hollow legs, swilling pints from straight glasses chased with neat whisky. It was also my introduction to Welsh hymn singing, as various taffies led us in drunken choruses of *Cwym Rhondda*, 'feed me till I want no more' seemingly appropriate to the occasion. Lionel, with his Jewish cultural background, was not a drinker and contrived to stretch a couple of beers to last throughout the session. He was wise, for that night the billet reeled as I lay on my bed and I swore that I would never drink again. Nature though, proved to have endowed me with a born resilience to hangovers and the vow was forgotten by morning.

During training we had been asked to select the trade we would like to follow during our national service, a farcical procedure for worthwhile skill training was reserved for those who were prepared to sign on for regular service. My choice of photographer, a skill that would have benefitted my career as a printer was ignored, and I was allocated for training as a clerk, an occupation for which I had neither aptitude nor inclination. Lionel, too, was designated for the same course, and having consecutive service numbers we shared the same posting to a training camp at Hereford.

Before relocating to RAF Hereford, we were given a short leave and I arrived home in uniform, feeling strangely proud of the wings on my shoulders and the gleaming brass badge in my cap. It was of course reflected glory, wearing the uniform of 'the few', a uniform that still marked the bearer as one of the 'Brylcreem boys' and the glamour associated with the popular image of Battle of Britain aircrew. Yet my feelings were contradictory, for I saw no glory in war, and had been shocked by some aspects of our battle training. During bayonet practice, where we were encouraged to scream like banshees and charge like Whirling Dervishes, we were taught to 'go for the stomach so that the blade does not get stuck in his rib bones', and when the victim was down to stamp on his face with the heel of one of our heavy boots and then twist it round, just to make sure that he did not rise. Angered by the insane violence, I wrote an account of our training in a letter which I sent to *Peace News*, the pacifist weekly paper which I had recently taken to reading. I was surprised to receive in response to publication, a letter from the Duke of Bedford, enclosing a wad of pacifist literature and I came close to declaring myself a conscientious objector. That I did not make the final leap of conscience was partly due to the fact that I could not persuade myself that pacifism would have halted the tyranny of fascism, and that only armed resistance had saved my generation from Nazi slavery and the concentration camps.

The training at Hereford in typing and filing was perfunctory, the billets often unheated and the food appalling to the point of often being inedible. It was left to a more spirited flight that followed us to make national news by going on hunger strike in protest against the swill they were ordered to eat. We had no opportunity of enjoying the beautiful Herefordshire countryside and after six weeks incarceration, the misery was ended as we were given our grades in a final examination and posted to our permanent stations. Lionel and myself passed out as aircraftsmen first class, just one degree higher than 'AC plonks' and once again were posted to the same unit. In the spring of 1949, we climbed into the back of a lorry and were driven to RAF Innsworth, a camp situated by a hamlet midway between Gloucester and Cheltenham. At last we felt like airmen, for at the entrance to the camp, just outside the gates by the guardroom standing as winged sentinels were a couple of Spitfires, embedded in concrete. That was as close as I ever came to aircraft during the whole of my service with the Royal Air Force.

The camp sprawled in the spring sunshine, nestling amid the rural landscape, a series of wartime wooden huts arranged in military rows, the roadways marked with whitened stones methodically placed at measured intervals. It was a large camp, housing regular personnel in married quarters, a few aircrew who appeared to have been posted there by mistake, for there were no operational aircraft on the base, hundreds of national servicemen and to my amazement and delight, WAAFS, their quarters absolutely out of bounds to all airmen.

Lionel and myself were allocated by continuing fate to the same billet, a narrow hut lined with two rows of iron bedsteads, heads to the walls, a dozen each side facing a centre aisle. The beds were separated by tall brown-stained plywood lockers, the windows of the hut were without curtains, the brown linoleum polished to a deep gloss and a solitary cast iron coke-burning stove in the centre of the aisle between the rows of beds the sole means of heating and the hearth and heart of communal life. This time, our fellow servicemen were a cross section of society, coming from the Rhondda, the Yorkshire dales, the northern counties, Worcestershire vales and various parts of Scotland. The lads came from widely differing cultural backgrounds although they were all basically working class, public schoolboys being carefully hived off for short service commissions as pilot officers. Our occupations in civilian life included a lobster fisherman, an engineer, the son of a shopkeeper, a clerk, a university student and a barrow boy from the Elephant and Castle.

For the next fourteen months we were to live as an intimate and artificially created family sharing a common ambition, to be demobbed. Service life resembled living in an institution, like a prison or a hospital. We got out of bed each morning at the same time, washed, shaved, paraded and had breakfast, worked, marched to the mess for dinner, went back to work, assembled for tea, enjoyed a few hours of free time, cleaned the billet and went to bed when the lights went out at the same time every night. Daily life was reduced to a monotonous unthinking routine with food, accommodation and clothes provided. There was no call for initiative, for we were told what to do by the minions of the officer class, corporals and flight sergeants who were in turn working to a routine laid down by the officers. The officers were seldom seen for they had their own quarters complete with servants called batmen, their own recreation area complete with tennis courts, a sport for gentlemen – other ranks played football – and their own

131

private offices for work. Class division extended beyond the confines of the camp, when officers journeyed their railway warrants were for first class travel, other ranks travelled second class. The Queen's Hotel, overlooking the Promenade in Cheltenham, was out of bounds to other ranks even if we could have afforded to dine there, which on service pay of thirty shillings a week (£1.50) was unlikely.

Officers when seen could be recognised not only by their insignia of rank, but by their sleek tailored uniforms and brown shoes, other ranks had rough standard issue and black boots. When encountered, officers had to be acknowledged by turning your eyes towards them and saluting. If they deigned to speak to you, which was rare, they spoke with condescension and upper class accents, usually to command you to do something, in the manner of prefects addressing their fags, 'I say Gorman, cut along to the orderly room with these files, quickly.' Class snobbery was personified when an officer asked my future wife, a WAAF, 'Where were you born', 'Plaistow, sir' she replied, pronouncing it as it is spoken by all who live there, 'Plarstow'. 'Oh yes,' the officer responded patronisingly, 'Playstow.' The exception to these stuffy prigs were the aircrew officers, remnants of wartime squadrons who had signed on for a few more years. They wandered around with their hands in their sheepskin-lined flying jackets, wearing white silk scarves and sporting luxuriant handlebar moustaches, exuding good humour and a cavalier independence. They were men apart from the pompous tailored dummies that commanded us.

I was put to work in a large office dealing with accounts, an absurd decision as maths was one of the subjects I had failed to pass in my final exams at school. We sat at brown oak desks arranged in rows, like a classroom, presided over by a WAAF officer who sat at a large desk at the front overlooking us in the manner of a schoolteacher. We worked in oppressive silence and I hated every minute of the interminable long days. Ahead lay the prospect of more than a year of boredom and at the end of the first week I considered asking for an overseas posting. Lionel, worked in another but similar office and was equally unhappy. With typical Jewish chutzpah he complained that he was unsuited for the work and asked for a transfer to another section. To the astonishment of everyone his request was granted and he was moved to take charge of the stationery store, a separated office at the end of a large section where he was left to work in splendid isolation. Although the work occupied him for only a few hours a day, he then asked the officer in charge, a tough Scots woman warrant officer, a wizened, bow-legged, sharp faced midget with the reputation of a martinet, if he could have an assistant. It was an absurd request, but Lionel always had a strong belief in his own ability to achieve anything on which he had set his mind and had a cunning but charming way of persuading people to accede to his demands. Against all probability, it was agreed that he should have someone to share the work. Having won the first hand, he then played his luck by specifically asking that I should be the one to join him. It was an audacious suggestion but for a reason that was never understood, the tough little Scots lady agreed. I was rescued from purgatory and together we were ensconced in the cushiest job on the whole station.

The stationery store was a quiet and private room lined with shelves and cupboards, a couple of desks, an oil stove, two ancient duplicating machines and a pre-war typewriter. The shelves and cupboards were stocked with thousands of forms, for the RAF ran a bureaucracy to rival Whitehall. Requests for forms and stationery would be brought to us in the morning, on the appropriate form of course, and we would have to have the order ready for collection by the afternoon. It was a task that on some days took minutes and never more than a few hours. Our only other obligation was to print the Unit Routine Orders on one of the duplicating machines. We had an endless supply of paper, pens and pencils at our disposal and the imaginations to make good use of them.

Billet living provided an education in life. I suppose that each of us thought that we all lived the same sort of lives, but communal living proved otherwise. Some were clean to the point of fastidious obsession, others slovenly, some were energetic and always active, others lethargic to the degree of sloth. Most smoked their cigarette ration, but others traded theirs for sweets, many drank at any opportunity, but the son of the methodist preacher had signed the pledge. While one lad spent his evenings reading Goethe in German, others plodded through Hank Janson. Muir, a lad from Orkney, where nearly everyone seemed to be called Muir, including their member of parliament, was innocent to the point of naivety. Prior to his call-up he had never left his island, had never seen a steam train, never been to a cinema or a city and had been solemnly warned of the evils awaiting him in the wider world by his minister. Bawdy barrack room life confirmed the

133

admonition that Satan was abroad and he constantly chastised us as 'wicked sinners.' Despite some uncharitable taunting for his Sunday-school-like fundamentalism he retained his integrity to his faith, ignoring the sniggers when he knelt in prayer by his bed on his first night to win eventual respect by his humility.

Discussion around the stove on winter evenings centred on sex, religion and politics, the first speculative for we were apparently all virgins. I argued for atheism and socialism, acquiring a reputation for being a bolshie, a barrack room lawyer hostile to authority. I urged passive non co-operation between us, the unwilling conscripts, and them, the regulars who wielded power. Support for my socialism came from the lads from Wales, where socialism was a religion and from the Scots and Geordies who came from the pre-war depressed areas and did not need me to persuade them of the realities of class war. Lionel too was sympathetic to the left, for he had a brother, Sam, a docker who had fought with the International Brigades in Spain, while he himself had witnessed the anti-semitic activities of Mosley's fascists in the East End. He had listened to the street corner Communist speakers in Stepney, especially the charismatic and handsome orator, Solly Kaye, and accepted the Communists as stalwart anti-fascists and champions of the poor.

My reputation as a 'red' grew when I returned from a weekend leave with a copy of Marx's *Capital*, loaned from West Ham Central Library. I had ordered the book, which was not stocked, and in filling in the form had to answer the question, 'Why do you want this book?' I wrote that 'I want to read it but cannot afford to buy it.' Although I called myself a socialist and supported the Communist Party on many issues, I was at that time not committed to the Party. I had asked for *Capital* because I had read in the *Daily Herald* that it was the most damning indictment of capitalism ever written and I wanted to learn more about the system of society which condemned most of its citizens to poverty. At the same time I was searching for political allegiance and my reading ranged across a wide spectrum of progressive papers and magazines. I read the Communist *Daily Worker* whenever possible, but I also read the *Daily Herald*, the newspaper of the Labour Party, the Co-operative *Reynolds News*, the Liberal *Manchester Guardian*, the weekly *Socialist Standard*, the organ of the tiny Socialist Party of Great Britain, the Fabian *New Statesman and Nation*, founded by the Webbs and Bernard Shaw, the *New Leader*, which had its origins in the Independent Labour Party,

Soviet Weekly and *Peace News*. All these were bought at random as the opportunity occurred and money allowed. My choice of reading was radical, but hardly catholic.

It was not long before my political views became known to the NCOs and officers, who for the most part regarded my preoccupation as eccentric and harmless. My Communist tendencies were first revealed to them during a routine inspection of the billet, when an officer made a rare appearance to accompany our flight sergeant on his weekly rounds. Our kit was laid out in regulation order on our beds and the hut bulled to glassy perfection when chiefy appeared at the door and shouted the standard order, 'Stand by your beds.' As they made their way along the rows of beds, pausing to inspect the prongs of forks and blancoed webbing belts for cleanliness, the officer started to open the lockers and peer inside them. These were not usually inspected and were crammed with personal belongings in disarray. Many of the lads adorned the inside of their locker doors with pin-up pictures of scantily clad film stars, not the nude shots that are splashed on page three of today's tabloid press or the centrefold of *Penthouse*, but publicity stills of film stars such as Betty Grable and Jean Kent, wearing copious twopiece bathing costumes and incongruous high-heeled shoes. These were passed without comment until my locker was reached. Opening the door, the officer gazed incredulously at the two pictures pinned to it, one of Karl Marx, with long hair and a suit with shiny lapels, the other of Stalin with drooping moustache and the uniform of Generalissimo. I imagine that the picture of Stalin had been clipped from a Soviet magazine for it was one of those awful retouched photographs that characterised official portraits issued from Moscow. The officer stood for a moment in disbelief, turned to the flight sergeant and murmured something I could not hear and then marched out of the billet.

The next day on parade, chiefy looked directly at me and then bawled in the manner given to flight sergeants, 'Come 'ere, Karl Marx, and hassume some hascendency over your fellow men. March this lot to the cook house.' It was a calculated move to place me in the invidious position of giving orders. From then on, whenever possible, the command would ring out 'Karl Marx . . .' Chiefy Askin, a jovial long serving regular, red faced and rotund, considered it a humorous response to my contempt for authority. Even more amusing, though not intended to be so, was when a warrant officer asked me to take a file to another section. As he handed it to me, he realised that it was marked 'secret'. He hesitated for a moment and than said aloud, 'Oh no, Gorman's a bit of a bolshie' and handed the file to another airman. The thought that anyone might have contemplated passing details of an officer's pay to the KGB I found hilarious.

Our days in the stationery store settled to a routine of doing crosswords, heating beans and toasting bread on the oil stove, reading books and magazines, talking, and marking the days off our demob chart as a prisoner crosses off the days of his sentence on his cell wall. We lived for release. The time occupied by actually working was minimal. Our days passed in indolence, wasted labour while the nation struggled for recovery from six years of war. Food, clothing and furniture was still rationed, cities scarred with bomb sites, tens of thousands homeless, millions of houses in a state of disrepair, and industry suffering from an acute shortage of labour. The government proclaimed to the people 'we're up against it' and campaigned for increased production, at the same time it sliced through the industrial training of hundreds of thousands of young men, consigning them to a year or two of idleness and effectively destroying the apprenticeship system. There was so much manpower within the armed services and so little to do, that officers vied with each other in the creation of meaningless tasks that would occupy the maximum amount of time. Polishing the insides of our coal buckets epitomised the insanity of conscription. The little real work that there was to be done was stretched to take as long as possible. We were trapped in an unreal world that was close to madness, a closed society based upon the profligacy of labour.

Neither Lionel nor myself were content to spend all our time in idleness and we both sought diversions from enforced boredom. Lionel whiled away some of his time by writing lyrics to popular tunes ridiculing aspects of life in the RAF. He had a clever way of rhyming unlikely words and squeezing long lines into short bars, a portent of his brilliant future as the best lyricist of the sixties. We sang the songs together and taught them to the rest of the unit in a spirit of satirical resistance. He loved to perform, and when our tyrannical WAAF warrant officer was away from the main section, he would emerge from the stationery store to act out his latest number to the delight of the airmen and WAAFs who worked in the outer office. He said that he had written his first song for the Victoria Boys Club, in Whitechapel, when he was twelve years old, evidence of his talent to string words together with an ease that matched his natural ability to draw and paint.

During national service however, his first creative love was art and he brought his artists materials into the stationery store where he sketched and painted. He did a crayon sketch of me which I kept for years, but sadly lost when I moved house many years later. In the evenings, he would make use of the social centre, a large hut that was seldom used, to hide himself away to paint. He worked on a full length portrait of a pasty-faced lad by the name of Kirkby. He entitled the finished work, 'The Pale Airman', entered it for the annual open show at the Whitechapel Art Gallery, where it was accepted, and subsequently sold to Lord Ismay for eight guineas, a sum I considered enormous. I often wonder who is the unknowing present owner of an original Bart.

His evening painting sessions in the social centre attracted the notice of a flying officer responsible for social activities and he asked Lionel if he would paint a mural to brighten the drab hut. Lionel agreed on condition that he could work on the mural during the daytime, a 'good skive' in RAF jargon, as he contrived to drag out the work for weeks. He chose as his subject a circus scene featuring two trapeze artistes, a man and a woman, swinging towards each other. His painting of the man appeared as a handsome and muscular figure, who from the size of the bulge in his trunks was obviously well endowed with the essential male attribute. The finished mural became the subject of artistic censorship when viewed by our squadron leader, a short, slight man, who may not have been so well blessed by nature. He prudishly argued that the size of the bulge in the man's trunks was too provocative to be displayed in a building that was also used by WAAFS. Lionel strongly defended his right of artistic freedom, but the issue was settled by the squadron leader using his authority to order Lionel to reduce the size of the offending bulge. There was no alternative but to comply and the great work was accordingly diminished.

Lionel continued to draw and paint, entering a poster for a United Nations competition, which he did not win, and securing the occasional commission to produce scraper board illustrations for the literary magazine, *John O'London*. He should have listened to his father's advice on the competition, for he would often counsel in his eastern European Yiddish accent, 'Lionel, don't go in for competitions, you might not win.' Competitions are about others being seen to lose, and who wants to be a loser. With Lionel producing artwork, I was anxious to resume printing and over a number of weekends I transported my equipment from home to the camp and set up a small hand-operated screen in a corner of the stationery store. To legitimise our activities we decided upon the production of a monthly magazine for the unit which we would jointly edit, with Lionel designing the cover which I would print. Official sanction was gained for the project, which I suspect was taken as evidence of a softening of our hostility towards everything connected with the service, and therefore to be encouraged. Although it was possible to screen print the cover in colour, the screen process was unsuited for printing the text. We decided to overcome the problem by obtaining estimates for printing the inner pages from a couple of local letterpress printers, one in Gloucester, the other in Cheltenham. This had the advantage of providing us with a valid reason for obtaining special passes which allowed us to leave camp during the day on unit business. Nobody questioned as to why it was necessary for two people to visit the printers, and we continued to make regular journeys like Siamese twins, contriving to make our visits last for an entire afternoon each time we left the camp.

One of our 'official' visits to Gloucester may have been instrumental in changing the course of British musical theatre. Having concluded our business with the printer, we sneaked off to the pictures to see an afternoon performance of *Oliver Twist*, starring Alec Guiness as a Cruikshank-like Fagin. It was a memorable film, and on our way back to camp Lionel said, 'One day, I'm going to write a musical based on that story and it will be better then any American musical.' It was an extravagant claim, even for Lionel whose imagination is untrammelled by the boundaries that limit other mortals, but ten years later as I watched the opening night of *Oliver!*, which won Lionel universal acclaim and adulation, I thought back to that afternoon of truancy and his prophetic words. Most musicals have a catchy tune or two, but Lionel's *Oliver!* was packed with singable songs combined with brilliant lyrics and a book treatment that created a new genre for stage musicals for decades to come. The clipped received English accents of earlier British musicals were replaced with raucous cockney and English as spoken with mid-European Jewish pronunciation. Gone were the Busby Berkely high kicking chorus lines, replaced with dance routines that had more in common with a good old East End knees-up. It was a musical that drew inspiration from the bubbling street markets of the East End, alive with colour, studded with working class wit and characters from London street life. There were to be many imitators.

Most weekends, we were granted a thirty-six hour pass, entitling us to leave the camp at noon on Saturday and return by midnight on Sunday. Those of us who lived in the south of England travelled home by coach, leaving the envious Scots and others behind. The coaches arrived at the camp just after twelve and we would dash from work to change into our civvies and scamper past the guard room as our passes were checked to escape for a weekend of freedom. It was like being let out of an open prison. The coaches which ran from the camp, and a number of other camps in the area, were part of a private and profitable enterprise organised by an astute national serviceman. He appointed agents in every camp to make the bookings in return for free travel, while he took a commission on every coach filled. The young entrepreneur was John Bloom, to make a fortune in the sixties by acquiring the Rolls Razor company and using the name to sell thousands of cheap 'Rolls' washing machines.

Lionel and myself made the journey to London nearly every weekend, and I enjoyed the fleeting panorama of the green and unspoilt English countryside as we travelled along the narrow A40 through Gloucestershire and Oxfordshire, a journey unmarred by motorways and the hideous red plastic of 'Little Chefs' and 'Happy Eaters'. On one such journey, Muir, from Orkney, made his first visit to London where he was to spend the night at the Union Jack Club which provided cheap accommodation for servicemen. He was almost delirious with excitement at the prospect of seeing the sights that he had only seen in picture books, especially looking forward to Buckingham Palace. As the coach reached Perivale on the Great West Road, we passed the Hoover factory with its art deco facade, gleaming white, emblazoned with a great 'By Appointment' royal coat of arms. 'Look Muir', said one of the lads, pointing to the factory, 'There's Buckingham Palace.' Muir expressed a doubt, but we all joined in 'Yes it is, look at the royal coat of arms,' and for a few seconds he gazed in wonder and belief before we all collapsed in laughter.

I used the weekends to change my library books, spending an entire Saturday afternoon browsing among the shelves, a retreat into sanity. In summer, sunbeams from the high windows caught the dust disturbed by the pulling of obscure titles from the shelves, in winter, the covers of books above the radiators curled in the heat and were warm to the touch. Poetry became a new passion and I risked derision by carrying volumes of Burns, Shelley and Walt Whitman back to camp for my weekly reading.

On Sunday evenings, Fred, John and myself would go to the People's Palace in the Mile End Road, often meeting with Lionel, to see a continental film. Well-meaning philanthropists had perceived the East End as part of a metropolis that, in the words of Sir Walter Beasant, 'Had no institutions of its own to speak of, no public buildings of importance, no municipality, no gentry, no carriages, no picture galleries, no opera.' The outcome was the opening in 1887 of the People's Palace, to bring culture to East London. The People's Palace was bombed during the blitz and rebuilt shortly after the war, but there were still no gentry in Mile End, for they merely lived off the poor, not with them. No matter, we availed ourselves of all the People's Palace had to offer, plays concerts, opera, and on Sunday evenings, foreign films. The price of admission was only one shilling (5p) for seats in the upper circle, and each week we devoured the social realism of French, Italian, and Russian films, sub-titled in English.

It was customary in theatres and cinemas to play the national anthem at every performance, and the People's Palace was no exception, a matter of some contention for many of the audience. The member of parliament for Mile End at that time was Phil Piratin, one of the two Communist MPs elected in 1945. Piratin enjoyed popular working class support in the East End, and it was mainly local people who packed the People's Palace for the Sunday evening film shows. As the anthem was played at the beginning of the performance, the audience, some sixteen hundred strong, should have stood, but row upon row remained firmly seated, half the assembly demonstrating their socialist republicanism with their bottoms. Enthused with the prevailing spirit, I joined the sitters in passive revolt against the establishment, an act of defiance made additionally satisfying if I happened to be in uniform.

After the performance, we would adjourn to the Bancroft Arms, opposite the theatre, for a quick pint, and then for Lionel and myself, a dash to Victoria to catch the coach back to camp. The coaches were not the luxurious monsters of today, but slow moving twenty-six seaters with a top speed of sixty miles an hour and low-backed hard seats that defied sleep. We would arrive back at Innsworth in the early hours, cold and cramped, to creep into

140

a dark and cheerless billet, reeking with the stench of sweaty socks, to snatch a few hours sleep before reveille.

Weekend release from camp was not always possible for you might be allocated a Sunday guard or fire picket duty. I turned the summer weekend internments to advantage by using Saturday afternoons to watch county cricket at the college ground at Cheltenham during festival week, or the Wagon Works ground at Gloucester. If there was no cricket at either ground, I would escape from camp before noon on Saturday and use the pulling power of my RAF uniform to hitch-hike to Worcester. There I could watch cricket at the beautiful ground by the banks of the Severn, seated in a deck chair with Worcester cathedral providing the backdrop to the most English of scenes. Cheltenham, Gloucester and Worcester were wonderful county towns, the very encapsulation of an England unchanged and untouched by war. Cheltenham was Regency elegance with the Promenade a blaze of flowers, its exclusive shops paraded by ladies in floral dresses, gloves and broad brimmed hats, accompanied by gentlemen in panamas. Gloucester was more plebian, but endowed with splendid medieval buildings, low beamed pubs and cosy tea shops. The surrounding countryside and villages presented an idyllic scene that might have been created for a tourist picture book. The pubs, villages, tea shops and cricket were all of a piece, a world apart from my Stratford, offering some compensation for involuntary exile.

In winter, the days at camp dragged as long as an English Sunday, time marked mostly by events in the wider world, for too many days followed a pattern that became a blur, one day indistinguishable from another. In theory, we were allowed out of camp for a few hours every evening, but in practice most of us were confined to camp by lack of money to spend. A diversion we could afford, was the camp cinema, a wooden hut that was evocative of the Splendid the seats hard and unbanked, the surroundings austere and the films chosen for popular appeal. We behaved like unruly adolescents, cheering the heroes, wolf-whistling the heroines and shouting ribald witticisms. At the end of the performance, a gramophone scraped out the national anthem and military police stationed at every exit would bawl out, 'Stand where you are', to preclude insult to king and country by an unpatriotic rush for the doors.

There was a pleasant pub within walking distance, the Hare and Hounds, but little else between us, Cheltenham and Gloucester. When funds allowed, a group of us would walk to the

Hare and Hounds to sit around the fire, making a couple of drinks last the entire evening. There was a companionship as warm as the fire as we talked for hours about our past lives and future hopes. One of the group that joined us from time to time was a Jewish lad from Stamford Hill, a personable Londoner who enjoyed the name of Alan Gershonblatt. I say enjoyed, because he was truly proud of his surname and insisted that it was really double barrelled, Gershon-blatt. From then on he was known to us as Gershonhyphenblatt. It rolled from the tongue with surprising ease. Back from one of his weekends at home he told us that Mosley was once again holding his fascist meetings in Ridley Road, a largely Jewish street market at Dalston Junction, not far from where he lived. He had taken part in an anti-fascist demonstration on the previous Sunday evening when four thousand ex-servicemen and women, mainly Jewish, had confronted several hundred fascists, who protected by large numbers of police had taunted the Jews by singing the Nazi marching song, *Horst Wessel*. It seemed inconceivable so soon after the war against fascism that our local variety of Nazis had emerged again to preach race hatred at one of their pre-war stomping grounds. Home on leave the following week I encountered a small group of fascists holding a street meeting and selling *Action*, the fascist paper, in Woodgrange Road, Forest Gate. I stopped to listen to the speaker who was in the midst of a tirade against the Communists, 'We have smashed the reds before' he cried, 'we smashed them at Olympia, we defied them at Cable Street, and we smashed them in Bethnal Green.' I could not resist the temptation for a provocative reply and shouted from the back of the small crowd, 'What about Stalingrad?' As a few burly stewards moved towards me, I fled.

In writing of Ridley Road, I am reminded of an old friend, Felix Scharf, a gentle and inoffensive Polish Jewish refugee from Nazism who fled to this country for sanctuary in 1938. He was found accommodation in a little turning off Ridley Road and on his first weekend in England, the home of democracy, feeling safe at last, he wandered into the market to familiarise himself with his new neighbourhood. To his astonishment he found himself in a seething crowd surrounding a fascist meeting. Unfortunately for Felix he was wearing a black shirt. Mistaken for a fascist supporter, the inoffensive refugee from fascism was set upon by three Jewish youths and given a pummelling before he could proclaim his race and allegiance. He was sufficiently acquainted with the English language to reflect on the aphorism about the frying pan and the fire.

There were many calls from trade union branches and other working class organisations for the banning of the post-war fascist marches and meetings, not an unreasonable position in light of the recent war. The Home Secretary, Chuter Ede, citing democracy in his defence, refused, and then made an extraordinary decision to ban all political marches in London for three months, making it clear that it would include Labour's traditional May Day march. It was an absurd decision by a Labour minister. May Day had been celebrated as international labour day since 1890 and was part of the cultural heritage of the British labour movement. Now, the right of the workers to march in solidarity with workers throughout the world was to be banned by a Labour government. Despite protests from the London Trades Council, the traditional organisers of the procession, Ede remained intransigent, insisting the march would be banned. The mass meeting in Trafalgar Square would, however, be permitted and I resolved to be there, in uniform.

I emerged from Charing Cross station to find myself wedged into a slow-moving throng of demonstrators, crowding across The Strand. Above the heads of the people the odd banner fluttered, while placards on sticks moved up and down as the wave of the assembly flowed inexorably towards Trafalgar Square. Then there was pandemonium, boos, roars and shouting, mingled with snatches of the *Red Flag* as the police launched a series of confiscatory sorties into the crowd, snatching and tearing at banners and snapping the sticks bearing slogans. A placard bearing the motto of the Electrical Trades Union, 'Light and Liberty', was raised higher out of reach, then, to a giant chorus of booing it disappeared from view, to be raised again, yards away to a burst of cheering as the marcher evaded the police. I saw a young constable trying to prise a little placard tacked to a broom handle from the fingers of an elderly woman. It bore a solitary word, 'Peace', painted in blue letters. She clung tenaciously to her proclamation and wrenching it free proceeded to belabour the policeman with the placard, the word 'Peace' rising and falling as she struck him repeatedly. I laughed inwardly at the irony as I was carried along by the sheer press of hundreds of bodies until at last the space of the square allowed some room to move freely. I positioned myself against the edge of a fountain and for an hour watched as thousands poured into the square, trade union banners, Communist Party banners and red flags raised in triumph as each new contingent broke through to join the thousands already massed.

At the end of the rally the word was passed that Harry Pollitt, General Secretary of the Communist Party, was to speak in nearby Cranbourne Street, and I joined hundreds of others, defiantly filling the full width of the road in marching to the meeting place. Pollitt stood raised above the heads of the assembly on a portable trestle-like platform, a solitary red flag fluttering alongside him as emblem and marker. Thick set, balding and dressed in a suit with a buttoned waistcoat, looking like the craft-skilled trade unionist he was, the former boilermaker stood proudly awaiting the crowd to form around him. I had often read articles by Pollitt in the *Daily Worker*, but this was the first time that I was to see and hear him. As he began to speak, the crowding hubbub subsided and his strong clear voice with its short northern vowels rang out, crisp and precise. He spoke quickly, without notes, a staccato condemnation of the banning of the May Day march by a Labour government yielding to a handful of fascists. His speech moved rhythmically to an attack on the right wing policies of the government and went on to expound Communist Party policy on wages, living standards and peace. His pace then increased as he talked with evangelical fervour of the first workers' state, the Soviet Union, and I was alternately mesmerised, exalted and finally moved to join in the thunderous acclaim as Pollitt outlined his vision of a future socialist Britain, a land where the creative and craft skills of the working class would be unleashed as we built a new society for ourselves.

With less than a year to serve, I finally decided to join the Communist Party. Political activity was officially forbidden in the armed forces but was impossible to suppress. I had openly argued the case for socialism since the day of my conscription and I now supplemented the arguments with a flurry of pamphlets and leaflets which were deemed subversive literature. The announcement that a General Election was to be held in February, 1950, marking the end of the post-war Labour government's term of office provided a platform for expounding Communist Party policy. Political discussion in the billet rose to a new level of intensity as everyone took sides in speculation as to the outcome. Allegiance was largely to Labour, with a smaller number of conscripts with middle class pretensions supporting the Conservatives and a smattering of Liberals holding the ground between the two.

I was encouraged in my lone protagonism of the case for Communism by news that the Party was to field one hundred parliamentary candidates and I was hopeful that the two Communist members of parliament, Gallacher and Piratin, would be joined by others. The candidate most likely to succeed was Harry Pollitt, standing for Rhondda East, a constituency that was already legendary in the folklore of the Labour movement with its incomparable record of trade union and socialist struggle. Pollitt had narrowly missed winning the seat in the 1945 election, failing by less than a thousand votes to beat the Labour candidate. Now, even the *Daily Express* was forecasting a victory for the Communist Party.

In the heat of the run-up to the General Election I persuaded the newsagent on the camp to stock the *Daily Worker*, much to the chagrin of the officers. The sight of the Worker being read at NAAFI breaks by young airmen was anathema to them, but the Party was an electoral force that could not be ignored. Our weekly education class, run by a genuine Liberal sergeant, became a forum for political debate and I would quote from the *Daily Worker* at every opportunity.

For me, the highlight of the election campaign was the broadcast by Harry Pollitt. With a hundred Communist candidates, the two main parties and the BBC were grudgingly forced to concede the Communist Party the right to be heard, if only to demonstrate the validity of British democracy. The solitary broadcast was restricted to eight minutes, at an off-peak time, but nevertheless offered Harry Pollitt a rare, if brief, opportunity to present Party policy to a national audience. Wireless broadcasts were relayed to the billets by a Tannoy system and on the evening of the Pollitt election address I ensured that our loudspeaker was tuned to the Light Programme. Most of the lads gathered to hear Pollitt, listening intently as he raced through Communist policy on wages, pensions, rents, housing, nationalisation, and the banning of nuclear weapons. It was a masterly condensation of the Party programme and his voice came into the billet as an ally in my isolated fight. The subsequent discussion raged until lights out.

On election night, I persuaded a corporal to let a group of us share his bunk room to listen to the election results as they came in on his wireless. In the stuffy, smoke filled room, we listened until the early hours, betting on the results from the better known seats. The first result came in at 10.30pm, a victory for Labour and I was elated, but it was to prove a misleading start. Soon the results alternated between Labour and Tory, with the monotonous repetition of the announcer, 'The Liberal and Communist candidates lost their deposit.' I went to bed long after midnight with Labour narrowly in the lead, full of doubt as to the final outcome. By mid-day the following morning the Labour lead was sixty-five, and without the sophisticated analysis that accompanies present day elections there was still hope of a substantial Labour victory. Gloom came during the afternoon with the news that Gallacher and Piratin had lost their seats and that Pollitt's vote had slumped to under five thousand. Although Labour polled a record number of votes, even more than they had in the 1945 election, they finished with a lead of only sixteen seats and the Communist Party was obliterated as a parliamentary party.

After the excitement of the election had passed, my thoughts centred on demob, just four months away. We were now old hands at playing the service game of dodging the column and impending release increased our disregard for the petty regulations of service life. Paying the Scots lads, who were too far from home to travel to and fro in a weekend, to do our monthly guard duties became common practice, ten shillings (50p) being the rate for the job. Lionel, who had an inborn aversion to domestic chores and an income supplemented by his father, regularly paid to have his bedspace polished and his equipment cleaned for weekly inspection, rather like a prison baron. We both laid in bed until well after reveille which was signalled by a siren, with Lionel singing to the tune of *My Happiness:*

> Air raid siren's just sound-ed,
> Got another hour in bed . . . .

More than once we appeared on parade with uniforms hastily pulled over pyjamas, creeping back to the billet during the morning to change, Orders from corporals, especially national service corporals whom we regarded as traitors, were openly challenged or simply disregarded. It was left to higher authority with the threat of jankers to enforce minimum discipline.

In London, the fascists had maintained their activities and threatened to march through the East End on the anniversary of the 'Battle of Cable Street'. On 4 October, 1936, Mosley had rallied his Blackshirts for an inflammatory invasion of the Jewish East End, but had been thwarted by hundreds of thousands of Londoners who blockaded the streets, led by the Communist Party with the anti-fascist slogan, 'They shall not pass'. The fascist plan to repeat the provocation, led to the Home Secretary, Chuter Ede, renewing his ban on marches in London, extending it to once again cover the annual May Day march. At home on leave for May Day, I joined with thirty thousand trade unionists as we marched in defiance of the ban, fighting our way into Trafalgar Square to hold a mass demonstration in solidarity with organised labour throughout the world. It was a massive rebuttal of Ede's ban, and despite reports in capitalist newspapers like the *Daily Mail* that the ban on the May Day march had been successful, my own participation and subsequent photographs in the *Daily Worker* nailed the lie.

Back in camp on the Monday morning I appeared on parade with a red London Trades Council badge in my buttonhole. It was soon spotted by our flight sergeant, who asked, 'What the hell is that, Karl Marx?' 'A May Day badge, flight.' 'Get the bloody thing off,' he ordered, with a wry look that said, 'I am being tolerant but don't push your luck.' With some humour he retaliated by including my name among those selected for the honour of taking part in the king's birthday parade. Apart from the dress rehearsal, the long hours spent in pressing my 'best blue', the uniform reserved for such occasions, the bulling of boots and buttons, and having my hair cut to the strictest regulation short back and sides, the ceremony was concluded with a compulsory church parade! Chiefy enjoyed every minute that 'Karl Marx' spent paying homage to God and the king.

With the end of national service only weeks away for most of us, there began a series of nightly demob parties as old friends reached the completion date for their intake. Impending release was celebrated by mass gatherings in a local pub where all good sense was abandoned in bouts of drinking that lasted until the call for 'time gentlemen please' and we were driven onto the pavements by a tired but richer landlord. On one of those jaunts, whilst walking with Lionel and some of my closest friends towards a chosen tavern, a running child tripped and fell, grazing his knees and howling with hurt. A WAAF, one of a party joining us for the evening, picked him up and consoled him with such tenderness that I was taken with the instant thought that if I ever married, and I had no such intention, that this was the kind of

147

woman that I would choose as the mother of my children. It was Pamela, a dark haired, brown eyed, soft spoken and shy country girl. During the evening we talked amid the riot of drink and song and I learned that she came from Faversham in Kent, but had been born in Plaistow, East London, and had spent some years of her childhood living in Stratford, just a couple of turnings from St James Road. Her grandfather's fourteen children had all gone to St James school, including her mother. Pamela too had started her schooling at St James and had been taught by Miss Forbes, before the family moved to Leytonstone. As infants we must have passed each other in prams and push-chairs. Once again, it was one of those rare coincidences in life as we were drawn together by chance and chemistry to produce, not just affection born from common ground, but that inexplicable mutual feeling between two beings that demands the sharing of life. A goodnight kiss sealed our instant love and in little more than a year we were married.

Lionel and myself held our demob party at the New Inn, Gloucester, where we packed more than a hundred into a private room, everyone chipping in to a kitty that raised enough money to drink ourselves stupid. That we were more than merry is beyond dispute. Those that lasted until closing time were left to jam the last double decker bus to Innsworth, singing the *Red Flag*, to be continued as I led a chorus of inebriated airmen in repeating the revolutionary hymn outside the guardroom. All reason and caution was washed away by a euphoria made from English ale floated with a surface dressing of cheap ruby port. The guard commander was asleep and the two national service bods on duty at the gate told us to 'piss off' before he awakened. Through the swirling mists of alcoholic stupor we grasped the words of reason and retreated in ignominious disarray. The next morning there was an inquiry that threatened to postpone our demob. We were blameless, for it was not the echo of rebel voices that had the camp buzzing but the action of some airmen from Station Headquarters who must have had even more to drink than us. They had been seized with the bright idea of sawing down the main flagstaff. That they had accomplished the task without injury was a remarkable feat, for they were very drunk and the pole was at least twenty feet tall. Apparently they were interrupted before they could finish sawing it up into logs but they escaped without detection and their achievement remained to become part of folk legend at RAF Innsworth.

I struck the last day from my demob chart with a final diagonal flourish and then proceeded to lace the filing cabinets in the outer office with Communist pamphlets which I inserted at random. I stuffed then into manilla envelopes containing dry records on officers' pay, buried them amid yellowing stacks of printed forms and pushed them into the drawers of desks. An archive of Communist literature was left like a time capsule for posterity. Over the years since I have often chuckled at the thought of an officer retrieving a file marked 'secret', or even 'most secret', to discover a flaking pamphlet by Harry Pollitt or Lenin hidden amidst those RAF documents. It was a final and youthful 'two fingers up' to the military.

As Lionel, myself and a few others packed our kitbags for the last time in readiness for our journey to a demobilisation centre in the Midlands, we made our goodbyes. Sleeping, washing, eating and working with others in a closed community creates a special relationship and our farewells were made with a mix of elation and regret. We promised to 'keep in touch', to write to Newcastle, Cardiff and Glasgow, confirming bonds of life-long friendship with those we left behind. Apart from Lionel and Pamela they were to vanish like ghosts to another world.

An airforce recruiting poster of the day depicted a young ginger-haired airman, smiling and waving, with the caption, 'Ginger's back! Join him in the RAF'. I had often returned from leave to poke my head around the billet door and call out the slogan, 'Ginger's back!', to be invariably met with a hail of boots and abuse. I left the billet after handshakes all round, closed the door and could not resist returning a few minutes later for a final 'Ginger's back!' I slammed the door quickly against the anticipated hail of missiles and walked away laughing. I was never going back!

CHAPTER 10
How's Business?

During our long hours together in the seclusion of the stationery store at RAF Innsworth, Lionel and myself had often talked of working together when we were demobbed, of working for ourselves, but the translation of ideas into action demands not only the will, but the means. I had no savings, neither did Lionel. The first prerequisite to becoming a capitalist, even of the petit bourgeois self-employed variety, is capital. It was not that I had any aspiration to become a capitalist, but I had a William Morris-like idea of working with my hands in my own craft workshop where quality counted for more than profit. Lionel said that he could borrow fifty pounds from his sister, Renee, and that if I could match it we should set up our own business as designers and printers.

I talked the proposition over with my parents who confirmed what I already suspected, that they did not have fifty pounds. My mother at that time was 'doing homework' to supplement her housekeeping, pinning shirts to cards, inserting celluloid under the collars and packing them in cellophane bags. She was paid about tuppence a shirt, (less than 1p) and that included ironing every shirt before it was packed. By working twenty hours a week she could just about make ten shillings (50p). Mum said that the only one of our relations who might have the money would be her brother Tom from South Shields. He had been apprenticed before the war as an upholsterer, but upon demob he had opted for greater security and joined the prison service. The memories of pre-war unemployment in Shields, an officially designated depressed area, led him to take a job that offered a house, a uniform, meals and a pension. It was a life sentence in Durham gaol, but he thought it preferable to the threat of the dole queue. Tom had managed to save some money and generously offered a loan of fifty pounds, a selfless risk, secured only by family loyalty. To have asked for the loan must have been hard for my mother, for like so many working class mums she avoided debt, even during times of severe deprivation, choosing to go without rather than borrow money.

I was still uncertain about taking the risk but the decision was settled for me by my employers at Display Craft. It had been understood that when I returned from national service I would be given a job in the studio, a step towards realising my ambition to become a commercial artist. Now they reneged on the agreement, insisting that I remained as a printer. I was a good printer and I enjoyed the satisfaction derived from printing by hand, but I could not see myself tied to the bench for the next fifty years. Apart from that, the denial of the opportunity, promised when I started work with the company, was so unfair. I was bitter at the refusal and I promptly responded by giving a week's notice. That evening I told Lionel that I was free to start business and that I could raise fifty pounds.

I collected my last pay packet and with another five or six pounds to top up the borrowed fifty, I was a business man with capital. Well, not quite, for the business was still only a shared idea. Our very first business decision was to choose a name for the company. With youthful conceit we agreed to base the name upon the initial letters of our surnames, Begleiter and Gorman? Gorman and Begleiter? The latter we felt had subtle connotations with Great Britain and after hours of wrangling the name G and B Art Service was settled upon. It was a clumsy name and some years later we abbreviated it to G&B Arts, to become known in time throughout the industry simply as G&B.

Neither of us had any experience of business, but with the help of an accountant introduced by Lionel's father, we registered the name as a partnership. The accountant, named Schiff, was a gross figure with a pin-striped covered paunch and black beetling eyebrows. Thick black hairs sprouted from his nose like two protruding brushes and his jowls spread so that his face was square, his large head sitting on his body without any visible neck. 'You mutht now open a bank account', he said, lisping the words 'I will come with you.' An appointment made, he said 'Leth take a cab.' I had never been in a London taxi and now felt as though I was embarking on an adventure, journeying into a world of commerce in the style of a business man. I soon learned that there is a price to be paid for style and watched with alarm as the meter relentlessly ticked up the fare from his office in the West End to a bank in Whitechapel. Lionel paid, tipping generously, and our capital had depreciated by seven and sixpence (38p). The bank was an institution with a public facade that fronted a closed world. I had never set foot inside a bank, nor did I know of anyone who had a bank account. Banking was for business people, not the working class. If workers contrived to save a few pounds, the Post Office Savings Bank was their recommended depository with its sixpence in the pound interest. To keep the masses from intruding into the privileged world of finance, the banks opened only when the workers were safely locked up in factories, shops and offices for the day, and closed before they were let out. Banks opened on Saturday mornings, but people worked on Saturday mornings, As the noon day factory hooters sounded, the banks promptly closed.

The interior of the bank was as solid as its stone columned exterior. The broad flat counters were of rich polished mahogany, the fittings solid brass, the tellers all male with stiff white collars, cufflinks and dark suits. The inkwells were brass with white ceramic liners and long pens scratched entries into thick ledgers. Even in my bespoke suit I felt shabby as Schiff asked the chief clerk for the manager. I glimpsed sight of more money than I had ever seen, coins were scooped onto the tall scales that stood on the counter with small brass shovels, pristine bank notes were handled in hundreds, each one as crisp as an ironed copy of *The Times*. The manager was questioning. 'What machinery did we intend to buy and how much would it cost?' My explanation that screen printing was a hand process and that my father would make a bench, screens and racks from second hand timber taxed his belief. Despite the improbability of such a venture succeeding, our enthusiasm, confidence, and the presence of Mr Schiff must have won qualified approval, for after our precious one hundred crumpled pound notes had been safely deposited, his soft pink hand shook ours in turn and we were wished success. Outside the bank, Schiff hailed a cab and left. We sat on the wall of a bombed building next to the bank scrutinising our pristine cheque book and paying-in book with curiosity, wondering how long would it be before we had a cheque to pay in?

The next task was to find premises and Lionel appeared with a copy of the *Hackney Gazette*, an East London newspaper with a large circulation, renowned for its classified advertisement columns. 'Av an ad in the 'Ackney' was its catchy and colloquial slogan. There was a listing headed 'workshops', mainly advertised as suitable for tailoring, but among them was 'two basement rooms and a scullery' for twenty-five shillings a week (1.25). Within hours we were in Elderfield Road, Hackney, descending down narrow wooden stairs into subterranean rooms probably intended for servants. Daylight entered the front room from an iron grating above, which allowed the light to filter through the grimy window panes of a pair of French doors that opened onto a tiny area filled with rubbish that had dropped through the grating. Off the room was a coal cellar, where coal could be delivered through a hole in the pavement by lifting an ornate cast-iron cover. The back room was smaller, light entering through another pair of small French doors leading to a bricked area. The scullery had the usual shallow stone sink, a single cold tap and a dilapidated lavatory. Above us, on ground level, was an old fashioned sweet shop run by a dear old lady who lived in two small rooms behind the shop, The two upper floors of the house were occupied by the Feldmans, German Jewish refugees from fascism. The basement rooms were tiny and dingy, but they were cheap. On 14 October, 1950, Lionel and myself signed an agreement to rent the premises, 'for business use only' and we were given a rent book. We were in business. Lionel said that from now on, whenever we met friends, they would not ask 'how are you?', they would say, 'how's business?'

Our first day in business became known to us as 'black Saturday'. We had resolved to clean the basement workshop in readiness for the installation of our first bench and drawing board and set to work with more vigour than we ever mustered for an RAF bull night. The floors were swept, windows cleaned, light bulbs fixed, the brass tap polished and the rubbish cleared from beneath the grating. It was then that we contemplated the coal cellar, a foot deep in fine coal dust, accumulated over half a century. We realised that the coal-hole as we called it, would make a suitable store for our inks and inflammable solvents, for apart from the wooden door, it was a room of brick with a roof of stone capped with London paving stones. Lionel went off to Chatsworth Road market and returned with a couple of potato sacks scrounged from a greengrocer. Carefully we half filled the sacks, for that was as much as we could carry, while trying to

SOUVENIR
of

1940

COPYRIGHT XPDOGRAPH

1   *As I was, in the blitz of 1940.*

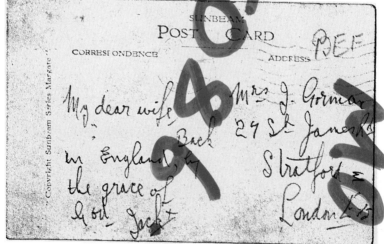

2 *Miss Jude, with her class at St James Road Church of England school, 1937. I am in the middle row, fifth from the left. We were, of course, dressed up for the occasion.*

3 *Back from Dunkirk. My father's pencil scrawled message on a seaside postcard from Margate.*

4   *Queuing for a meal at the British Restaurant in Water Lane, Stratford, 1941. My first experience of dining out.*

5   *Studio photograph of my mother, my sister Dorothy and myself, taken in 1943 to be sent to my father on active service.*

6   *My father, 1943, somewhere in North Africa.*

7 *Outside our billet at RAF Innsworth. I am standing next to the flight sergeant, on his right. Lionel is on his left, holding the forage-cap.*

8   *The poster that haunted me throughout my time in the RAF. I was never going back!*

9 *With Lionel, outside the entrance to our basement workshop, at 53 Elderfield Road, Hackney, 1950. Note the sole of Lionel's right shoe, parted from its upper.*

10 *Screen printing in our basement workshop on a Sunday morning. The hideous wallpaper reminded me of Oscar Wilde's words as he lay dying, 'My wallpaper and I are fighting a duel to the death. One of us has to go.' We went, evicted by order of the Hackney Borough sanitary inspector.*

11 Pamela, centre in white sweater, on her government secretarial training course, 1949. She passed with the highest marks.

12 With Pamela, posing for our wedding photograph in the backyard of our home in Stratford, 1951. The corrugated asbestos roof on May and Alf Giles' scullery was a temporary repair for the slate roof blown off by a V2 rocket in 1944. Her tin bath survived the blast.

13 Halcyon days. Pamela with our son and a friend, on our summer holiday, 1956.

14 *Programme cover designed by Baron Moss for the 1951* Daily Worker *rally at Harringay Arena. Speakers included John Campbell, the Dean of Canterbury and Harry Pollitt.*

'I GOT A PROPELLING PENCIL. WHAT DID YOU GET?'

15   *Street party for kids, gathered outside Sarah and Jim Blackshaw's house, Coronation Day 1953. Our son John is sitting on the pavement, talking to a young chef.*

16   *Gabriel's Coronation cartoon for the* Daily Worker.

17 'Peace for our Children', my first limited edition screen print, for the Communist artist, Sheila Dorrell.

TENANTS
PUBLIC MEETING

THURS., MAY 5th 8 p.m.

St. James' Road School

■■

SPEAKERS :

Mr. W. T. WILLIAMS, M.P.

Cllr. F. C. JORDAN (West Ham)

Mr. J. GLOVER

(Sec., West Ham Tenants Campaign Committee)

CHAIRMAN :

Mr. J. GORMAN

(St. James' Road Area Tenants' Assoc.)

Repeal The Act

18   *United in fighting the 1954 Housing Repairs and Rents Act.*

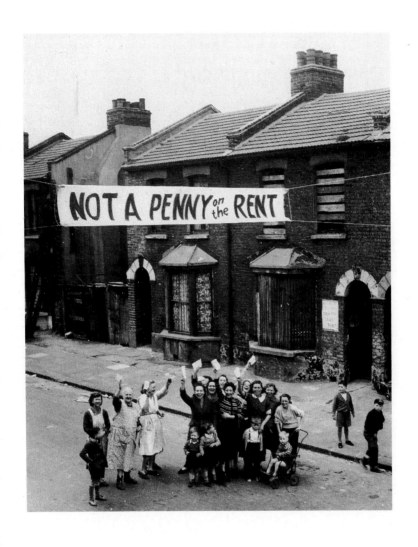

19 *April 1954. Tenants in Biggerstaff Road, Stratford, wave their 'certificates of disrepair'. The banner was painted in my studio at Dalston.*

Pay	Wk/Mth Date	Hol. Pay	Reg. Hrs.	Rate	Over Time	Rate	Amount										Gross Pay Week/Month		
							£	s.	d.	£	s.	d.	£	s.	d.		£	s.	d.
	6/6/69		40	2/9			5	10	0								5	10	0

Total Deductions			Gross Pay Less Deductions						Total Amount Paid			No.	NAME
£	s.	d.	£	s.	d.	£	s.	d.	£	s.	d.		
	11	8	4	18	4				4	18	4	15	J. Gotman

20   My father's penultimate pay-slip. The reward for a week's work after a lifetime of skilled labour.

21   Pamela and myself, some time after our resignation from the Communist Party in 1956.

prevent the clouds of coal dust from spreading to the freshly cleaned rooms. To dispose of the dust we agreed to dump it on one of the many bomb sites in the surrounding streets. We hoisted the sacks upon our shoulders, and leaving a fine trail of coal particles sieving through the sacking, we made a crouching journey to a site a few turnings away. After a couple of hours and half-a-dozen journeys, with stretched arms and aching backs we emptied the last sack against a fence at the back of the site.

As I straightened up I was grabbed by a furious red-faced man with a yell of 'Gotcher'. 'I'm fed up with people dumping their rubbish next to my garden', he shouted, 'This is not a rubbish dump, now I've caught yer I'm g'nner send for the law.' I had a fleeting vision of a court with a serious judge, 'determined to make an example . . . anti-social . . . vandals . . . against the bye-laws . . . fined twenty-five pounds.' I saw our working capital slashed before a print had been taken. We pleaded with the red-faced man but our pleas were fiercely rebuffed. It was obvious that rubbish dumping on the site was the bane of his life and now that he had a culprit in his grasp he would surrender him only to the police. I considered wrenching myself free and fleeing, but realised that even if we escaped now we would be bound to encounter him again. From a safe distance, Lionel put a proposition, 'we will take all the coal dust away.' 'Oh no, yer not g'nner ger away like that' and he tightened his hold on my arm. Lionel countered, 'alright, you keep hold of him while I go and fetch something to take the coal away.' The man was unsure, but while he wavered Lionel was off. The man loosened his grip and I sat on some rubble while he stood guard over me. Where Lionel had gone to and what he had in mind I could not imagine. I believe that both the red-faced man and myself were beginning to doubt if Lionel would return when he appeared, pushing a costermongers' barrow, hired for five bob from the market. We spread the sacks on the barrow and heaped the dust high to form a huge coal tip. By now we resembled a couple of minstrels from the Hackney Empire and with final apologies to the red-faced man we heaved and grunted our way back to Elderfield Road. 'At least we will not have to carry it down those stairs' Lionel said, 'We can push it down the coal hole.' We lifted the patterned cast-iron cover, and started to bucket the coal from the barrow to the hole in the pavement. After a while we sat on the kerb for a rest, two sweaty, tired and blackened figures, the object of some curiosity from passers-by, when my father appeared from around the corner. 'Hello, I thought that I would come and see how you were getting on with your first day in business.'

My father built our first printing bench using timber from the old railway fence that ran along Forest Lane. The fence was being replaced after sixty years with a concrete barrier and Dad was quick to ask the workmen if he could have half a dozen of the planks. They were ingrained with soot, and he sweated with his heaviest jack plane to turn the rough sawn, railway blackened wood into smooth clean boards. Our workshop slowly took shape, Lionel's drawing board set up on an old kitchen table, wooden racks made for drying the prints, shelving fixed to take the tins of printing ink, silk stretched taut on the wooden printing frames, and squeegees made in a variety of sizes. Lionel painted a sign for the street door, 'G and B Art Service, commercial artists and silk screen printers'. We had business cards printed by a jobbing printer in Jubilee Street, Stepney, and bought an invoice book from Wilson and Whitworth, the stationers in Stratford High Street. What we lacked were orders.

We had launched our venture oblivious of the times in which we lived and the difficulties we would face. Britain, still recovering from the war, was now embroiled in another war, in Korea, and the shortage of materials of every kind, already acute, was now exacerbated by the demands of the military. Printing paper was in short supply and allocations were made only to established accounts. We tramped the length of Upper Thames Street, Blackfriars, a street of paper merchants, pleading for some double crown poster paper. In desperation we crossed the palm of a counter clerk with a florin (10p) and emerged with two reams, staggering back to Hackney by bus and foot. Showcard board was as scarce as bananas in wartime and we were faced with a dilemma, did we seek orders and then search for materials or did we anticipate the character of non-existent orders and search for the stock we might need?

A further setback came when we tried to obtain a telephone. We were in an area where demand was high, the materials for new lines in short supply and the waiting list a year, even for businesses, which were considered priority. There was no phone in my home, in fact there was only one phone in the whole of St James Road, and that belonged to a bookmaker. Working people did not have phones. However, Lionel's parents had recently moved to Stamford Hill, and his father with his little tailoring business had a phone in their new house. We could use that, but who would answer the calls? Lionel's Galician born mother, who had migrated to Britain at the turn of the century, never did come to terms with the instrument. If Lionel rang in from a call box to ask if there were any messages for him, the conversation, half of which was in her middle European accent, sounded like a comedy act: 'Hello mum, it's Lionel.' Holding the 'phone at arms length Mrs Begleiter would reply, 'Lionel's out.' 'Mum, this *is* Lionel.' 'He's not at home.' 'Listen mum.' Lionel would speak slowly and clearly, 'This *is* Lionel, are there any messages for me?' 'I'll tell him you called.' Click.

We tried using the Begleiter phone to solicit orders, but it was a 'party line', a line shared with another subscriber, a common practice during the post war years of shortages. In the middle of a conversation explaining our services as designers and printers I was likely to be interrupted by the hysterical woman who shared the line, 'Will you get off, I've been waiting ages to make a call,' she would scream. Nothing could be said that would persuade her to leave the line, and an amazed prospective client would hear a furious exchange of abuse before deciding that his company could not do business with a mad-house. Between our attempts to seek business, Lionel's mother would keep us supplied with food, a constant supply of bagels and chicken soup, treating me like one of the family, 'Come on John, have some more chicken soup.'

The communication problem was partly solved when we discovered that the waiting time for phones in Stratford was only a couple of months, for demand in the area scarcely existed. Assuring my mother, who managed the family budget, that the firm would pay for the installation and rental, we arranged to have a phone in my home, an acquisition that carried enormous prestige in the street. In the meantime, we solicited for work from a public call-box in Mare Street, Hackney. Our pockets filled with heavy copper pennies we would work our way through the commercial directory. While I explained our services to prospective clients, Lionel would stand in the background making noises like a printing machine, 'Shoosh-er, shoosh-er, shoosh-er', a serious act of comic and doubtful deception. We would be interrupted at frequent intervals by impatient and angry people waiting in a growing queue to make calls. More than once in the middle of a sales pitch I had to contend with a rumpus as the door was wrenched open with a shouted demand, 'How much bloody longer are you going to be?' while Lionel tried to fend off the intruder.

The eventual arrival of the telephone in St James Road was an event that aroused the interest of the entire street. It was a status symbol to rival a motor car. My mother proudly showed the black Bakelite object to a steady stream of neighbours, all of whom made a note of the number. If they did not have a phone themselves, they knew people who did. Calls came at all hours, 'Sorry to trouble you, but would you knock at number seventy something and ask Mrs so-and-so if she could come to the phone.' On cold winter evenings this often meant running half way up the street in the pouring rain.

Two months passed without an order. With the payment of rent, the purchase of a minimum of necessary supplies and odd pieces of equipment, our capital was dwindling. We drew just two pounds a week each to live on and depended on the support of our parents for food and accommodation. We brought sandwiches from home each day for our mid-day meal, supplemented by a cup of tea in a local 'caff'. Lionel's shoes wore through and he could not afford to have them repaired; when he called at my home my mother would cut pieces of brown paper to stuff inside the soles to help keep out the water as he squelched through the rain. When we went to the workshop each day, we looked more like tramps than businessmen. As Christmas approached we had secured just one order, a single piece of artwork from Lionel's old contact at the *John 'O London* magazine which earned the business four guineas (£4.20) It promised to be a poor Christmas.

My WAAF girlfriend, Pamela, had left the airforce a couple of months after my demob and we had kept in touch by letters. Some time before Christmas there was a turn of fate that brought her from Faversham to live in London. She had secured a place on a government training course with living accommodation in a hostel in Sloane Gardens, Chelsea. The hostel was a grand building but the interior was bleak, the food almost uneatable and her allowance mocked the wealthy area in which she was boarded. Men were barred from the all-woman hostel and we would meet at Sloane Square underground station on Sunday afternoons, where penniless, we would walk the streets in search of free galleries, museums and lectures, furtively exchanging kisses behind stone pillars, Egyptian mummies, and holding hands during long lectures on British-Czechoslovak friendship. We enjoyed walking arm in arm along the King's Road, Chelsea, with its second-hand bookshops, antiques, and grocery stores whose windows were filled with exotic foods unknown to us. We speculated as to how you ate aubergines, peppers and celeriac. Smart restaurants displayed menus without mention of 'meat and two veg', listing incomprehensible foreign dishes, 'Minestrone, Cervelle Milanaise, Zabaglione', with prices that took the appetite away. Main courses cost around ten shillings and the cheapest wine was offered at a staggering two and sixpence a glass, the cost of two pints of beer. In the surrounding streets were colour-washed houses with artists' studios and the first brightly painted front doors we had ever seen. We nudged each other as we passed men with beards and open sandals worn without socks, accompanied by women with swirling gipsy skirts, beads and flowing unpermed hair. It was all very strange to us.

On Pamela's first Saturday in London I contrived to raise enough money to take her out for a meal. I had never eaten out in London, apart from using a British Restaurant during the blitz, and I chose a cafe that I used to pass on my way to night school when I had worked at Waterloo. It was in Villiers Street, just off the Embankment and we had egg and chips, a slice of bread and butter and a cup of tea, but we were so happy we could have been dining at the Savoy.

Just before Christmas G&B secured its first order, to produce ten large banners for a clothing wholesaler in Houndsditch, a firm called Silverclad. I had imagined when we started the business that Jews were part of a business Cosa Nostra, and that Lionel would be able to open doors to a fraternal world of Jewish business contacts, as helpful to each other as Freemasons. I soon learned that 'business is business' and that my concept of an ethnic old school-tie network was unfounded. This time, however, for whatever reason, Mr Silver took a shine to Lionel, liked the design he submitted and accepted our price for printing, a grand total of thirty-seven pounds. While Lionel drew up the artwork to size, I searched for some banner linen, scouring London, for clothing had only recently been taken off ration and all types of fabric were in short supply. Our families and friends were pressed into the hunt, and as we were about to give up, my mother found some heavy white material in Robert's store in Stratford that would just about pass for banner linen. From Lionel's artwork, I cut the stencils, printed the large banners in small sections, had them hemmed and eyeletted and we delivered the banners by bus, asking Mr Silver if we could be paid before Christmas. For a discount he paid cash. For the first time in my life I handled five-pound notes, twice the size of one pound notes, boldly printed in black on crisp white paper that rustled at a touch. Real folding money.

The printing of the banners had brought another unforeseen problem. The smell of the printing ink and cellulose solvents rose to permeate the building. The odour of acetone may have passed for pear drops in the sweet shop, where the dear old lady, Mrs Simons, was uncomplaining, but the pungent odour made the Feldmans ill, and they protested loudly. In broken English, Mr Feldman would shout down our stairs, 'The schmell it is everywhere, in our bed, on our clothes, in our chicken. My wife she is sick,' and he imitated the sound of spewing. There was nothing we could do and the daily verbal assault continued. As we printed, Lionel responded to Feldman by composing his own lyrics to the chorus of a hymn, 'All good things around us,' singing loudly, 'All good schmells around us are meant for Feldman above.' It was unfeeling, but humour was our only response to an impossible situation. The unfortunate man would stamp on the stairs in rage, 'I can hear you making singing jokes.' We thought him unreasonable.

The phone in my home made canvassing for orders easier and with persistent effort work began to trickle in. We accepted anything, including work for which we were not really equipped. Lionel secured an order for a short run of gramophone labels from Monty Sunshine for the Crane River Jazz Band, which we designed and printed but were unable to cut to the necessary circular shape. With inspired salesmanship he persuaded them that square labels would be an innovative design feature. If any of those old 78rpm records survive, they must be collectors items for the labels alone. We tackled hand written posters, though for all Lionel's artistic skills he was no poster writer. On one such order we agreed to include the cost of billposting the posters on Waterloo station in the price. I borrowed my father's wallpaper-hanging brushes and armed with step ladders we became billposters for a day.

Although we existed on small local orders we persisted in seeking orders from the largest companies, boldly ringing multi-nationals for appointments to show our few samples. The break came after six months with an order from the British Bata Shoe Company for a series of showcards designed by the well known Swiss artist, Herbert Leupin, to be printed in several languages. The job was technically extremely difficult, involving half-tone colour printing, which was still in its infancy for the screen printing process. It was an order that would have deterred many firms in the industry, but we accepted the work with alacrity. By using the facilities of the London College of Printing, which I still attended, we coped with making the necessary photographic stencils which I transported in their wet state in large screw top jars filled with water, carrying them by bus to our workshop. We sweated through the work and at times were close to desperation as we struggled with primitive plant to produce an acceptable job. When the printing was finished, we trimmed the cards on our small hand guillotine, fitted them with card struts and delivered the English versions to the Bata head office in Old Bond Street as instructed. We made the delivery by packing the cards in two old suitcases and humping them to the West End on a number twenty-two bus. The buyer praised the quality of the work and we were elated, then he dropped his bombshell; he wanted to visit our premises. The following day I spruced up the basement workshop while Lionel painted cupboard doors with signs like 'Darkroom, keep out', in a desperate effort to make the business look larger and better equipped than it really was. Fortunately, the proposed visit was cancelled at the last moment.

There was more work from Bata, and with other odds and ends, including posters for the *Daily Worker*, we were busy. Each morning I travelled by the single deck bus that ran from Maryland Point to Hackney, leaving home at six-thirty, usually carrying two new wooden drying racks made by my father the previous evening, for we needed hundreds of them. After six months, the regular conductor could contain his curiosity no longer. 'Why do you carry those wood frames wherever you go?' he asked, convinced that I was an eccentric compelled to carry them as a cross through life, not realising that they were two different frames every day.

We often worked from seven-thirty in the morning until the last bus left at night, sustained only by a few sandwiches and a couple of cups of tea. Combined with the physical activity of printing, my weight dropped below eight stone. The ceiling to the basement was low, just above my head height, there was little natural light and I lost an entire summer from my life. The walls were covered with an oppressively heavy floral wallpaper and after printing for fourteen hours or more I used would recall the words of Oscar Wilde as he lay dying in the run-down Hotel d'Alsace, 'My wallpaper and I are fighting a duel to the death. One or the other of us has to go.' On some evenings my labours would be lightened when Pamela would arrive from Sloane Square by bus to rack the prints for me, her presence coming like sunlight to cut through the gloom. The long hours, lack of food, the fume-laden claustrophobic atmosphere and sheer fatigue took their toll, one evening as Pamela was working with me I collapsed at the bench from sheer exhaustion.

I kept the workshop spick and span, in the manner of a true craftsman, for I never did believe that good clean work could be produced by working amid rubbish in a state of disorder. That may have been Morris-like, and there was certainly nothing in the workshop that was not useful, but the vision of producing only work of the highest quality was at that stage as utopian as *News from Nowhere*. Unlike Morris, I did not have a private income and the first necessity for the business was survival. We accepted work lacking in artistic merit and for any price so long as it helped to pay the rent.

Among the work we accepted that had no aesthetic value was an order to apply glitter to ten thousand greetings cards, an enormous run at that time for production on a hand operated screen. The process involved printing gum onto the cards, and while they were wet, shuffling the cards in a tray filled with glistening metallic particles. I printed while Lionel shook the cards in the tray, the glitter adhering to the wet gum. Soon the whole workshop began to twinkle as the silvery flecks were shaken into the air to settle where they fell. At the end of each day we would wearily travel home, our clothes and hair sparkling, anticipating the appearance of pop stars of the future. We looked like fugitives from a cheap musical.

We worked hard but made no profit. Our clothes became shabbier and impregnated with the daily absorption of ink and solvent fumes. After finishing a day of printing with PVC, a particularly pungent and obnoxious ink used for printing on plastics, my odour became the subject of discussion by the entire upper deck of a bus as I travelled to meet Pamela. 'What's that smell?' a woman asked her companion. 'It smells like petrol, I wonder if there is a leak?' 'No, it's paint,' replied another, joining in unasked. Soon speculation was rife. A man with a briefcase on his knees gave his opinion. 'They've been coating the top of the bus with a sort of bitumen,' he said with authority. 'They have to do it every so often to keep it weatherproof.' While the surrounding passengers sniffed, I sank lower behind my evening paper, remaining silent, hoping to avoid detection.

We repaid some secondary loans when the Bata cheque arrived, but our resources then sank to a new level. At the lowest ebb, early in 1951, we were reduced to drawing just fifteen shillings a week for our subsistence. It was at this time that Lionel began to demonstrate his strange and lasting cavalier attitude to money. We were just about to go out from the workshop one Monday morning when we encountered a woman who told us that she was taking a street collection for flowers, for old Mrs Simons who had died over the weekend. We had pooled our money for the week, which stood at exactly one pound, and it was in Lionel's wallet in the form of two ten shilling notes. We expressed our sadness at the news and then, with a flourish, Lionel pulled out his wallet and took out one of our precious notes. I expected him to ask for change, contributing the customary shilling or two. To my dismay he offered the note, 'here you are,' he said quietly, 'This is from us.' When the grateful and surprised woman had left, I remonstrated with him. 'How are we going to manage for the rest of the week? A couple of bob would have been enough.' Lionel offered no rational explanation, merely saying, 'We will get by.' A few weeks later, while still struggling to exist on a weekly fifteen shillings, we went to the caff one Monday at mid-day for a cup of tea. To my utter astonishment, Lionel ordered a dinner, which he followed with a substantial pudding and a second cup of tea, saying that he was hungry and just had to eat. I knew that we had no money coming in and that his parents were unlikely to give him any as they were already starting to complain that he was making no contribution towards his keep. 'I will worry about that later,' he said. By Thursday he asked if I could lend him a shilling. In the sixties when his income was to be measured in thousands of pounds a week, Lionel with an extravagant lifestyle claimed that he was dyslexic with figures, especially money. There is perhaps an element of truth in his assertion, for he has been known to receive a cheque for ten thousand pounds and claim that it was for a hundred thousand pounds. At times I suspected exaggeration, but often it proved to be genuine confusion. Beneath it all it seemed that Lionel did not feel that he should have to worry about calculating, and that money was just there to be spent.

When Pamela had finished her training course and qualified as a shorthand typist, we married. Secretaries commanded higher wages than craftsmen and she had secured a good job with a firm of lace manufacturers with offices in Carthusian Street, Clerkenwell, at a salary of six pounds a week. Together with my income, which had climbed back to two pounds a week, we were no worse off than most working class couples, and better off than

163

some. Of necessity, we followed East End tradition, starting married life by living in two rooms, in my parents' house, sharing the scullery with its tiny gas stove for cooking and a single cold water tap for washing. Pamela was back in the area where she had lived as a child.

We were married at West Ham registry office, on a weekday afternoon, and I went to work that morning, going home at midday to change into my suit, bought when I was sixteen with the 'tools for the trade' insurance money. Lionel was the best man, and we walked to the registry office, strolling through West Ham recreation ground on our way to West Ham Lane. My mother cried, we had a wedding breakfast with ham and beer in our house in St James Road, our photographs taken on a Brownie box in the back yard by the dustbin, and then I escaped with my bride, travelling by bus and train to Faversham for a three-day honeymoon, having the use of Pamela's former home while her parents were on holiday. I had married on five pounds, spent thirty-five shillings on a ring, twenty-five shillings on the train fare and was left with two pounds to spend. It was idyllic, for Faversham was a sleepy, unspoilt rural town and we were on our own, two young people very much in love.

The volume of work in the business increased and it became clear that we needed additional help. If I was printing and Lionel was designing, I had to rack the prints myself. We were often working fourteen hours a day and a helper would increase my speed and cut down the hours of work. We advertised for a boy to learn the trade and engaged our first employee, a local lad named Ken Hall, for a wage of three pounds a week, a pound more than either of us were taking. The current working week in the industry was forty-four hours, but as a good trade unionist I resolved to implement the growing demand for a forty-hour week, eliminating Saturday work. With our first employee, we became the first firm in the industry to introduce the forty-hour week. We also promised full pay for sickness. I knew from experience the hardship caused by illness and loss of earnings to working class families and I was determined to operate the working conditions that I was fighting for as a Communist and trade unionist.

On his first morning at work, the young lad addressed Lionel as Mr Bart, which amused and puzzled us. He explained that our names were on the sign on the front door, misreading it as Gand Bart Service. He thought that the two partners were Mr Gand and

Mr Bart. It has always been my contention that when Lionel changed his name from Begleiter to Bart, that he remembered the incident and was influenced in the choice of his new name. Lionel says that he took the name from Bart's Hospital, but it is a moot point.

We were beginning to make some progress in the business, when an eviction order arrived on the authority of the Hackney Borough Sanitary Inspector. It seemed that our business stank. With a sweet shop and residential accommodation above us, the premises were deemed unsuitable for printing because of the smell of the fumes from the printing inks and solvents. We were given one month to get out. Mr Feldman had won his battle. It was a terrible blow, for we had just four weeks to find another premises and move. The difficulty was compounded when Pamela, who was pregnant, was told that she must leave her job. Her employer, a millionaire who spent each winter in the West Indies, did not want a pregnant woman in his office and gave her two weeks' notice. There was no protection in law, no maternity rights and no trade union to take her side. The loss of Pamela's earnings combined with the enforcement order threatened to end the business. Pamela was totally supportive, saying that we had to hang on and that she would try to find another job and work until the baby was due. Six months pregnant, she applied to office after office and then tramped the industrial length of the foul Carpenters Road, calling at every factory . One look at her rounded figure brought the constant reply, 'Sorry, no vacancies.'

I talked the matter over with Lionel, saying that I must start to take five pounds a week from the business, that being the least on which I could manage. Lionel took the news calmly and said that we should carry on, borrowing more money if necessary. It was obvious to me that a substantial sum would be required if we were to survive both the move and the increase in wages and we decided that once again I would approach my uncle. This time I asked for three hundred pounds, and he agreed. If we could find suitable premises, we were still in business.

We were lucky. Our first search among the columns of the *Hackney Gazette* led us to a studio at Dalston Junction, offered at two pounds a week. It was a dream. Situated in a small yard, the studio was built on top of a workshop occupied by a firm of surgical instrument makers, and looked as though it had been taken straight from the first act of *La Bohème*. It had a great sloping north light window reaching to a height of fifteen feet, calling to the sky. After the oppressive low ceiling and gloom of the basement, the light was dazzling and I felt as if a burden had been lifted from above my head. In my imagination, I was a Bohemian artist. It had a small office and a clear floor space of four hundred square feet. The studio had been built in Victorian times and was complete with gas bracket lights and a small cast-iron stove. I fell in love with the studio as soon as I walked up the dusty stairs and saw the window.

Managing on five pounds a week was closer to existence than living. I was wearing the clothes bought with my demob money, and they were wearing beyond threadbare towards disintegration. I stitched leather patches on the elbows of my jacket, not for style, but to stem enlargement of the holes, and sewed little strips of leather on the bottom edges of my turn-ups to stop further fraying. For appointments with clients, I wore my only suit. Travelling to Dalston every day entailed journeying on two trolley buses, with a consequent increase in fares. I got through the week on a pound, leaving Pamela with just four pounds for rent and housekeeping, including provision for our expected baby. Her clothes, and they were few enough, were also becoming unwearable, for a different reason. The buttons on her coat were strained by the growing life in her womb, the edges of the coat gaping in a series of dark open mouths. She is a naturally shy person and the rounding of her girlish figure made her self conscious of her appearance. Pregnancies were concealed, not flaunted in the fifties and a winter maternity coat became a necessity. Pamela had to make do with the cheapest and thinnest of coats and I felt frustrated and helpless at my inability to provide the essential needs for her and the baby. She managed to save for a new pram, but had to settle for a second-hand cot, bought for fifteen shillings. Sarah, our former lodger, then living in another house in St James Road understood our plight; warm hearted and compassionate she would sometimes slip me half a crown, saying, 'Take Pamela to the pictures.' They were special treats, never to be forgotten.

After a year of incarceration in the gloomy basement, working in the studio became a pleasure. We cleaned the long panes in the great window and ripped up the worn linoleum from the floor, reading, as we went, the yellowed newspapers from the time of the First World War which had been laid as lining on the floor boards. We scrubbed the boards, blackleaded the stove, and with the help of my father moved in our equipment. We found that it was possible to get a phone installed and within a few weeks we had two second-hand chairs and a typewriter in the office and a phone number on our business cards. We showed off the studio to friends and relations and felt that we were finally established. Our accountant may not have agreed, for after one year our turnover amounted to just over four hundred pounds and our loans had grown to four hundred and fifty pounds. We owed too much money to turn back.

I was printing in the studio on Christmas Eve, aiming to finish a colour on a long run of showcards for the De La Rue company, when the phone rang. It was to tell me that the baby was on its way, a month earlier than expected. My mother and Pamela had been pegging out washing on the clothes line in the backyard, hanging heavy wet sheets, when Pamela had reached up to pull the line down and the stretching had precipitated her labour. Mum had walked her round to the Sick Home and then phoned to tell me the news. There was no question of being allowed anywhere near the birth, as much as my instinct was to rush to Pamela immediately. The birth of a baby was considered to be an intimate event concerning only women, and husbands were kept well away. Visiting was not allowed until seven in the evening and so I finished my work and cleaned up before leaving for the hospital. I was there at seven on the dot, just in time to see our son carried out of the ward to be washed. I was permitted a momentary glimpse of his red and wrinkled face and then had to don a mask and white coat before being allowed into the ward.

I was fortunate to have arrived as our baby was being taken from the ward, or I would not have seen him until the following day. The baby was taken from Pamela, who was allowed a brief cuddle after the birth, and not returned to her until feeding time, a thoughtless cruelty to both the mother and the child. The next day the hospital staff invited the new fathers to a Christmas party, an hour of tea and buns taken in celebration with the three other women in the small ward, all cheerful mums with names that sounded like a music hall act, 'Doll, Beat and Ede'. Pamela was in the hospital for twelve days, the normal period of a confinement in those days. It was a practice that served working class mothers well, for return home meant an immediate resumption of household drudgery, cooking, scrubbing, washing and ironing as well as looking after the other kids.

In mid-January I went to the Sick Home to collect Pamela and the baby, walking home with the little bundle in my arms.

Together in our small room we put him in the new pram and sat looking in joy and wonder. It was the start of a new life for all of us.

Pamela, who had a religious upbringing, was keen to have our son christened, but I refused to have anything to do with the church. When Pamela went to see the vicar of St James, he was difficult, saying that it was essential that both parents should be present if the child was to be christened. After some pleading by Pamela, he relented, but promised that he would call on me to discuss the matter over a drink, a remark that I considered more patronising than well intentioned. I would have welcomed the confrontation, but he never managed to walk across the road to our house. Before the birth, we had decided that if it was a boy he would be called John, after myself, my father and grandfather. On the day of the christening I stayed indoors, while Lionel, a good Jewish boy, joined Pamela, family and friends at the font. He said that he enjoyed the hymns!

It was a year of unremitting penury as we struggled to stay in business. Some weeks there was not enough money to draw the five pounds target wage and Pamela had to juggle with her meagre housekeeping allowance just to feed us. There was no family allowance for a first child and as so often happens in working class families, Pamela often went throughout the day without food for herself so that she could feed the baby and myself, the so-called breadwinner of the family. She never complained. In her gentle and quiet way, Pamela possessed a deep reserve of inner feminine strength and was resolved to give me all the love and help she could. A demanding partner would have destroyed the business in its infancy.

At work, as winter bit with long dark hours and freezing temperatures, I started each day by standing in a long queue for the trolley buses to Dalston. Without warm clothing, I arrived already chilled to the bone, to the studio, which with its large area of glass was as cold as an ice box. We could not afford to buy fuel for the stove, and I would bring a couple of shovelfuls of coal from home each day to supplement the rubbish which we burned in a futile attempt to keep warm. After a while, I had to stop bringing coal as it was needed to keep our room warm for the baby. We were reduced to scrounging broken boxes from the stalls in Ridley Road market.

Pamela endured the winter in her thin maternity coat, but my baggy corduroy trousers finally had to be replaced. I bought a pair of ex-army fatigue trousers from an army surplus store for twelve and eleven (65p) and considered them a bargain. The crepe soled shoes that I wore became affected by spilt solvents at work and the soles turned into a sticky sponge that squelched at every step. If I had to stand up on a bus, the soles welded themselves to the rubber floor. When I went to move, it was as though I was stuck in melting tar.

I liked to smoke the occasional pipe, and being unable to afford tobacco turned to experimenting with 'herbal smoking mixture', a shilling sack of dried herbs that burned at tinder speed, showering sparks with each sudden movement or gust of wind. It smelled like burning autumn leaves and I became a walking bonfire, a fire hazard hidden in a cloud of peculiar fumes. The upper decks of the buses, where smoking was allowed, were always filled with men creating a tap-room fug of cheap shag and Woodbines, but the smell of my herbs was more pungent than the strongest tobacco and was often the subject of disparaging comment.

That we survived the next twelve months was due solely to tenacity. Work was spasmodic, the circle of friends from whom we could loan money exhausted, overdraft facilities at the bank refused and credit from our suppliers cut off. We lived from week to week on a cash basis and our watchword was frugality. One desperate Friday, unable to raise the three pounds for the wages of our lone employee, we turned to another 'uncle', pawning our typewriter.

Our fortunes improved at the end of the year when I succeeded in getting an order from Sainsbury's, the grocery chain. Their shops were still counter service stores, with marble topped counters, patterned tiles, and men in long white aprons patting butter with small wooden paddles, but the company was moving ahead, promoting cleanliness and quality as the spearhead of its sales campaign. Their graphic designer was the distinguished Leonard Beaumont and we grasped the opportunity of working with a top flight designer, producing work of the highest standard. It was our first opportunity to work in liaison with a recognised designer and to use our skills as creative printers. It was the first of many close working relationships that we were to forge with designers, working partnerships that were to be the basis to our future success.

After a while, Beaumont retired, and was succeeded by a young designer, Ray Hadlow, appointed as design manager to continue the high standard of design initiated by his predecessor. I never

169

deigned to conceal my political views in conversation and soon found that like myself, Ray Hadlow had strong socialist beliefs. He lived in a community of progressive artists in a country mansion called St Julians, set in wooded acres, just outside Sevenoaks in Kent. It appeared to be an up-market commune, where the wealthy, famous and artistic among them took their turn by rota at performing the household chores of cooking, washing up and cleaning. We became friends as well as business associates, sharing a mutual enthusiasm for design and print. There was no direct business advantage in our shared political outlook, but it made work all the more pleasurable.

On my regular visits to Sainsbury's head office, at Blackfriars, Hadlow introduced me to the artist and illustrator, James Boswell, who worked on the Sainsbury house magazine. A large, cheerful and generous man, Boswell had been a founder member of the Artists' International Association. Formed in 1933, the Artists International had aimed to mobilise progressive artists against the threat of 'imperialist war against the Soviet Union, Fascism and Colonial oppression.' That was the language of Communism, but the threat of war and fascism was real. Under the chairmanship of Misha Black the AIA attracted many well known artists of the period, including Augustus John, Stanley Spencer and Duncan Grant. Wider support for AIA exhibitions in Britain came from world famous foreign artists, among them, Leger, Miro, Masreel and Picasso. I recalled that during the war I had visited an AIA exhibition in the bombed out basement of John Lewis in Oxford Street, though I had no understanding at the time of the political thrust of the show.

Jim Boswell always had a friendly word for me as I passed his drawing board when collecting work from the Sainsbury studio, and on one occasion he presented me with a signed copy of a book that he had illustrated. I had been nervous and somewhat overawed on my first visits to Sainsbury's, dealing with smart-suited executives at the hub of a multi-million pound enterprise, but my discovery that the business world included men like Ray Hadlow and Jim Boswell came as a revelation and inspired me with confidence.

The amount of work from Sainsbury's, although regular, was not all that great in value and we still relied on small orders from local business to keep us going. One morning, a market trader appeared in our studio, a cloth cap pulled sideways over one ear and a knotted muffler at his throat. Could we print on foam rubber? He had a sample of the cheap pink material, about the size of a small mat, in his hand. His idea was that we should design and print a pair of footprints in black on the foam rubber, and he would sell them as novelty bath mats. He said that he would bring in a thousand pieces of foam rubber and asked if we could print them for a shilling each. I had serious doubts about his ability to pay, but before I could discuss payment, he said that he would pay cash, and he meant cash, not a cheque. It was a gift, fifty pounds for one day of printing. I saw him selling his mats on Kingsland Waste the following Saturday, and like most market traders, he was a talented salesman. He had his trousers rolled to his knees and a bowl of water beside him on the pavement. He would stand in the water, and then leap out onto the mat, placing his feet on the footprints while extolling the absorbent qualities of the foam rubber. At ten bob a time they were selling like the proverbial hot cakes, and his profit must have been about eight hundred percent on each mat. For five or six weeks we coined in the cash, printing a thousand mats a week, then suddenly it stopped. It transpired that the low quality foam rubber disintegrated after a few weeks of use and customers were beginning to look for him in the market to ask for their money back. I saw him again a few months later, selling hula-hoops in Petticoat Lane. They were made from a length of garden hosepipe, formed into a circle and fixed by a piece of dowel pushed into the open ends and made secure with a couple of office staples. At ten bob a time he was still operating on his normal mark-up of eight times the cost of production.

Another casual caller, to become a regular client for the next ten years or so, was Lou Bell, a toy manufacturer in a small way of business with a shop in Lower Clapton. He made children's playsuits – cowboys and Indians – and wanted us to produce designs and print them on pre-cut sections of flocked material from which he made up the suits. He gave his playsuits names, like 'Shooting Sheriff', 'Brave Warrior' and 'Indian Chief' and had also secured the rights to print under licence, the names of Hollywood cowboy stars, Tex Ritter and Gene Autrey. He dreamed of creating a mass market with a new generation of children clothed as squaws, braves, cowboys and cowgirls. Lionel dutifully made drawings of sheriff stars, bucking broncos, lassoes, tepees and braves with feathered head-dresses which I then printed onto the material Lou Bell supplied. The work was cheap, but it was regular and the studio was seldom without a pile of cowboy trousers or Indian smocks. Lou Bell liked to haggle over prices, and aware that we needed the money would bait us down on price by producing a large cheque book which he always carried, offering to pay us cash on delivery, for a discount. He counted his pennies and every piece of material, making deductions for any pieces spoiled during printing. His big day came when Tex Ritter came to England on a stage tour and the sales of endorsed cowboy suits soared. Lou told us with a knowing chuckle that Tex Ritter and all his cowboy troop were Jewish, rather like the thirties band of 'Felix Mendhelson and his Hawaian Serenaders', most of whom came from Whitechapel.

Dalston Junction, where our studio was situated, was a busy and cosmopolitan market area, packed with traders and small workshops. We use to take our tea-breaks in a small caff next to the railway station and at midday we would wander among the stalls in Ridley Road market, where Lionel revelled in the raucous sounds and colourful bustle of East London street life. There were five pubs close by the studio, four of which were virtually unchanged from the time of the First World war. They had large public bars with high nicotine-stained ceilings, chocolate brown woodwork, sawdust on the floors and few chairs and tables. Drinking was a bar standing activity, with bitter and mild served from large wooden barrels. One pub, the Tyssen Arms, was a well known haunt of local fascists and we never ventured inside during the three years we spent in the locality. A local newspaper seller who had his pitch on a corner of the junction was one of the Mosleyites who used the Tyssen Arms. A surly individual with a large beer gut, he refused to sell me a newspaper when he saw that I had a copy of the *New Statesman & Nation* tucked in my jacket pocket. His refusal hinted at violence and I would give his pitch a wide berth when crossing the junction.

Half way between the news pitch and the Tyssen Arms was a cab rank. Without any transport of our own, we often used the black cabs for deliveries, and we became well known to the cabbies, most of whom were Jewish. One of them, Aubrey Morris, who came from Cable Street, and had taken part in the famous 1936 battle against Mosley and his fascist followers, was a Communist who was to stand as a parliamentary candidate for Stoke Newington. When Lionel joined the Communist Party in 1951, it was Aubrey Morris who was the secretary of his branch at Stamford Hill. Aubrey, to become a lifelong friend, was to give up cabbing within a couple of years to build a successful career in the travel industry. As chairman of Thomson Travel in the 1970s, his brass licensed taxi drivers' badge used to hang on the wall behind his imposing desk, a reminder of those days on the Dalston rank.

Behind the cab rank in Ashwin Place, we had a rival firm of screen printers, Print Processes. Well, hardly rivals, for they were large and established, their business housed in a substantial four storied Victorian building that was the original premises of Reeves, the famous manufacturers of artists colours and materials. The managing director of Print Processes, was Sid Chillingworth, another stalwart Communist. Strangely, we never actually met, although we both printed posters for the *Daily Worker*.

The Dalston shops supplied many of our day-to-day needs. Among them was an old fashioned builders merchants, an emporium that sold nails by weight, ovals, wires and pins of every size, weighing them on large metal scales and wrapping them in newspaper. Their catalogue of ironmongery ran to thousands of items, all in stock, kept in worn wooden drawers. The men who served knew where every item was, what they were used for and what they cost. The store sold methylated spirits and turpentine, filling our own cans by the gallon from huge drums in the yard. These were the days before DIY 'toyshops' packaged a few nails or screws in plastic and cardboard packs to sell at extortionate prices and dispensed turps substitute in medicine sized bottles with fancy labels. Dalston junction with its Cooke's pie and eel shop, workmen's caffs, cheap clothes shops, market traders, a flea pit cinema where disgruntled kids had chalked, 'don't go to this pictures' and a surgical shop that appropriately sold trusses in the Balls Pond Road, became a second community to me, as close and friendly as Stratford.

Slowly the business grew until we had a staff of four crammed into the studio, including two older and experienced craftsmen, Alf Paulding and Charles Try, leaving Lionel and myself more time for selling. A major problem was that the world of advertising operated from smart West End offices with carpets and chromium, staffed by fashionably dressed account executives, smooth and affluent. By comparison, we had the sartorial appearance of starving artists and looked too young to be capable of handling the work of national advertisers. Lionel insisted that we must improve our appearance and try to look older, persuading me that on receipt of our next substantial cheque we must take money to buy clothes. Reluctantly I agreed, feeling guilty that Pamela, who was also in desperate need of new clothes, would be excluded. We drew thirty pounds and took ourselves to Dunns, a gentlemen's outfitters in Kingsland Road, a long way from Savile Row but more suited to our purse. We emerged with long, double breasted and belted crombie overcoats and hats. My hat was a conventional trilby, but Lionel bought a broad brimmed hat of velour, the first of a series of stylish and often exotic hats that were to become part of his public persona. The long coats could hide shabby clothes beneath and the hats added years to our ages. I allowed my moustache to flourish and Lionel sported a razor trimmed beard. With leather briefcases and shiny new shoes we must have looked like anarchists posing as insurance men. Lionel was to write a song for an amateur review about two city business men, 'Mr Prendergast and Mr Smith.' A line in the song went, 'You'll see us on omnibus, on underground and tram, our briefcases hold sandwiches which usually hold jam.' That was us.

Ever the actor, Lionel would insist on rehearsing our roles before we went on appointments to meet new clients. I was unconvinced, but he would say, 'I will be the client. You come into the office and tell me what you are going to say.' We acted out the charade and he would criticise my approach. Then we would change roles. Unfortunately, no matter how many times we rehearsed, the client never kept to the script! There was one occasion when I deviated from our set replies. I had called at the advertising agency of Auger and Turner, in Gerrard Street, and was asked by the receptionist whom I wished to see. I had the name of one of the directors and asked for Mr Auger. 'Oh, you mean Captain Auger', she replied haughtily. 'Who shall I say is calling?' I resented the unwarranted use of a military title, it was the old officers' and other ranks' act. I decided to respond in kind. Using my former RAF rank, I said, 'Tell him it is AC 1 Gorman.'

One evening, Lionel said that he must have a serious talk with me. I speculated that he was in some sort of trouble and needed advice or help. With a solemn face, he told me that he had joined Unity Theatre. Was that a problem? Yes, for three nights a week and weekends, he would be unable to work. It created an immediate hiatus, for we were still in debt and had to work whenever there was work to be done. We had been so close, sharing our money, sharing the hardships, sharing the work and the fun. The business dominated our lives, now Lionel was saying that there was something that was more important to him than our work together. He wanted to be involved in the theatre, painting scenery, acting, and writing songs. There was no point in trying to dissuade him, for he had made an irrevocable decision, as though he was seeking to fulfil the needs of an inner compulsion. He was to work in the business with me for another ten years and remain a close friend, but he no longer had a total commitment to the firm, for his heart was somewhere else.

Lionel's association with Unity Theatre drew him into the Communist Party, for it was the Party that was the driving force behind the theatre. The Communist Party had theoretical direction concerning culture and the organisational skills to translate theory into practice, with Communist fractions meeting within the broader structure of the theatre's democratic management. Already sympathetic to the Party on many issues, Lionel readily joined the Communists, directing his creative and youthful energy to painting scenery, designing posters – which we printed at cost – writing songs, scripts and performing. Whether appearing as an ugly sister in a political version of Cinderella, singing '*Any Old Iron*' for old time music hall or writing for a revue, he immersed himself completely in the life of the theatre. His new friends, Communist writers and actors like Alfie Bass, Bernard Goldman, Eric Paice, and John Gold among them, all came to our studio at various times, often to sit huddled around the stove with Lionel, late into the night, working on ideas for shows. Twice Lionel travelled abroad with Unity to Communist sponsored International Youth Festivals, firstly to Bucharest in 1953 and again to Poland in 1955, where he appeared in an excerpt from *Twelfth Night* in the role of Sir Andrew Aguecheek From Warsaw he brought me a present, a fine etching of two coal miners, which hangs in my studio at home to this day.

Although Lionel's activities with Unity Theatre cut into the time he spent in the studio, he still worked with enthusiasm at designing and selling. Towards the end of 1953, we were employing six people and had reached the point where we could hardly move to print the work. If we had a large poster to print, we had to clear a space to make sufficient room to spread the sheets on the floor to draw the design to size, for there was nowhere to fit in a large drawing table. We talked of moving to larger premises, but we had no reserves. We had yet to repay all our debts and Lionel and myself were still only able to take a wage of seven pounds a week, about half the wage we paid to our skilled stencil cutters. Also, the nature of our work was such that we fluctuated between working all hours or having no work at all.

Advertising work is invariably rush work, meeting deadlines tied in with dated promotions. We would work all weekend, printing throughout the nights, and then find that we had no work for the next couple of days. There was no continuity and we took each day as it came, elated when we were busy and filled with gloom when we were slack. 'Up and down like Tower Bridge.'

What we needed was a regular flow of work, with sufficient staff and space to cope with the special panic demands inherent in advertising. The break in our fortunes came when we secured Marks & Spencer as a client. Getting the first order from M&S was not really luck, for we had a policy of trying to work for the largest companies. Yet, it involved one of those strange coincidences that have followed me through life. It was on one of my regular phone sessions seeking new clients that I rang M&S head office and was put through to their design studio. A charming man with an Irish lilt in his voice answered the phone and I made my sales pitch. He invited me to call the following day with samples of our work. His name was John Oxenbould, and when I told Lionel the good news, he said that the unusual name was familiar, that there was an Oxenbould at Unity Theatre. Could it be the same man? I thought it improbable, but Lionel suggested that he should keep the appointment, just in case it was the Unity man, and a common interest might give an edge. Lionel, with overcoat, hat, and an artist's folio stuffed with samples of our work, took a bus to the Marks & Spencer studio in Orchard Street, just opposite Selfridge's. A few hours later his swift run up the stairs to our studio and the smile on his face signalled success before he spoke. John Oxenbould was indeed involved with Unity Theatre, he was also a Communist. The degree of coincidence stretched further. John Oxenbould should never have answered the phone in response to my call. He really had nothing to do with placing orders for print, for he was the editor of the Marks & Spencer house journal, *St Michael News*, and just happened to be by the phone when it rang. The buyer was out of the room at the time and John answered to be helpful. He was interested in what I had to say about our company and had made the appointment with a view to introducing me to the buyer. As it was, Lionel was given a friendly introduction and returned clutching an order. It was the start of a client-supplier association that was destined to span four decades.

John Oxenbould, a red-head with high brow, who resembled a shorter version of Bernard Shaw, became a good friend and business associate. He had an easy Irish charm and was a cultured and witty journalist, an extrovert who loved the theatre and was a first class chairman for old time music hall, not only at Unity, but also for the Players Theatre. As a Communist, he was far removed from the cloth capped stereotype, but he had a fierce loyalty to the working class. When he canvassed the *Daily Worker* from door to door, smartly dressed in Donegal tweed, with a broad knotted red tie, he would raise his hat if a woman answered the door, greeting her with a smile, 'Good morning madam, I wonder if I could interest you in buying a copy of this splendid paper?' Some time during the 1960s he left Marks & Spencer to become the public relations officer of the London Co-operative Society, an act of political faith, as he strove to change the public image of the Co-op to match a changing society.

With regular work from Sainsbury's, Marks & Spencer, a few agencies and various local advertisers, we outgrew the studio and a move to larger premises was imperative if we were to cope with the work. This time it was Lionel who came up with a source of capital to finance our next move. A friend of his, Jack Averton, was a handbag manufacturer and market trader, producing the bags in a back room and garage at his house in Stamford Hill and selling them from the back of a battered van at London street markets. He had asked Lionel to paint him a 'flash', a signboard to hang in the back of his van when working the markets, proclaiming himself as 'Jack the handbag King.' Despite his scruffy appearance, his cockney talk, his garage sweatshop and his veteran van, Jack was a shrewd operator and always had cash. Lionel negotiated a loan of a thousand pounds from him, high risk capital for which we had to agree to pay fifteen percent interest, a usurious figure when the bank rate stood at four percent. Nevertheless we staked our future on the loan and were poised for our next move.

CHAPTER 11
A Factory As It Might Be

The factory was a sound two-storey brick-built building with a corrugated asbestos roof, situated in a quiet cul-de-sac off Homerton High Street, Hackney, backing onto a railway line. Our neighbours were a piano factory, a welding business, a grim-looking pub and a corner shop. The shop sold general provisions, and on its side wall was a vitreous enamel sign that read, 'Milk delivered in sealed bottles.' On the opposite side of the street was a high wall that protected the rear of a box-making factory. The rent was five hundred pounds a year for a thirteen-year lease, an eternity and a daunting commitment, but in the summer of 1954, we signed, Gorman and Begleiter pledging to pay one hundred and twenty-five pounds every quarter day until 1967.

The following Sunday, we went to the factory together with my father, to plan the building of an office and a studio within the open floor space. When we arrived at eight in the morning it was as quiet as a cemetery, without a person or a car to be seen. When we left after four hours of measuring and debate, the road was jam packed, nose to tail with private cars. In those days, when there were comparatively few motor vehicles, we were astonished by the sight. Why were they there, and where were the drivers? The other factories were locked and silent. It was a mystery solved when we went to go into the pub for a quick drink before going home to our Sunday dinners. I had trouble in pushing the door open because of the press of bodies against the door. The pub, which was practically empty all day during the week, was filled to capacity.

179

The pub was the Deuragon Arms, referred to by locals as the 'Dewdragon' and a rendezvous of homosexuals from all over London. Homosexuality was illegal, queers were regarded as queer indeed and a subject beyond the agenda of public debate. Yet here was a compere on stage, known to everyone by his pseudonym of 'Gaye', with gorgeous wavy hair and a heavily powdered face, wearing a white silk blouse and the tightest trousers I had ever seen, openly camping his way through a routine of *double entendre* patter as he alternated between singing and introducing the next turn. Radio stars, Ronnie Ronalde and Carol Levis appeared, as did a variety of drag queens. I had never been in a pub like this one. During the weekdays it was a mausoleum, serving the odd glass of Worthington to a wheezing pensioner, but for two evenings a week and on Sundays it was transformed by a pulsating gathering of bizarre characters who found their way to this quiet backwater in East London. Rosina Street, where our factory and the pub was situated, was a little known road, even to the locals. If you asked a taxi diver for Rosina Street, you invariably beat his knowledge, but we soon found that you could hail a cab in the West End, ask for the 'Dewdragon', and be driven there without giving further directions.

The working space in the factory amounted to two thousand square feet, evenly distributed between the two storeys. With rows of windows along either side, the light streamed in throughout the day. The floors were of a smooth hard composite, uninterrupted by divisions or pillars and the roof rose in a high triangle, providing an airy upper floor ideal for printing, allowing the fumes to rise above working level. Built in the thirties, the factory was neat, without adornment, severely practical, constructed of good red bricks and solid woodwork.

I had read William Morris's essay, *A Factory As It Might Be*, and was enthused by his vision. Morris, in describing a factory in a socialist society, envisaged it set among beautiful gardens. There was nothing that I could do about that aspect, for our factory had been built according to the dictates of capitalism, by landlords seeking to extract maximum profit from the land without regard to the environment. As many factories as possible were crammed together for rent, spacious grounds being reserved for the homes of the factory owners, their upkeep, as Morris explained, paid for by the factory workers. However, the building met Morris's requirement that it was reasonably 'beautiful with its simplicity as a workshop', and I was determined that our working environment would not be a dirty, cramped, degrading slum, like so many workplaces. Light, air, order and cleanliness would prevail. We would produce good work to a 'true standard' as Morris would have wished, work which would give satisfaction to the maker and pleasure to the beholder. My aspirations to meet Morris's dream were restricted by circumstance, but if we could not adorn the workshop with art and sculpture as he described, then our walls would be hung with framed copies of our finest printing. If we could not operate a twenty-hour week, we would strive to offer the shortest hours in the printing industry. I wanted to work happily as part of a team of crafts people, in pleasant conditions, producing work of the very best quality, well rewarded, but not driven by the desire to accumulate wealth at any cost.

We painted the walls matt white and the woodwork a glossy grey, a decorative innovation when cream, chocolate brown and bottle green predominated as the colour scheme for public buildings, offices and factories. My father spent his summer holiday erecting the studded framework for the office and studio, and over following weekends clad the lower parts of the partitions and glazed the upper parts with fluted glass. His work continued for months during weekends and evenings, making drawing tables, printing-benches, plan chests, and building a reception area with a giant vertical book-like display, whose leaves could be turned to display examples of our work. He gave freely of his labour, entering into the spirit of creating civilised working conditions for a union workshop. The factory smelt of newly sawn wood, fresh paint and printing ink and gradually order emerged from chaos. As the work progressed we enjoyed unaccustomed luxuries, angle poise lamps and swivel seats at the drawing boards, intercommunicating phones and space to move freely between the racks of newly printed work, the racks lined in regimental rows as straight as beds in a barrack-hut.

Lionel and myself still worked on the shop floor, designing and printing, but we also had an office with a modern metal desk, a single padded boss's chair, a filing cabinet and a typist's desk. Soon, my sister Dorothy joined us as a receptionist, typist, book-keeper and general factotum. When customers 'phoned we sounded like a real business, 'Mr Begleiter, yes, hold on, I'll put you through.' For the first time we encouraged clients to visit us, proudly displaying the pristine workshops and letting them see their work in production.

I would have liked to have built a canteen where we could take our tea-breaks, but that was not to be for some years. Instead, we had a tiny kitchen beneath the stairs and followed the usual workshop practice of drinking our tea and eating our sandwiches where we worked. By tradition, the youngest boy made the tea for everyone. One lad, on his first morning at work was told of this chore. 'Can you make tea?', I asked. 'Oh yes, my mum has shown me.' That morning, at tea-break, the tea he served was as thick as glue and almost black. Amid the roars of complaint I asked him to explain precisely how he had made the tea. 'I did like my mum said. I warmed the teapot and put in one spoonful for each of us and one for the pot.' There were eleven of us!

While the tea was being made, another boy would be sent to 'Lil's', the local caff to bring back food for the staff, bacon sandwiches for those who could afford them, bread and dripping or jam sandwiches for the rest of us. This was the task of a young Teddy boy from Hoxton, Mick Holt, who came to work wearing thick crepe-soled shoes, drain-pipe trousers, a long black jacket with a velvet collar, his hair greased and combed into a 'DA' style, a 'duck's arse' haircut. He was witty, sharp and streetwise. Stopped on one occasion by a policeman as he was carrying the food back to the firm in a cardboard box, he was asked with some sarcasm, 'What have you got in there, the crown jewels?' Without hesitation, Mick looked at the copper and said, 'Why, are they missing?'

Mick's confident nature and his cheeky sense of humour manifested itself when we were visited by an important potential client. Prior to his arrival I had told Mick that should he have to come into the office, he was to knock first instead of just walking in as he usually did. I explained that this was not snobbishness on our part, but necessary as part of our effort to win a customer. He could still address us as John or Lionel, as all the staff did, but that a 'Sorry to trouble you' preceding his interruption would help to create a good impression. The client arrived for his appointment at 9.30, shortly before Mick started his round to take the orders for tea-break. I was doing my best to play the part of the sophisticated businessman when there was a measured knock on the office door, bomp, bomp, bomp. 'Come in,' I called. Mick's greased hair and velvet collar appeared around the slightly opened door. 'Excuse me sir, I am sorry to trouble you, sir,' the emphasis firmly on the 'sir', 'What would you like this morning, drip, jam or marm?'

Our client list grew. Apart from the regular work from

Sainsbury's and Marks & Spencer, we added two more multiple retailers, David Greig the grocers and the London Co-operative Society. I had a political allegiance to the London Co-op and I warned the publicity manager of the progressive retail policies of Sainsbury's and Marks & Spencer, but they were swept aside with the contemptuous comment that the Co-op sales of bread and milk alone exceeded the total London sales of Marks & Spencer. Tip Top cleaners, with more than a hundred branches, May and Baker – the pharmaceutical company that manufactured the wonder drug, M&B tablets – and a number of advertising agencies, including Baron Moss Advertising, run by a former publicity manager of the *Daily Worker*, made for a steady flow of work. Lionel and myself still took less wages than our senior staff, but we began to repay my uncle's loan in dribs and drabs. Cash flow, however, remained a problem, and I became a master at extricating money from the bank when our balance was nil. Drawing the wages on a Friday I would go to the bank at mid-day when the chief clerk was out for his lunch. He had been at the bank for years, and knew to the penny the current position of every doubtful customer without reference to his ledgers. Avoiding the chief clerk was paramount and I would seek out the youngest and most inexperienced counter clerk, talking to him non-stop to divert him from checking our balance as I presented the wages' cheque. The moment the money was in my hands I fled from the bank, arriving back at the office where a message to ring the bank at once invariably awaited me. The manager would castigate me for putting our account deeper in the red without authority, but it was too late, the wages were safe for another week. Red was to be the predominant colour of our bank statements for many years to come.

The work we printed was commercial, not fine art, but our craft standards were high, meeting the quality vigorously demanded by Marks & Spencer, whose studio manager was a talented designer in pursuit of perfection. If a colour varied a fraction of a shade from his original artwork the entire job would be rejected and he brooked no argument. His imposed quality control pushed us to new limits that stood us well in later years when we worked with creative artists producing limited edition art prints. Although we always worked conscientiously for all our customers, inevitably mistakes occurred from time-to-time, each one a tragedy that cost us lost production, and threatened our growing reputation. One of the more amusing errors was the transposing of two letters on a window poster for the David Greig grocery chain. The poster was advertising loin chops, but the inadvertent switching of the 'o' and the 'i' in loin when preparing the artwork, led to the posters reaching the shops reading 'Lion chops 2/4d lb.' It was not until a guileless customer enquired if the lion chops came from Africa that the error was revealed.

Perhaps the nearest we came at that time to printing the sort of work of which Morris would have approved was an order for wallpaper. Lionel, who had moved from his parents' home in Stamford Hill to a rented room in Gloucester Place in the West End of London, had a circle of theatrical and artistic friends. Among them was an interior designer who was decorating the London home of Lady Moorea Hastings and was seeking a French wallpaper of a pattern that was unobtainable. Lionel said that we could hand-print the paper, and obtaining a small sample was able to work out the repeat pattern. We screen printed a dozen rolls in soft pastel colours and the cost seemed colossal compared to the few shillings a roll that we paid for home decorating, the price working out to about twelve pounds a roll. Evidently the cost was immaterial and it gave me a glimpse of how some people lived.

Meeting with business people gave me an insight into the life-style of the middle class, revealing the tremendous social differences between us. Chatting to a couple of buyers in a Marks & Spencer office, I listened in wonder as one of them was asking the studio manager for advice on matching the colour of the front door of his home to the colour of his new car. I had neither a house nor car and could hardly comprehend the seriousness with which they discussed the problem. A further revelation came in my dealings with a wealthy entrepreneur, Albert Goodman, owner of an electrical sign-making company. He was an Edwardian gentleman, an immaculately dressed septuagenarian who drove a Mark VII Jaguar and lived in Maida Vale. I hardly ever saw him without a large Havana cigar clenched in his teeth and he would make a great play of producing his cigar case and rolling a selected cigar between his fingers, close to his ear, to judge by the sound if it was right for smoking. A widower, he treated me kindly, often giving friendly advice about business, rather like a father talking to his son. He had given us a steady flow of work throughout the year and I thought that it would be a nice gesture, as well as sound business, to buy him a Christmas present. What to buy him was a problem, for he had nothing that was cheap, from the gold rings on his fingers to the gold hunter in his waistcoat pocket. Cigars seemed the answer, but what cigars? My knowledge of cigars was confined to the packet of two Mannikins that Pamela would sometimes buy for me as a special treat. I decided that the best solution would be to let him make his own choice. Shortly before Christmas I said to him, 'Albert, you have been a good customer throughout the year and we would like to buy you a box of cigars. Meet me tomorrow morning and I will take you to Fortnum and Mason's and let you choose a box.' I said Fortnum and Mason because it was a Piccadilly store where the rich shopped and I knew that they sold cigars. He took his thick cigar from his mouth, looked at me and said in his throaty voice, 'John, you don't buy your cigars from a bloody grocer's.' The following day he took me to Dunhill's in Jermyn Street where we were taken into a humidified room. After a knowledgeable discussion between Mr Goodman and the manager he selected a box of Monte Cristo, leaving me stunned by the price.

A significant advance in our business was made with our decision to buy a vehicle. We were still pushing print work for finishing to a trade house half a mile away in Morning Lane by barrow and sending boys to deliver small orders to customers by bus. For larger orders, we had a dodge of persuading van drivers who were delivering goods to us, to re-route their rounds to enable them to also include our deliveries. A ten-bob note worked wonders. When that failed we hired taxis or vans but we had reached the point where hiring was inconvenient and uneconomic. Deciding to buy a vehicle was perhaps the easiest part, for neither of us could drive. We booked a course of lessons with the Elite School of Motoring at Upper Clapton and three times a week we would sally forth to the distress of the instructor and with considerable risk to other road users. Neither Lionel nor myself had been cyclists and we had no road sense at all. I had little feel for things mechanical, and double-declutching on a crash-gear-box was an art that I did not acquire easily, the instructor wincing with each metallic rasp of the gears. Hand signals were obligatory and at one time Lionel had his left hand on the gear change and his right arm stuck out of the window signalling right. With no hand with which to hold the steering wheel he meandered ahead to the consternation of the car driver behind and the dismay of the instructor.

The vehicle we bought, on hire purchase, was a Ford Escort shooting-brake, though the term shooting-brake was merely the invention of an imaginative copywriter, for it was little more than a standard five-hundredweight Thames van with two windows in the rear panels and a back seat which folded flat for carrying goods. But it was new, when most vehicles on the road were pre-war rusting wrecks with balding tyres, and it was ours. Lionel and myself shared it during the day for making deliveries and travelling to appointments, taking the car home for our personal use on alternate weeks.

I had rarely travelled outside of London, seldom journeying further than it was possible to travel by bus or tube. Now, the car brought a new freedom. On free summer Sundays, Pamela would pack up a picnic and we would drive with our five-year-old son to beaches on the south coast, arriving early and spending long and glorious days of happiness, far away from the smoke and stress of the city. Each journey was a joyous expedition of discovery as we explored the Kent and Sussex countryside, driving narrow lanes amid hop gardens and orchards, enviously admiring centuries-old cottages with their gardens of hollyhocks and revelling in the charm of villages that seemed lost in a time warp. Pamela was liberated from housekeeping and I escaped from the relentless pressure of work. They were days of sheer and simple pleasure which we shared as a family, playing beach cricket, paddling and walking for miles. In the winter we visited museums and castles and sought out quiet tea shops run by elderly spinsters. The alternate weeks when the car had to be handed over to Lionel for his turn, filled us with gloom as we were restricted to London and travel by bus. Motoring retained much of the flavour of the thirties, indeed most vehicles on the road were of that vintage. Some cars struggled to climb the gentlest of hills and breakdowns were frequent. Warned by the sight of forlorn families sitting by the wayside as the driver poked about with desperation and hope beneath a raised bonnet, we speculated four pounds and joined the Automobile Association. We sported an AA badge of yellow enamel and chromium, and when we passed an AA patrolman on his motorcycle combination he would give a smart salute with a gauntletted hand which we acknowledged with waves and smiles. In our gleaming new vehicle with its rounded corners and curved bonnet, we felt smugly superior to the upright and angular cars that chugged along leaving trails of oily exhaust fumes.

Both Lionel and myself were young and inexperienced in the ways of business, but Lionel was always more worldly than myself. He had some grasp of how businesses functioned and he was driven by ambition to be successful. Now that we had a car he said that we should take our Marks & Spencer clients out to lunch. This was beyond my experience; for the working class, social eating was restricted to Christmas Day, birthdays, weddings and funerals. Entertaining, by eating outside of the home or family, was unknown. When I told Pamela that Lionel and myself were going out to lunch with clients, she could not understand. Why, when a dinner would be ready for me at home that evening?

My knowledge of food was limited to the meals we had at home during the thirties, the war years of rationing – which extended in some form until the 1950s – canteen eating in the RAF, and the meals Pamela made for me from basic foods bought on a tight budget. I had never actually gone without food as a child, but there were many times when I had been hungry. There was no eating between meals, apart from a ha'porth of sweets or an occasional watery 'ice cream' and there was no refrigerator in the kitchen to be plundered at will. Our food had been kept on two small shelves in a cupboard in the kitchen, and without refrigeration it was bought in small quantities for daily use. Even so, in hot weather there was the chance of curdled milk, rancid fat and sweaty cheese. The shelves held only essentials, bread, margarine, jam, tea, cocoa, milk, condiments and cooking fats. Luxuries like biscuits and fresh fruit were bought only on special occasions. When I was about six-years-old, I remember my mother crying when she spilt a pint of milk because she could not afford to buy another. They were tears of poverty, and young as I was, they were tears that ran into my heart.

Coming from the north of England my mother had inherited a tradition of baking and during the good times she would make us a pie for our dinner, a rabbit pie perhaps, or my favourite, steak and kidney, the crust baked to an undulating crisp golden brown on top, with white soggy and succulent pastry underneath, the centre of the crust propped up in the enamel pie dish with an upturned egg cup. We had a small roast joint on Sundays, with Yorkshire pudding, roast potatoes and cabbage, the best meal of the week, and she would save enough of the joint for a cold meat dinner on Mondays. In the winter, she would make Irish stew, filled with pearl barley and huge suet dumplings. For 'afters' there might be more suet pudding with treacle or custard, or perhaps a rice pudding and arguments with my sister as to who should have the crispy brown skin. Chicken was an expensive luxury, a meal we had once a year, on Christmas Day. Even until

187

the 1950s chicken remained an annual treat in our home, and I had been amazed to find that Lionel's family ate chicken several times a week. Before we went to bed we would have supper, a piece of bread and marge, mousetrap cheese and cocoa made with hot water. Working class diet was food which provided bulk at the lowest cost, and any delicacy was likely to be put into a sandwich to give it necessary bulk.

During the war we lived on our rations, unlike the wealthy who supplemented their diet by dining at restaurants. The rations varied from time to time, but in 1944 they were two ounces of cheese and butter a week, two pints of milk, two ounces of tea, four ounces of bacon, eight ounces of sugar, one and twopence worth of meat and one egg every other week. You could have put the whole lot on one dinner plate. The weekly ration of cheese would make one decent 'doorstep' and an egg shared with my sister for a meal was not unknown. We lived in a siege economy where oranges and bananas were never seen for years and foods like canned fruits, tomatoes, tinned peas, biscuits and sweets were rationed by a points system. We supplemented our diet with the few foods that were off-ration, as and when we could afford them. Offal was off-ration, and I can still recall the rubbery tubes as I cut into a baked sheep's heart. Sausages too were off-ration, made from unsavoury scraps and tasting as if the butcher had included the sawdust sweepings from his floor. Egg substitute and Spam, a tinned meat from America, were popular, but we never tasted the off-ration grapes that sold in West End stores at a guinea a bunch.

Rationing continued until long after the war, and in 1946 bread was added to the foods already controlled, nine ounces a week for a man, unless you were a factory worker, in which case it was fifteen ounces. Women and children received less. Bread, potatoes and jam were rationed until 1948, the meat ration in 1951 was down to tenpence-worth (4p) a week and tea and sugar remained on ration until 1952. It was not until 1954 that rationing was finally abolished. When I was a child I had been told that it was polite to 'leave the table feeling as if you would like a little more', that was an affectation originating from the better off who were in danger of eating too much. I often left the table feeling that I would like a lot more.

It was against this life-long experience of frugality that Lionel and myself invited Clive Lloyd, the studio manager of Marks & Spencer, and Arthur Hawes, their print buyer, to lunch. They suggested the restaurant, the Chez Auguste in Soho, close to

Marks & Spencer's new studio and offices in Poland Street. As the door of the restaurant was opened, it was the threshold to a different world.

The waiters were dressed in black dinner jackets, the first men I had actually seen wearing dinner jackets apart from cinema managers, with stiff white shirts and bow ties, looking like tailor's dummies. The floor was carpeted to the walls and the seats covered in red velvet, the lighting was soft, the ambience quiet and opulent. Once seated, a waiter asked if we would like an apéritif, and I wondered what that was. Our guests nodded in the affirmative, and fortunately they ordered for themselves, both chosing a Campari and soda. Without any idea of what it was, I said that I would have the same. It tasted like a fizzy cough-medicine. Menus were brought, the size of small posters, and I studied mine without comprehension. It was in French, and might just as well have been in hieroglyphics for I had little knowledge of the language and even less of *haute cuisine*.

As we made polite conversation with our guests, who were as strangers to us apart from our business dealings, I was inwardly petrified by my ignorance of the menu. How could I order what I did not understand? They discussed the selection of *hors d'oeuvre*, and I was mystified. Lionel had recognised the *saumon fumé* as smoked salmon and made that his choice. I followed his lead, 'Yes, I will also have the salmon.' Tinned salmon was a working class delicacy that we sometimes had for Sunday tea and I felt smoked salmon must be similar. It proved to be dead cold fish, rubbery and almost tasteless. Where was the vinegar? I did not dare ask. The whole meal was a gastronomic education and a stomach churning ordeal as I emulated our guests, ordering what they ordered, closely following their use of a bewildering array of cutlery spread on the starched white linen. Crusty bread was offered from a basket, not slices, but hunks, together with enough butter to have been a week's ration for two people not long ago. To my consternation I was handed the wine list; I had once had a glass of Keystone Burgundy at Christmas, and that was the extent of my knowledge of the wines of the world. I pretended to study the list, murmuring approval as my eyes scanned the incomprehensible pages. I nonchalantly passed the list to Clive, 'You choose,' I said, which was accepted as a magnanimous gesture. The wine waiter hovered. 'A bottle of Châteauneuf du Pape, I think,' said Clive, looking to me for approval. 'That's fine,' I replied, happy that I did not have to try and pronounce it by name.

My palate was assaulted by unfamiliar tastes, a bloodless white meat served with a fried egg topped with strips of salty fish, sprinkled with strong tasting hard green objects that looked like crinkled peas, an introduction to escalop Holstein with its anchovies and capers. The sliced and fried potatoes were acceptable, sauté, they called them, but I had never tasted spinach or had little peas cooked with ham. It was accompanied by a salad, dripping with a dressing base of olive oil, the greenery largely unrecognised with its mix of peppers and spiky leaves, quite unlike the water-washed lettuce and tomato that was the salad we had at home. I washed the taste away with gulps of the deep red wine.

The orgy of eating continued. A silver trolley was wheeled to the table, rich with a mysterious assortment of sweet dishes – the desert trolley – laden with green figs, rum baba, *crème brûlée*, a host of the uncustomary together with the spoken offer of *crêpes suzettes*. I settled for the trifle, although my mum's trifle had never been laced with liqueur and flooded with thick cream. Would we like coffee? Of course. Coffee to me was made with a teaspoonful of Camp coffee from a bottle, mixed with boiling water and topped with a splash of milk. What was served was strong and black, a bitter tasting liquid served in a cup that looked as if it had been taken from the dolly's tea set that my sister had as a child. Brandies were ordered and served in large balloon glasses, each one warmed in the flame of a contraption heated with methylated spirit as the waiter twirled the glass. This performance concluded my first business lunch.

The bill came to eight pounds, a figure that exceeded my weekly wage. The whole experience left me feeling as if I had taken part in an immoral act, the obsequious service, the excessive choice of dishes, the ritual, of allowing the wine to breathe, the generous portions, the profligate lump of butter, the number of courses and the indulgence of the liqueurs. Above all, the time and the cost. We had eaten for two hours and spent as much per head as an old age pensioner had to live on for a week.

The lunch proved to be a seduction, for in time I was to succumb to the pleasures of the table with the passion of a lover, each meal bringing satisfaction without destroying my appetite for the next. I was encouraged in yielding to the temptation by two colleagues, Charles Try and Ray Bernard. Charles, our production manager, had lived and worked in Paris and had acquired the Gallic attitude to food, that eating should be for pleasure, to be lingered over and never rushed. Ray, the Central London area organiser of the Communist Party had taken part in the invasion of France in 1944. During the first weeks of the battle he had been holed up for a few days on a farm in Normandy, in a barn containing several thousand ripe cheeses. He gained a love of Camembert which ripened into a love affair with French food as the battle moved across the peasant countryside of northern France. Both Charles and Ray were practical gourmets who loved to cook, talking of food with reverence and understanding. For them, the ritual of the table was close to a religion, the spreading of the white cloth on the sacrificial altar, candles lit, bread broken and wine sipped.

Ray Bernard would talk endlessly of food, of unusual dishes and how to cook them, drooling over every ingredient. He saw part of his mission as a Communist to raise the standard of eating among the working class and was scathing in his criticism of our fish and chip culture. It was from Ray that I first heard the name of Raymond Postgate, the socialist historian, a foundation member of the Communist Party of Great Britain and founder of *The Good Food Guide*. Ray saw no conflict between socialism and the love of good food. Although he was impecunious, living on a Party wage, he would save up to take his wife out for meals at the cheaper continental restaurants, Schmidts and Bertorellis in Charlotte Street or Gennarios in Soho. If he was in funds, he would head for the Au Jardin des Gourmets in Greek Street, where he would indulge in four or five courses and recount every morsel in mouth-watering detail the next time we met.

In time, business lunches and dining out became a central part of my life-style, the world of advertising revolving around expense account entertaining, but in the years to 1956 opportunities were few. Pamela and myself still regarded beans on toast at Joe Lyons a treat, and ravioli and chips at the Rex Cafe in Mare Street as an adventure into foreign food.

Parallel with working at G&B, Lionel was making strenuous efforts to further his career in the theatre and no aspect of it appeared to be beyond his ambition. At Unity Theatre he had been a co-writer on the revue, *Turn It Up,* and he had also painted the scenery and designed the poster, which we printed. On the stage, he had appeared in the pantomime, *Cinderella,* and he once auditioned for music hall at the Metropolitan Theatre in Edgware Road, without success. With ambition to become a script writer, he wrote to Spike Milligan, offering his services, only to receive a letter of refusal which began, 'Dear monstrous lad.' He was undeterred. Prompted by the rise in popularity of coffee-bars, he wrote a song entitled, *Oh For a Cup Of Tea*, which he sent to the well-known band leader, Billy Cotton. This time he scored, and it was played one Sunday morning on the *Billy Cotton Band Show*. It was the first Bart song to be broadcast.

His friends from the theatre arrived at our factory from time to time, bringing Bohemian colour to an already colourful business. A young and aspiring actor, Ivan Berg, made regular visits, roaring up on a cerise painted Vespa, while the stage designer and director, Bernard Sarron, came with his Siamese cat on a gold chain. The actor, Alfie Bass, by contrast, was not flamboyant, but a warm hearted and ardent Communist whose connection with Unity went back to pre-war days. When we were busy, Lionel would offer casual employment to unemployed actors whose willingness to perform repetitive and menial tasks was marred by their inability to get up in the mornings. They would stumble in around ten o'clock, full of apologies and lame excuses. Lionel too was finding it difficult to get in on time, for he was now a night bird, spending half the night playing in a skiffle group at a coffee bar known as the 'Two I s'. Playing a wash-board in a Soho basement may not have been a likely springboard to fame, but it fortuitously brought Lionel into contact with a young merchant seaman named Tommy Hicks, playing under the name of Tommy Steele. Lionel introduced him to me, saying that Tommy was 'Britain's king of rock and roll.' Lionel was given to hyperbole, and as I had barely heard of rock and roll, and never of Tommy Steele, I took the claim as evidence once again of Lionel's unbridled imagination.

Before long, Lionel, who had changed his surname to Bart, was writing songs for Tommy Steele and our office phone was ringing, not with enquiries for printing, but with calls from a coterie of show business promoters, managers, publishers and agents. The transition was fast and the names of John Kennedy, Larry Parnes, Peter Maurice and Ian Bevan became as familiar in the office as the names of our clients. Tommy Steele signed a recording contract with Decca and Lionel a contract with the music publisher, Peter Maurice. When Tommy Steele appeared on the new teenage television programme, *Six-Five Special*, performing *Rock with the Caveman*, a number which Lionel had written for him, Lionel, was invited to appear on the show for an interview. Television was still regarded as a wonder, sheer magic, a medium that was changing the culture of entertainment. To be seen on television carried enormous prestige, setting you apart from the masses that merely watched, and bringing instant recognition. When Lionel went into our local fish and chip shop the following day, the owner asked, 'Didn't I see you on television last night?' Fame can be as a drug, and Lionel, who had an obsession to become famous, was hooked. His professional career in the world of show business was moving ahead, fast.

If Lionel had been nervous about his first appearance on television, he was confidently in charge when a reporter from the *Daily Express* came to interview him at our office. Lionel sat in the padded swivel chair behind the desk, acting out the role of the business man who could also write songs while travelling on the top deck of a bus or sitting in the bath The reporter may have been amused by the brash youngster, but within six years Lionel would be voted by the Variety Club of Great Britain as 'Show Business Personality of the Year.'

People have often asked me if I was surprised by Lionel's success as a composer and lyricist. Not really, for he was gifted as an artist in the widest sense. He was markedly different to most of us, possessed of a mix of inspirational genius and ambition. He would work with enormous enthusiasm and creative ability towards any goal he set himself, and for Lionel there were no limits. Intelligent and imaginative, he had a childlike charm that drew people to him, yet the same qualities could produce dramatic tantrums if he was thwarted and our relationship was at times tempestuous. Fortunately, they were passing moments, forgotten by him as quickly as they arose. If anything surprised me about Lionel, it was merely the speed with which he achieved the fame he sought.

Lionel's life-style changed. He was able to indulge his love of stylish clothes, to spend hours at the hairdressers, where they razor trimmed his beard and scented him with cologne. In conversation, he invariably referred to well known stars in the world of show business by their first names. The effect of Lionel's burgeoning success upon my own life was a mixture of advantage and disadvantage. Benefit came as soon as Lionel received his first cheque from his publisher, for he promptly put down the deposit on a new car, an ice-blue Zephyr convertible with a power operated hood. For Lionel, it was a conspicuous and potent symbol of success. For me, it meant that I now had sole use of the firm's Escort. It also profited the youngest of our lads in the firm, for Lionel would extravagantly pay him five shillings to wash his car during his dinner hour. On the debit side, the time that Lionel spent at G&B diminished in direct proportion to his increasing involvement with the theatre. In some ways this suited me, for I was free to make my own decisions, but there were times when I missed having him around to share the minute-to-minute problems which are inherent in any business.

Any thoughts that Lionel's new found fame would directly benefit the company financially were dispelled when the bank bounced a cheque that we had issued to one of our suppliers. We went to our bank, then a branch of the Midland Bank in Kingsland Road, and Lionel played the Tommy Steele name as hard as he could, talking with enthusiasm of the tremendous opportunities in writing popular music. Unfortunately, the bank manager, a little grey man, was not given to watching teenage programmes on television, asked who Tommy Steele was, and in any case could not see what it had to do with the business. Lionel immediately closed his newly opened private account and we transferred our business overdraft to a city branch of the Westminster Bank.

One of my reasons for going into business on my own account was a search for independence. I had no ambition to be wealthy, setting my goal to earn perhaps twice as much as I would have done as an employed printer. That would bring relief from the constant worry of buying food, clothing and paying the rent. More importantly I wanted to be in a position to work in my own way, producing work that I would enjoy. I also wanted to be free to have time to spend with my family, without being tied to the endless treadmill of work as a necessity for survival. From my first day at work I could not reconcile myself to the idea that to toil from dawn till dusk, five or six days a week for fifty years, was an acceptable way of life, unless that work was pleasurable and freely chosen. To be shut in a factory, workshop or office for half a century, working merely for subsistence is the theft of life. I set myself the goal of being free to chose my work and the way I would live by the time I was thirty-five.

After five years of self employment, I had failed on all accounts. I did not take higher wages than a good printer, I took less, although I did have the benefit of the car. I did not print the work of my choice, but rather the work I could get, and it was all rush, rush, rush. I did refuse one job, an enquiry from the Ministry of Defence for printing on plastic which was to be part of a bomb sight. I wrote a letter explaining that I was more interested in construction than destruction. I never received a reply from the Ministry, but I did receive a personal letter from a sympathiser within the department who told me that the letter had created a furore. As for my hours of work, they fluctuated with the volume of work available, but often ran late into the night and bit into the weekends. The company was still in debt, and the prospect of being able to live a more leisurely life was distant.

However, I was able to print some jobs that gave me a special satisfaction, including posters for the *Daily Worker* and the Communist Party. I had also produced my first limited edition print, an image of peace, depicting a child holding a dove, designed by a Communist artist, Sheila Dorrell. At the same time, I started a working relationship with another Communist artist, Ken Sprague, making a screen printed version of his lino-cut illustrating the tale of 'The man who stole the goose from the common, and the man who stole the common from the goose'. Within a few years there was to be a succession of posters for Joan Littlewood and Gerry Raffles at Theatre Workshop in Stratford East, and the first of hundreds of posters for the Royal Shakespeare Company from that other Stratford, work which was to give enormous satisfaction.

Ahead, I was to enjoy years of working with some of the best graphic designers in Britain, George Mayhew, Henrion, Abram Games, Alan Fletcher, Peter Dixon, and Gordon House among them. There would be printmaking too for many of the better known names in the fine art world, from Kenneth Armitage to Edward Paolozzi, work where the sole criteria was technique and quality, before time or profit. This special work apart, I took pleasure in every job we printed, especially the difficult work which I regarded as a challenge to our craft skills, driving us to extend the boundaries of the process. But even the simplest jobs were rewarding, for I took pride in producing work that was crisp and clean and derived an aesthetic satisfaction from the solid intensity of colour produced by the screen printing process.

I strove to build 'a factory as it might be', making our workshop a pleasant place where we produced the finest work. We were a trade union house, a closed shop – scorning those who would happily share the benefits of organisation without paying their dues – providing the best wages and working conditions in the industry. With a team of talented designers and printers, we won every major award for fine screen printing, both at home and overseas. Guided by Morris's vision, I tried to create a workplace where there was pride in the work produced and dignity in the labour of production. Yet despite the fulfilment of many of my aspirations, including a degree of prosperity, I was trapped by the very system of capitalism. Independence and security were illusory and I was not my own master, for my masters were the large companies that were my customers, themselves driven by their shareholders in the pursuit of profit. Loyalty and integrity had little place in big business when the bottom line on the balance sheet fell below the level demanded by the city. For the most part our work was produced under pressure, the anxiety of salaried executives transmitted downwards to insist on the saving of another penny or another hour, men and women in vast office blocks shuffling papers that affected all our lives. To achieve the dream I shared with Morris it would be necessary to build a society based not upon competition, but upon co-operation, a society where labour was 'honourable and honoured', a commonwealth where men and women would rejoice in their labour and share the wealth produced, wealth created for common use, not private gain. For a factory to be as it might be, the goal was socialism.

CHAPTER 12
Comrades and Friends

'The poverty of the poor is not an accident, a temporary difficulty, a personal fault. It is the permanent state in which the vast majority of the citizens of any capitalist country have to live.' These are the opening words of *The Town That Was Murdered*, Ellen Wilkinson's searing history of Jarrow. I read these words when I was seventeen while standing at a bookshelf in the West Ham Central Library. Written in 1939, the book is a damning account of capitalist acquisition and exploitation, with indecent wealth and power for a few, callously plundered from the many good citizens of that ancient town. Jarrow has passed into our language as a word synonymous with Britain in the thirties, unemployment, dereliction and hunger. The 'Jarrow Crusade', the march of two hundred thin-faced men from Tyneside to Westminster, with their blankets, ground sheets, and a field kitchen lent to them by the Boy Scouts, has become a legend, a march representative of all the millions of hungry and unemployed in that desperate decade before the Second World War, when skilled workers like my father were driven to the charity of soup kitchens. The Jarrow march had touched the conscience of millions, but not the heart of the Bishop of Durham, who wrote a condemnatory letter to *The Times*. Perhaps he was following local ecclesiastical tradition, because an earlier Bishop of Durham had loaned his stables to the local constabulary for the imprisonment of three hundred striking miners, when the gaol and House of Correction were full.

I borrowed the book and read it at a sitting, enthralled by 'Red Ellen's' account of the rise of a town virtually owned by one man,

Charles Palmer, with its Palmer's shipyard, a Palmer commemorative tablet in the Town Hall, a Palmer portrait in the council chamber, photographs of Palmer's works decorating the corridors, the Palmer Memorial Hospital, the Palmer's library, and streets named after Palmer's directors and managers. Even the mayor's gold chain had been given to the town by Palmer. Jarrow was Palmerstown, a town to be consigned to the scrapheap when it stood in the way of larger financial interests.

The Town That Was Murdered presented a cogent case for socialism, for the consideration of community above private interest. It was a book that was to be a seminal influence in my conversion to the cause of socialism, a book that I link with three others which together led me to join the Communist Party. They were *Adversary in the House*, a story of the life of the American socialist, Eugene Debs, by Irvine Stone, *The Ragged Trousered Philanthropists*, a tale of working life in the building trade by Robert Tressell, and the first volume of Karl Marx's *Capital*.

I bought myself a copy of *The Town That Was Murdered* shortly after reading it for the first time, a Left Book Club edition, and sometime in the early 1950s I lent it to Lionel. It came back with the salient points marked in pencil, for he had considered making the story of the Jarrow march into a musical. That he did not pursue the idea is a loss to the English stage, for it would have made a valuable contribution to working class theatre, much in the way that Miles Malleson did with *Six Men of Dorset*, a stage version of the story of the Tolpuddle Martyrs. The idea of writing a musical about a march, must have buzzed around in his head for years, for in the 1960s he conceived the idea of writing a musical based upon the Aldermaston march, treating the subject as a modern version of *The Canterbury Tales*. Sadly, that too remained unwritten.

Reading socialist literature developed a class conscious attitude to life, providing the economic theory of class, but the instinct for class solidarity was nurtured by my environment. I did not need Marx to understand that the society in which we lived was divided between the wealthy, who did no productive work, and those who grafted all their working lives and owned little or nothing. That is a simplification, but in essence it was true. If the rich 'worked', it was to use their money to make more money, earned for them by wage workers.

For wage workers, there was no accumulation of wealth. This truth was poignantly demonstrated when an old widow in our street died. Her husband, who had predeceased her by a few years, had been a hard-working man, a good husband, father and neighbour. Their children had married, moved away from the street, and the old woman lived alone, cared for by her nearby relatives and neighbours. When she died, the house she had rented for fifty years had to be cleared, as the landlord had a new tenant waiting to come in. The children shared a few personal trinkets and arranged for the furniture and effects to be removed, a dealer giving them a paltry thirty shillings for the lot. On the day of the clearance, a few days after the funeral, he sorted out several pieces which he took away on his cart, and left two rag and bone men to clear the rest. The accumulated possessions of a lifetime amounted to a few sticks of furniture, kitchen utensils, crockery and some worn linoleum. Unceremoniously, the contents were thrown from the upper windows of the house, the old fashioned wardrobe smashing as matchwood upon the pavement. The bed in which her children had been born was dismantled and slung out as old iron, the bedding for rags. Women stood at their doorsteps, arms folded across their pinafored breasts and watched in silence. Within minutes, without dignity, all trace of a home that had been loved for more than half a century was hauled away as worthless rubbish.

Working for wages was a trap, designed to keep the poor *poor*, in their place, at the bottom of a class structured society. Tory shareholders were fond of talking of 'a fair day's work for a fair day's pay', but what was fair? The hardest, dirtiest, most dangerous work rated the lowest pay. Before the Second World War, landed dukes drew more money in royalties for each ton of coal mined, than the miners who hewed at the coal face. Skilled craftsmen, after seven year apprenticeships, considered themselves aristocrats of labour, but they earned less than a stockbroker's clerk fresh from college. It took twenty years to become an engine driver, responsible for the safety of hundreds, but they were rated on the pay scale below a secretary in an insurance office. For the most part, wage-work meant eking out an existence from pay-day to pay-day.

The brunt of making ends meet was born by women, for they had the management of the weekly pay packet. Mums worked economic miracles to feed their families, but a quarter of all our children in the 1930s lived in homes where there was no more than four shillings a week per head to spend on food. They juggled the housekeeping to pay the landlord, buy coal and clothes, while scrubbing and polishing to keep a 'respectable' home. Women darned, patched and mended to keep the kids 'decent', scrimped to have boots repaired, and if they were lucky, had their hair permed once a year. The poorest took in washing, or homework, turning their already cramped living rooms into rent-free sweatshops. My mother, a fast and proficient knitter, answered an advertisement for home knitting, and sat for long hours making babies' bonnets with Angora wool, until she choked with the amount of fine fluff produced. She then turned her hand to making tassels for curtains, setting up the wooden frame on our kitchen table, but as deft and nimble as she was, could only earn shillings at an hourly rate that was akin to slave labour. A neighbour made up cardboard boxes, her house reeking of glue, with every room and even the passage piled high with finished cartons. Homework was among the worst forms of exploitation of female labour.

A week of illness or unemployment for the breadwinner wrought chaos with the budget, a prolonged period of enforced idleness brought debt that might take years to clear. This did not stop the wealthy from prattling on about the virtues of thrift, of 'saving for a rainy day', to make provision for sickness or old age. They made their provision by carving a biblical inscription in stone above the Stock Exchange, proclaiming, 'The earth is the Lord's and the fullness thereof', and proceeded to rob the poor of the full value of their labour.

The plight of the working class was compounded by poverty. Shoes that let in water, unheated bedrooms, cheap thin clothing, and waiting for trams and buses in all weathers aggravated common colds, leading to chest complaints and rheumatism. Men and women dragged themselves to work when sick, for they could not afford to lose a single day's pay. My father scarcely took a day off throughout his working life. Getting to work meant walking, waiting at bus stops, or pedalling a push bike, winter and summer alike. Arriving at work, often to work in wet clothes, conditions were grim, large workshops sometimes heated by a single stove. Lavatory facilities were basic, and in the factory where my friend Ken Sprague once worked, the doors to the cubicles were removed by the management to discourage malingering for a crafty smoke. Industrial disease and injury were prevalent in a wide range of occupations, from deafened boiler-makers to myopic seamstresses, as the many toiled to provide a cosy life for the few. Almost ten thousand miners were killed in pit accidents between 1930 and 1940, and there were more than one and a quarter million injuries, as profit was weighed against safety. Despite the daily carnage, mine owners resisted every demand for higher wages or shorter working hours.

The illnesses, diseases and infirmities caused by relentless manual work in arduous conditions often had to be endured without proper treatment; and what could a panel doctor say to a woman worn out by childbearing, undernourished and worried sick because her husband was out of work? 'Take a month at a convalescent home in a warm climate, we will look after the children.' The likely treatment, frequently prescribed by our doctor, was a bottle of tonic, a mysterious red liquid used as a panacea for anyone who was 'run down'.

Children with rickets, their legs in metal callipers, were a common sight in West Ham during the 1930s, yet attempts by Labour politicians to introduce legislation for the provision of free milk and dinners in the schools were fiercely resisted by well-fed Conservative politicians, ably supported by our lords spiritual and temporal who saw the provision of welfare as undermining 'family values'. This at a time when Sir John Boyd Orr reported that thirteen million working people were 'gravely undernourished'. School clinics strove to cope with the ill health of poor children, but adults had to manage as best they could, paying into hospital associations, or going 'on the panel'. My mother's weekly coppers paid to the Hospital Savings Association were a priority that ranked with paying the rent. Self-medication was endemic. Bad eyesight was tackled by the simple process of trying on pairs of spectacles at a market stall or from a counter at Woolworth's, a hit or miss affair until apparently suitable lenses were found. Rotting teeth resulting from poor diet were generally treated by pulling them out. Women, their teeth further affected by childbearing, frequently had all their teeth extracted by the time they were thirty. My mother had twenty teeth extracted at a single sitting, when she was twenty-nine.

Working people had the worst of everything, shoddy clothes, sub-standard housing, tied cottages, primitive health care and limited education. For slum dwellers, the 'red army' meant the swarms of bugs that infested their rotting homes, to be fought with paraffin. It was the working class that bought cracked eggs, skimmed milk, margarine and bruised fruit, a life of bread and scrape, their children shorter in height and lower in weight than the children of the well off. If workers travelled by train, they rode third class, if they went on holiday, they stayed with relatives or in boarding houses. I did not taste fresh pineapple, peaches or grapes until I was twenty, and did not spend a night in a hotel until I was twenty-five. My father summed it up neatly:

> Britain is a free country,
> Free without a doubt,
> And if you haven't any money
> Then you're free to go without.

The rigid structure of class society manifested itself in every aspect of life. The professions were closed shops to the school-leavers of the poor whose full time education ended at fourteen, turned out to sell their labour for dead-end jobs in offices and shops, fields and factories. The administration of the law was firmly in the hands of a cosy all male, middle class fraternity of lawyers and judges. There were no High Court judges drawn from the working class, (are there any yet?) for their role was the defence of property. Officers in the armed forces, the brass hats, were drawn from the public schools, as were the senior officers in the police force. The three police Commissioners prior to 1945, were a Field Marshall, an Air Vice Marshall and a Marshall. The higher echelons of the permanent administration of the state, the Foreign Office, for example, was an old boys' club, its members again culled from the major public schools, guardians of the Empire, wealth and imperial rule. The Church of England too was class ridden. Jesus may have been the son of a carpenter, but there was never any chance that I could have become the Archbishop of Canterbury.

Class snobbery was pervasive, permeating downwards from a wealthy clique of royal families, dukes, duchesses, lords and ladies, acting out useless lives of wealth consumption, but producing nothing. They not only lived different lives from the mass of the people, but they talked differently, their accents aped by the middle class who looked down on regional and local accents as belonging to a lower social order. Their class snobbery was especially bigoted with regard to the accents of those living in the industrial cities. A cockney accent was derided as comic and indicative of ignorance, a formidable barrier to better jobs, hence the futile attempt of our English teacher at West Ham Secondary School to 'improve' our speech. Pre-war British films make the point clearly, portraying cockneys as chirpy ill-educated wits or petty thieves. Despite a pretence of democracy, control of the state was firmly in the hands of landowners, capitalists and the aristocracy.

My steady conversion to socialism was influenced by a growing awareness of the absolute unjustness of our society. It was not a case of envy, but of reason. The distribution of wealth, created by millions, was inequitable, and for me, unacceptable. Even before the war, Britain produced enough to ensure that no family lived in want. There seemed no logical reason why the producers of the nation's wealth should not have their share. Yet, production for profit, not use, meant that building workers were unemployed while millions lived in houses without bathrooms, textile workers unemployed while children were dressed in hand-me-downs, people hungry, while food was dumped. We lived in a society that condemned the majority of its people to live out their working lives as second class citizens. There had to be a better way.

The war shaped my political development, for it brought social change and proved the efficacy of a society where private interest gave way to the public good. Rationing and price controls were a fairer way of distributing the limited food resources available to the nation. Of course the greedy rich punched holes in the system, dining in expensive restaurants that dodged the controls, and buying from the black market. The rich still had their luxuries; Evelyn Waugh was able to write in his diary for 1942, 'A good year . . . drunk three hundred bottles of wine and smoked three hundred or more Havana cigars.' But for most of the people, rationing ensured that no family went without necessities and that shortages were shared. Indeed, there is evidence that a majority were in favour of rationing and price controls continuing after the war, for despite a restricted diet, millions were in fact better fed and consequently healthier than they were during the thirties. In waging the war, production was not left to a free-for-all scramble for profits. Needs were determined and industry directed to the production of the materials and weapons necessary for the successful prosecution of the conflict. It was state planning that guided Britain to victory over fascism.

Few predicted Labour's overwhelming victory in the General Election of 1945, but the prevailing mood was for change, no return to the bad old days between the wars. Labour's election programme recognised the needs of the people, a nation ravaged by war who demanded food, homes and jobs. The Tories, led by Winston Churchill, posed as champions of freedom, urging the lifting of wartime controls and restrictions, but Labour explained that the price of so called 'economic freedom' for the few was too high if bought at the cost of idleness and misery for millions. Labour stood for freedom, the freedom of trade unions, denied by the vindictive Trades Disputes and Trade Union Act, passed by the Conservatives in 1927, after the General Strike. Labour said that it 'would not tolerate freedom to exploit other people, freedom to pay low wages and to push up prices for selfish profit, freedom to deprive the people of the means of living full, happy and healthy lives.' The Tories misread wartime support for Churchill, assuming that his role as the architect of victory would also guarantee popular leadership in peacetime. To most workers, Churchill was a warmonger, virulently anti-working class, the man who sent troops to quell striking miners, the epitome of class oppression.

Before the election, I bought and read the Labour Party's declaration of policy, *Let Us Face the Future*, with its V for Victory cover, a document of inspiration and hope. Its words proclaimed, 'The Labour Party is a socialist party, and proud of it. Its ultimate purpose at home is the establishment of a Socialist Commonwealth of Great Britain, free, democratic, efficient, progressive, public spirited, its material resources organised in the service of the British people.' To ensure that the basic industries would work in the interests of the people it pledged the public ownership of fuel and power, transport, iron and steel and stated its belief in the nationalisation of the land. Together with the restructuring of key industries, Labour, promised a programme of social security that would end 'the mean and shabby treatment which was the lot of millions while Conservative governments were in power for long years.' This would be achieved by introducing an all-inclusive programme of social welfare, with benefits for children, expectant mothers, the unemployed, the old and the sick, the basis for a new egalitarian society, sweeping away the old Poor Law that treated the poor as paupers, subjected to the loathsome means test. Labour planned to implement a National Health Service – where the criteria for treatment would be need, not the ability to pay – and a system of social security including child allowances, maternity benefits, free milk, and fruit juices. Underpinning the reforms would be a policy of full employment. It may be said that Labour's programme of social security was based upon recommendations contained in the wartime Beveridge Report, so it was, but it was derived from socialist philosophy. Labour had received the report with enthusiasm, while Churchill and his followers accepted it grudgingly, with reservations. Conservative ideology led them to claim, 'Provision by the state of complete social security can only be achieved at the expense of personal freedom and by sacrificing the right of an individual to choose what life he wishes to lead and what occupation he should follow.' They could not understand that without economic justice, people have no choice. It is the theory that we are all free to dine at the Ritz.

Labour proposed the creation of new Ministries, for Health, Housing, and Town and Country Planning, but more than that, Labour had vision, projecting a society with concert halls, civic centres, modern libraries, day nurseries and health centres, the creation of a truly free society where people had the health, wealth and leisure to lead fulfilling lives. Labour's programme contrasted with the Conservative concept of profit-grabbing freedom for the few, with unemployment, insecurity, landlordism, and exploitation leading to private wealth and public neglect. It was Labour's plan for social justice that captured the hearts of the people. In the 1945 election, Labour polled more votes than any other party in our history. Old people wept with joy, there were bonfire celebrations in parts of London's East End, while in the House of Commons, triumphant Labour MPs sang *The Red Flag*. It seemed that the long, long night was over and that dawn would bring the sunshine of socialism.

My parents had of course voted Labour, as did practically everyone else in our street, and indeed in the whole of West Ham, where the votes cast for the Conservatives were derisory. After six years of war, my father took up his tools again and started to rebuild his life, not waiting for the War Damage Commission to start repairing our house, but doing most of the interior work himself while we awaited a new slate roof to replace the one blown away by a rocket. He resumed his monthly attendance of his trade union branch meeting, was elected to the committee, and in time was delegated to represent the branch on the West Ham Trades Council. As a family, we were 'solid Labour', or as Sarah described us all, linking our families together, 'red hot Labour.'

The Labour government inherited the huge debt accumulated during the war, depleted national resources, millions of homes destroyed or bomb damaged and industry geared to war production. It tackled the problems as pledged. Rationing, price controls and restrictions continued as part of a planned return to peaceful reconstruction, demobilisation of the armed forces was controlled and methodical and there was no return to the mass unemployment that followed the end of the First World War. Despite enormous difficulties, Labour pushed ahead with its legislation to build a fairer Britain. Many of its promises were kept, including the founding of the National Health Service. It took three years of hard negotiation with the doctors, and often the opposition was powerful and vociferous as sections of the medical profession sought to defend private practice. One doctor described the proposals relating to the voluntary hospitals as 'The greatest seizure of property since Henry VIII confiscated the monasteries.' Accepted now as part of the structure of our society, it is hard to understand the logic that sought to keep hospitals dependent on charity, selling flags to help support their existence, a proposition that would never have been acceptable in relation to the armed forces. There was plenty of talk among doctors about freedom and the constrictions of state control, but freedom in a capitalist society meant that the rich had access to the finest consultants and treatment, while the poor took pot luck. A *laissez faire* system had resulted in there being plenty of doctors in wealthy areas and few in the densely populated districts of the poor, just where they were most needed. Labour's state control envisaged health centres in every community with first class medical care for all. Aneurin Bevan fought with passion and skill for the creation of the National Health Service, a fight during which he was constantly mocked and vilified by the right wing press, but Labour was resolute, and despite concessions, the greatest socialist measure this country had ever placed upon the statute books became effective in July 1948. Just how much the service was needed is evidenced by the fact that in less than a year, more than five million pairs of spectacles had been dispensed, another three million were on order, and more than eight million people had been accepted for dental treatment.

While steadfastly supporting Labour, reading the *Daily Herald* and *Reynold's News* and arguing on the factory floor in favour of nationalisation, I also became a regular reader of the *Daily Worker*. The *Worker* had a fine books' page and my reading in the public library centred on the political as I devoured books by Jack London, Upton Sinclair, Sean O'Casey and Bernard Shaw. I grappled alone with books on Marxism, trying to understand dialectical and historical materialism without much success, and persevered with the books of Marxist writers like Christopher

Caudwell, Ralph Fox and Jack Lindsay. I was searching for an understanding of the society in which I lived, but I was wandering along a broad path without a map. By 1949, it was to be the Communist Party, with its critical analysis of monopoly capitalism and a Marxist theory of the historical inevitability of socialism that was to provide direction in my life for the next seven years.

My decision to join the Communist Party, 'the Party', as it was known to all who embraced its cause, was no sudden leap of faith, but the result of a steady move to the left, nurtured by my reading of the *Daily Worker* and my increasing identity with Communist Party policy. As the Labour government allied itself with the foreign policy of the United States, and the chill of the Cold War began to turn to ice, it seemed that the Labour Party was losing its impetus towards the building of a socialist commonwealth. The need for a strong Communist Party to give direction to the working class in the fight for socialism appeared crucial.

I made my application for Party membership during my military service, by sending in a recruiting form snipped from the *Daily Worker*. Within a few days, the local branch secretary, Hymie Miller, was knocking on my door in St James Road, giving the shocking news to my mother that I had joined the Communists. Hymie had made the journey from his home near West Ham park, with great difficulty, for he was stricken with osteoarthritis, and found walking a laborious and painful exercise. He was bent forward from the base of his spine, and walked with his arms extended, clutching two walking sticks, his limbs supported as in a Salvador Dali painting. With considerable tenacity he had inched his way the mile or so from his home to meet the new recruit. My mother, shaken by the news, and apprehensive of letting a Communist stranger into the house, uncharacteristically sent him away without inviting him in for a cup of tea, merely taking his name and address.

On my next leave, I called on Hymie, to make my first official contact with the Party. He lived with his wife, Evelyn, in a ground floor flat of a small house in a tree-lined road leading to the park. Hymie had raven black hair, brushed back, penetrating brown eyes that gleamed as the black lashes of his eyelids blinked behind rimless glasses perched on a beak-like nose. A diamond polisher by trade, he was a soft-natured man, imbued with kindness, never complaining of his considerable disability. His welcome was at first cautious, his questions probing, with what I later realised was the mild paranoia that gripped some Party members, ever watchful for infiltrators, harbouring the same sort of suspicions that racked the Soviet Union, encircled as it was by enemies. When satisfied that all was well, he warmed, calling me comrade, which was both welcoming and strange. Evelyn made tea, and Hymie gave an analysis of the current political situation. With what I considered undue concern for my welfare, he thought it best that he should retain my Party card until I was demobbed, and I was rather disappointed, for it made me feel that I was not yet a true Communist. However, he sold me some of the party pamphlets he had shown me during our talk, 'lit', he called them, using party jargon that was soon to become familiar. I wanted the pamphlets to take back to camp, to spread the message of socialism, for in joining the Party I was eager for converts.

On my return to civilian life I collected my Party card and avidly read the small print. 'Party members should regard it as a duty to buy and study the *Daily Worker* every day, and when possible, *World News and Views* weekly (4d), the *Communist Review* monthly (9d) and the *Labour Monthly* (1s 6d) every month.' I was to learn that the key words were 'duty' and 'study', Communists had duties towards the Party, and to the working class. Communists did not read literature, they studied it, and the Communist Party produced more printed matter than any other political movement in the world. Other duties included, 'with the assistance of the Party', the improvement of your political knowledge and understanding of Marxist-Leninist theory, membership of your appropriate trade union or professional body, and membership of the Co-operative Society. It was also a duty to observe Party discipline and carry out the policy and decisions of the Party and 'to fight against everything which is detrimental to the interests of the Party and the working class.'

The further aims of the Party as set out in the membership card were lengthy, as were most Party statements, but they were precise and unequivocal. The first aim was to 'replace capitalism with a socialist system based upon the social ownership of the means of production and exchange.' Socialism, it said, 'creates the condition for the ultimate goal of communism, based on the principle, "From each according to his ability, to each according to his need".' Other aims were equally laudable, 'the removal of all discrimination based on race, class, sex or religion', and support for the struggle of the peoples of the British Empire for national independence. There was much more, including an explanation of democratic centralism – the organisational structure of the party – and the claim that the 'Communist Party is the vanguard of the working class, guided by Marxist-Leninist principles', uniting within its ranks, 'all those who are prepared to work for the achievement of socialism.'

My Party card brought a sense of pride, purpose and commitment. I was now an agitator, expected to be able to give a lead in the daily struggles on the streets, the factory, my trade union, the Co-op and the broader Labour movement in the fight for socialism. It was a role I was eager to accept and fulfil.

Communist Party life was all embracing, political, social and cultural, for Communists were a driving force, rooted in the working class, yet separated from them by a resolute dedication to the pursuit of political influence and power. My introduction to this new way of life was the branch meeting, held once a fortnight in a bare-boarded and cheerless room at a local school. We met at eight in the evening, giving us time to come home from work and have a meal. At my first branch meeting there were about a dozen men, mostly in their thirties, drably dressed in working clothes. These were the most active members of the branch, a hard core who turned up to every meeting. We sat on school chairs, facing a table where Hymie sat, flanked by two members of the branch committee. I was formally introduced, 'a new recruit, Comrade Gorman', and I was filled with pride by the title. Amid a haze of tobacco smoke, Hymie and the other comrades of the branch committee expounded the Party line on the issues of the day and organised political action within the Stratford area for the coming week.

'Organised' and 'active' were key words, constantly used in relation to the Party and its work. We talked of the 'organised working class' and recognised organisation as central to the attainment of political power. Stalin had laid down sound guide rules to successful organisation, which we endeavoured to follow. They were simple and effective. First, 'take the decision, secondly, allocate the responsibility, thirdly, check to see that the decision had been carried out.' At branch meetings, the decisions of the branch committee were explained and discussed, commitments made, responsibility allocated for carrying out the decisions, and checks made that earlier decisions had been acted upon by those responsible for agreed action. The meetings started on time, for as Harry Pollitt had pointed out, if they did not, then those who were late would not know that they were late. Proceedings were formal, minutes read, and we followed an agenda drawn up by the branch committee. The final item on the agenda, 'any other business', led to political discussion on specific issues, when any questions on policy were convincingly answered by an exposition of the correct line. The meetings finished on time and we promptly dispersed as the rather hostile caretaker, anxious to go home, walked into the meeting and started to stack the chairs. There was always a meeting after the meeting, as we stood in a group on the pavement and continued the political discussion, finally drifting away at ten-thirty or eleven.

The Party brought me a new circle of friends, comrades, bound together in a close fraternal association, dependent on each other for mutual support, a society within society, like a secular religion. In many ways they were different from the friends I had made at school, in the RAF and at work. Communists were serious, dedicated idealists, claiming the moral high ground in the fight against rapacious capitalism, ever concerned with social issues and constantly involved in political struggle, 'the mass struggle' as it was called. Their homes, even the poorest, and there were plenty of those, invariably contained books, for books yielded knowledge, and knowledge was power. In many Party homes, books took priority over new furniture. While other workers saved for a new three-piece suite, Communists very often spent precious shillings on adding to their library. Much of it was Party literature, heavy political tomes, the works of Marx, Engels, Lenin, and the *History of the Communist Party of the Soviet Union (Bolsheviks)*, a foundation text second only to *Capital*, printed by the Foreign Languages Publishing House in Moscow and sold throughout the world at a subsidised price. Along with the *Communist Manifesto*, other books might include the writings of Communist leaders past and present, Dimitrov, Leibknecht, Rosa Luxemburg and inevitably, Stalin. Dotted among the shelves were the soft orange covers of the Left Book Club, a recurring favourite being Strachey's *The Coming Struggle for Power*. Pamphlets and booklets were collected as school children might collect stamps, with unbroken runs of *Labour Monthly*, reports on party congresses and CPGB publications covering every industrial front, mining, docks, engineering and building, wherever the party was engaged in struggle. Party language was the language of war, class war. Areas of conflict were described as 'fronts', workers were 'mobilised', there were 'assaults' on the capitalist system and the world was divided into the socialist and capitalist 'camps', with the socialist countries leading the 'fight' for peace. Books were 'weapons' in winning the 'battle of ideas', a war ceaselessly waged in 'winning the masses' for the principles of socialism.

The Party had a Marxist position on every aspect of culture, and books were read that buttressed the concept of socialist realism, a counter to bourgeois ideology. If a few volumes of Dickens were on the shelves, *Hard Times* was sure to be included, if there was poetry, *The Rubaiyat of Omar Khayyam* and works by Robert Burns would be found. H G Wells, Mrs Gaskell, especially *North and South*, William Morris, Zola and Gorki all found favour. British working class writers like John Sommerfield, Ralph Bates and Edward Upward were popular, as were American revolutionary novelists like Jack London, Upton Sinclair and Howard Fast. Most collections included John Reed's *Ten Days that Shook the World*, and Harry Pollitt's autobiography, *Serving my Time*. Added to the books that were almost obligatory reading, Party members displayed their own diversity of special interests, with books on education, art, theatre, music and history. Soon, I began to accumulate a few precious volumes, housed in a glass-fronted bookcase, made for me by my father. I had little to spend and tended towards the cheap books printed in the Soviet Union, early purchases including Marx's *Capital*, the *History of the CPSU*, Engel's *The Condition of the Working Class in England*, a biography of Stalin, and a book of poems by Nikola Vaptsarov, a Bulgarian worker hero who had been shot by the Nazis. Other books I had already culled from second hand bookshops, including, *The Iron Heel*, *The Ragged Trousered Philanthropists*, *Adversary in the House*, and a beautiful Nonesuch Press edition of selected poems and essays by William Morris. Paperbacks had their place, *The Last Frontier* by Howard Fast, *The Case for Communism* by Willie Gallacher, and some of the plays of Bernard Shaw among them. I bought *Women and Communism* for Pamela, and when our son was born, invested in a hardback on the education of children by Makarenko. My total commitment to the Party could be measured by my purchase of *How to be a Good Communist* by Liu Shao Chi. Frivolous reading, that is for no better reason than pleasure, gave way to reading that would help me to become a good revolutionary. With time for reading limited by work and a full programme of party activity, my reading was dominated by Party pamphlets, but there is no doubt that many who had no previous habit of reading were introduced to the world of books upon joining the Party.

From my first branch meeting I was drawn into street activity, canvassing for signatures to the Stockholm Peace Appeal, issued by the World Peace Council from its meeting in that city the previous year. The Party it seemed had a passion for collecting signatures to petitions, not because they were efficacious, but as a means of involving the masses in a political act and useful for making contacts with sympathisers. This was to be the first of countless petitions that I would badger my friends and acquaintances with over the next six years. The demands of the petition were reasonable enough, 'The prohibition of all atomic weapons with international control and inspection', a reference to branding the first nation to use the bomb as war criminals, and a demand for an all-round reduction in armaments, to be agreed by the great powers. It appeared to offer an easy introduction to my first experience of 'going on the knocker.'

We worked in pairs, walking from door to door along the streets of narrow terraced houses, pens and petitions in hand, ringing at bells, tapping knockers, and flapping at letter-boxes where unwelcoming doors were blank of knocker or bell. We ignored the occasional sign, 'No hawkers, canvassers or circulars', for it was a matter of life or death. Doors were sometimes opened by children, 'Mum, there's a man to see you,' yelled down the passage. An irritated reply, 'Who is it, what's he want?' The child would relay our response, screeching to the disembodied voice, 'It's about the atom bomb.' That was unanswerable from a distance, and a curious mum would stop making the tea and hurry to the door. The lone and elderly pulled at net curtains to see who was calling, while large men opened the door wide to fill the frame with confrontation. Most signed readily, for war was a recent memory and the start of another conflict in far off Korea had renewed old fears. Some argued. One man, shaving in the late evening in readiness for the night shift, came to the door with his face half-lathered. He thought we were wasting our time, we countered his objections at length, and the shaving soap congealed to a cold blancmange before he finally signed. Kindly mums said 'Not today, thank you,' a polite, stock, and very English reply to unsolicited callers of all kinds. Too often the reply from married women was, 'I will have to ask my husband.' If he agreed, they both signed. It was rare for a woman to sign if her husband refused, and it had more to do with obedient subjection than a reasoned difference of opinion. Few were hostile or rude and the petition sheets were filled evening after evening as we systematically covered our branch ward. On Saturday afternoons, if I was not working, I joined the other comrades in Stratford Broadway, accosting busy shoppers, awkwardly signing as they grappled with handbags and shopping baskets. The petition was always with me and I pressed relations, friends and workmates to sign, proudly handing in the filled sheets on branch meeting night. The *Daily Worker* regularly reported the world-wide growing number of signatures as if giving the latest score in a test match.

Popular support for the Stockholm Peace Appeal in the summer months of 1950 was boosted by the decision of the Attlee government to increase the period of military conscription to two years, followed soon after by the issue of registration papers to a quarter of a million 'Z' class reservists. The cabinet prepared plans for mobilisation, and suddenly the remote Korean conflict seemed nearer home. A peace rally in Trafalgar Square brought thousands onto the streets, blue and white banners fluttering their slogans, 'Not a Briton for Korea' and 'Hands off China.' Pamela, Lionel, my father and myself joined the demonstration to hear the Soviet writer, Ilya Ehrenburg, make a powerful plea for peace, recalling the twenty million dead that the Soviet Union had lost in the war against fascism. Together we cheered Arthur Horner, the pugnacious Communist General Secretary of the National Union of Mineworkers, as he proclaimed the international solidarity of miners and pledged the support of British miners for the cause of peace. I left the square determined to resist any recall to the RAF.

May Day in London, 1951, brought the opportunity for us to join another heartening march and demonstration, more than thirty thousand packing Trafalgar Square, bringing a sense of unity and strength to comrades scattered in small branches throughout the capital. Among the many banners carried in the spring sunshine that day, bobbing amid the historic colours of the dockers and engineering unions, was a hand made slogan banner with a simple message of peace, 'Shake hands – don't shoot.' For me, it summed up the way to resist the men of war. Pamela marched in the demonstration as one of a group of five young women, each holding a giant cut-out letter spelling the word 'PEACE', proudly holding her 'E' in line with the others. Lionel and myself were banner bearers, though its message is forgotten. When we passed the offices of an advertising agency from whom we were seeking work, Lionel with a grin suggested that we should

213

lower the banner to obscure our faces lest we were seen by our prospective clients and victimised.

A few days after the rally, the national press was headlining the news from Korea of the terrible casualties suffered by the Gloucestershire Regiment in defending a lone hill against the Chinese. Praise for the 'gallant Gloucesters' was matched by vituperation against the Communists. Going on the doors that evening the response was hostile, for we were seen as the enemy. At any moment I expected to call on a household where a son was serving in Korea and to be faced with family wrath. That I sustained the canvass was as much due to the physical presence of the comrade I was working with, a sixteen stone ex-serviceman, as to my political convictions.

At the height of the crisis in Korea, Harry Pollitt came to Stratford to speak on the war. The town hall was booked for the meeting and we whitewashed streets with the message, 'Pollitt speaks', giving the time and date of the meeting. This was my first venture in daubing the streets and it was with excitement and apprehension that I joined the small group of comrades who had volunteered for the task. We set off as darkness fell, brushes and buckets of whitewash in hand, a band of clandestine revolutionaries. The cover of darkness was chosen to avoid becoming involved in time-wasting arguments, and also because the traffic was lighter. We painted our slogans across the full width of the roads, choosing major junctions for maximum impact. It is an indication of just how little motor traffic there was that we were able to work in the roads without any real fear of being run over. West Ham was an old Labour borough and there was said to be a bye-law which permitted the whitewashing of messages in the roadway to advertise political meetings. It was certainly the argument we used when approached by a policeman. 'Now then,' he said in a stentorian voice, 'what are you up to?' Wally Barnes, an experienced comrade and the leader of our group, explained that which was self evident. 'Who gave you permission?' asked the constable. Wally told him of the bye-law. The officer looked doubtful, pressing the point, 'But who gave you permission?' With some exasperation, Wally replied, 'Alright, the mayor.' 'The mayor,' repeated the officer with astonishment. 'Yes,' answered Wally, boldly, 'The mayor.' The policeman departed slowly, making an entry in his notebook as he left. Laughing, we continued our whitewashing round of Stratford's streets.

We did our work well, for the meeting at the Town Hall was packed, late-comers being unable to gain admission, crowding the pavement outside. Pollitt, a skilful orator, with a burning faith in the working class, lashed the Labour government for its support of the Americans in Korea, spelt out the dangers of such a policy for the British people, and argued for the banning of the atomic bomb, an all-round reduction in armaments and an increase in spending on housing and the social services. He ended with an impassioned appeal for people to join the Communist Party, and twenty-seven responded when stewards passed the application forms among the audience, including Pamela. I was overjoyed, for our love was now bonded by comradeship. La Pasionaria, the inspirational Spanish Communist had written, 'Your wife should be your comrade who shares with you the sorrows . . . the troubles and also the joys of the struggle.' So it was to be.

By now, I was accepted as an active member of the branch and my life outside of work centred on the Party. Communists were a close-knit group within society, insular and interdependent. Comrades tended to recruit their relations and friends and to work and play in the company of other Communists. In time, my sister and my brother-in-law both joined the Party, but I never succeeded in winning my parents away from their loyalty to Labour. 'Evolution, not revolution' was my father's argument, which I rejected as reformist. Through the Party, I met professional people for the first time as equals, and made good use of their services. The optician I consulted was a Party member, Max Hillel, who had a small practice in Woodgrange Road and loaned the attic rooms above his shop for Party meetings. We discussed my eyesight and he gave advice as a comrade and friend. In business, our solicitor was Barry Amiel, a member of the Communist Party Lawyers' Group, an astute and well-loved man who was widely known within the Party. For Pamela and myself, the active branch members became our close friends, Jenny and Joe Edkins, whose grandfather had been a socialist associate of Keir Hardie; Edith and Alf Myers, Alf had been a staunch Communist while in the army during the war, and would regale us with hilarious stories of skirmishes with his officers; Peter Jackson, a student teacher who lived in a permanent state of penury in lodgings in Tower Hamlets Road, whom Pamela would endeavour to feed, sharing the little we had; and Wally and Eileen Barnes, stalwart comrades, Wally had been imprisoned for inciting people to march on the banned May Day demonstration in 1949, and Eileen had left the calendar in their house forever fixed at the date of his release. Others included Cyril Woolf, a young Communist whose father was a Labour councillor, Gerry Cassidy, a flaming haired Irishman with a fondness for drink, rare in our ascetic circle, Paul Weiss, whose wife was Norwegian, and Ernie Lytton, who with his brother, owned a men's outfitters in Forest Gate and ran a stall in Petticoat Lane. We thought the Lyttons well off, for they left lights burning in their home when they went out in the evenings, an unheard-of extravagance, for at home we would turn off lights as we moved from room to room.

There were many others, with whom we shared party work from time-to-time. The Ball brothers, two bachelors whose tiny kitchen was piled high with old copies of the *Daily Worker*, dangerously heaped to the ceiling each side of the kitchen stove. There was Joe Tossa, a Maltese, with a strong accent that I could barely understand; Frank Goddard, a low-paid building worker with a large family, who struggled for survival, and an old comrade, worn with toil who worked in the sewers for a pittance. Bert Finch, our literature secretary, had a small business repairing invalid cars, single seater three-wheeled death traps that condemned the disabled to journey alone. Some of the comrades in the branch were well known for their work in other fields, which left them little time for local activity; Julius Jacobs, Secretary of the London Trades Council, Cliff Giles, a former President of the National Union of Teachers, and Trudy and Joe Stern, actors with Unity Theatre and the BBC, were among them. Well known or rank and file, including those whose names I have forgotten, we were as one in believing that the future was ours.

Our social activities in the branch invariably had a multiple purpose, to raise funds, involve sympathisers, 'raise the cultural level' and to simply enjoy ourselves. Perhaps the most popular of our group pleasures were the trips to Unity Theatre, filling a coach to combine support for the theatre with an evening out. The theatre, at Mornington Crescent, was intimate, that is small, cold in the winter and hot in summer, shabby, and ours in the sense that it was part of the Labour movement. After weeks of selling tickets for our block booking, we would descend on the theatre bubbling with the good spirits generated by comradeship. Before the performance we would browse at the book stall, perhaps buy a beer or a cup of tea, and see if we could spot any 'names' among the crush. The faces that we could recognise were likely to be trade union leaders, though I did once spot Krishna Menon, the Indian High Commissioner, struggling through to the stalls. Some shows, like the play *The Ragged Trousered Philanthropists*, played to full houses, but at other times the audience might be sadly sparse. Whatever the performance, a musical review, a play, or old time music hall, we thoroughly enjoyed ourselves. At the height of the cold war, we roared approval at the anti-American songs of the review, *Here Goes!*, shed tears for the noble George Loveless in *Six Men of Dorset* and were moved to anger by the royal betrayal of the English peasants in *The Word of a King*. Unity had a wonderful atmosphere where ruling class values could be ridiculed, exposed and attacked in a way unknown in the West End theatre, and we would come away entertained and uplifted.

In smaller groups, we would go to the Scala Cinema, just off Tottenham Court Road to see Soviet films. One of the more memorable, brilliantly satirised royalty, at a time when any reference to royalty by the media in Britain was invariably sycophantic. The film was an animated cartoon in which the king was depicted as a puppet, with the puppeteer a capitalist, providing the voice and pulling the strings. Perhaps the scriptwriter had in mind the words of Thomas Paine, 'It requires some talents to be a common mechanic, but to be a king, requires only the animal figure of a man, a sort of breathing automaton.' The film appealed to our republican sympathies and we recalled it with mirth for years to come. Another Soviet film remembered was a propaganda epic of the Second World War, the Great Patriotic War as the Soviets named it, with Stalin portrayed as a father figure of presiding military genius. The famous Red Square speech in which Stalin, invoking past Russian glories, rallied the citizens of Moscow to repel the Nazi invaders when they were at the threshold of the city, I accepted with uncritical acclaim. The dramatic filming of the great moment when Soviet troops triumphantly raised the red flag over the Brandenburg Gate, moved me with emotion. What Pamela found difficult to accept, however, was the Soviet obsession with images of happy peasants, finishing their day's work by dancing through fields of golden corn singing revolutionary songs; 'The corn is glistening around us ... as we go forward, forward, forward ever forward ... ,' a contrived portrayal of work that was awkwardly embarrassing. Whatever misgivings we may have had about the idealisation of the representation of agricultural labour in the

217

Soviet Union we kept to ourselves, for to criticise would have been to ally ourselves with anti-Soviet elements, and loyalty to the Soviet Union, the first workers' state, was paramount.

An activity that Pamela and myself found an ordeal was the contrived gathering together of comrades, friends and sympathisers for a social, an event designed to raise funds and draw people into contact with the Party. Held in a school hall, with chairs pushed back to the sides of the wall to form a concourse, we were obliged to make friendly small talk with non-Party members that we hardly knew. Neither Pamela nor myself were dancers and there was no licensed bar to stimulate conviviality, they were tea and cakes affairs with dancing and entertainment redolent of a children's party. Perhaps we were unsocial socialists, but it was hardly our idea of a fun evening. On one occasion, Joe Edkins had the bright idea of booking a woman accordion player for a solo spot of entertainment. At least we laughed when we saw the heavily bosomed woman strap on her accordion and prepare to play, for the likely loss of her dignity was easy to imagine. In the event, she survived without mishap as she squeezed and swayed, while we endured her medley as an act of political faith. Looking back through an old copy of our Branch News Letter, I am amazed to read that three hundred people attended that social in Water Lane School.

At a time when few working people had television, we would sometimes arrange a film show, borrowing a projector and hiring a film from Plato Films, a left wing organisation with strong Party links. In a blacked-out school hall, with uncomfortable wooden chairs arranged in rows, we would show films depicting the achievements of peaceful reconstruction in the USSR. With a drive to sell shilling tickets, we might attract twenty or thirty people to watch a flickering black and white story of the bringing of electricity to a remote farming community in Uzbekistan, for as Lenin had said, 'Communism is Soviet power plus the electrification of the whole country.' As the village was finally lit up, the film would assuredly end with joyous workers singing 'Soviet land, so dear to every toiler . . . ,' the sound track crackling its message to the faithful and sceptical alike. Naive and amateurish it may have been, but our sincerity and passion for the cause blurred the reality of any shortcomings. With a captive audience, the opportunity was never missed to conclude by speaking about the Communist Party, appealing for non-members to join, taking a collection, and advertising our next meeting.

After a year or so in the Party, I was co-opted onto the branch committee as membership organiser, to be responsible for ensuring the regular payment of the weekly subscription of sixpence a week by every branch member, and for leading the campaign to build the membership. The objective was the annual re-registration of every member and to increase membership over the previous year, setting ourselves a Stakhanovite target. Better-off members would pay monthly, but the majority paid weekly, which meant calling regularly on those who for various reasons did not attend branch meetings. It was a continual fight against the accumulation of arrears, but it enabled me to have direct contact with every comrade in the branch. As some members worked shifts, and others were out most evenings of the week on trade union work, it was not an easy round. Without transport, every call was made by walking, tramping around the ward, evenings and weekends, a dismal circuit when it was raining. It was at this time that I bought myself an umbrella, a bank manager's icon, steeling myself against the ridicule it was to provoke from some of my class-conscious comrades.

Sent to call on a new recruit, I found him to be a newly arrived immigrant, among the first of the West Indians to come to Britain in the 1950s. This was at a time when there were few black people living in West Ham, the only one that I recall being a doctor with a practice in Romford Road. The newcomer was living alone in a miserable bed-sit in a tenement, and realising that he was broke, I said that if he did not have sixpence I would pay his first stamp for him, and he could repay me when he had found work. He said that I was the first person he had met in England who appreciated that even sixpence might be difficult to afford and it showed that Communists really understood the plight of the working class. That understanding bonded us as comrades and friends.

CHAPTER 13
All For The Cause

Our work in the branch constantly moved forward to keep pace with the ever changing political situation, as one campaign was succeeded by another. The international issue of peace dominated our work, and we fought against the military strategy of the Western powers. We were active in opposing the war in Korea and Britain's colonial wars in Malaya and Kenya. We campaigned against the North Atlantic Treaty Organisation, German rearmament, and the building of US air bases in Britain. 'Don't be Yanked into war' was our blanket slogan to cover most aspects of US imperialism. During those years, in the early 1950s, my life became a continual round of work, branch meetings, branch committee meetings, sub-committee meetings, AGMs, Co-op quarterly meetings, public meetings, street activity, dues collecting, jumble sales and selling the *Daily Worker*. Unlike other political parties, the Communist Party did not restrict its campaigning to once every five years; working class agitation was ceaseless.

On the home front, we were busy publicising the new programme of the Communist Party, *The British Road to Socialism*. Published in January, 1951, the cover of the pamphlet was printed in a shocking pink, amusingly described in *The Daily Telegraph* as being a case for 'Hammer and Cyclamen.' The programme contained a foreword by Harry Pollitt, and Pollitt had in fact drafted the original document. It included a new policy statement on the attainment of socialism, rejecting revolution as the only path to political power. It postulated the theory that each nation would find its own road to socialism, depending on the conditions prevailing in each country. Britain, it said, 'could transform parliament, the product of our nation's historic struggle for democracy, into a democratic instrument of the will of the vast majority of her people, creating a People's Government, uniting the working class and its allies.' About this time, Lionel designed a poster for a Communist Party meeting celebrating the anniversary of the Easter Rising in Ireland in 1916. He painted a powerful illustration of raised arm, bearing aloft a rifle, but the design was rejected on a direct order from Harry Pollitt as conflicting with the new Party policy of peaceful transition to socialism.

To help promote the new programme, the London District Committee of the Communist Party sent us a fiery and experienced orator, Solly Kaye. We planned a big public meeting at Park School, seeking to draw in as many Labour Party members as we could. To this end, we set about all our usual methods of advertising our public meetings, including the production of thousands of leaflets, laboriously cranked out on an aged Gestetner duplicating machine on Joe Edkins' kitchen table. These we poked through every letter box in the ward. To attract the maximum attention for the meeting we decided to whitewash the streets with details of the event, and Joe and myself undertook to organise the whitewashing teams. For some reason, probably to save spending money on whitewash, I said that I would provide some old white printing ink from my factory, that we could thin down with turps substitute to a suitable constituency for painting. 'The British Road to Socialism. Solly Kaye speaks', together with the venue and date, was duly splashed across all the key crossroads in the area. I had given little thought to the permanency of screen printing ink, and the message remained ingrained in the tarmac for the next two years!

Solly Kaye was a spellbinding speaker, forceful, yet persuasive, leaning into the audience, finger stabbing as he made his points with a passion that was imbued with humanity. For enemies of the working class, his invective was devastating. In answering questions he was direct, never evasive. In coping with hecklers, he was quick witted and humorous. I envied his talent in the way that youth admires a sporting hero, and in my day-dreams I imagined being able to hold an audience as he did. We counted the meeting a success, with some fifty or sixty copies of *The British Road to Socialism* sold and a few new members made. Perhaps some of the Labour supporters left enthused by the meeting, but as far as

I recall, our contact with the ward Labour Party remained unofficial and distant.

Although I disagreed with many aspects of Labour Party policy, and thought many of the entrenched Labour councillors in West Ham to be reactionaries, I regarded Labour Party workers as fellow socialists and natural allies. I had long been proud of the borough's links with Keir Hardie and Will Thorne, and saw the Communist Party as true heirs to the militant tradition of the pioneers of Labour. Within my own family, my uncle, Bert Gorman, a former engineering shop steward, was a Labour councillor in Greenwich, later to become its mayor. My aunt, Elsie Gladwell, of East Ham, had been in the Labour Party since 1916, and was to be honoured at the age of eighty-five with a merit award presented by Harold Wilson for her life of service to Labour. My mother's family from South Shields – where no Conservative has ever been elected as a member of parliament – were staunchly Labour, and Labourism was part of my cultural heritage. I accepted the need to criticise the policies of the right wing leadership, but often felt uncomfortable with the vehemence of the attacks upon the Labour Party made by some Communist Party comrades. For myself, *The British Road to Socialism* presented the opportunity for discussion and debate with Labour Party workers on how to achieve socialism, and how to retain power once it was won. I felt that too many Communists saw the Labour Party solely as rivals to the leadership of the working class.

As Communists, we attended the larger Labour Party public meetings in our area, partly to support a working class activity, partly to hear and question Labour policy, but also to make our presence public. We would stand outside, selling the *Daily Worker* and party pamphlets before a meeting started, and then take our seats to make use of the opportunity to put our case before a large audience at question time. Many of the well known Labour leaders came to West Ham, Barbara Castle, Manny Shinwell and Aneurin Bevan, among them. I remember Shinwell speaking at West Ham Municipal College when a group of fascists who had occupied the front seats began to heckle, holding up copies of the Mosleyite paper, *Action*. Shinwell, a tough East London Jew who had spent his youth in South Shields and Glasgow, rolled up his sleeves and offered to meet any one of them outside the hall. I do not think that he was bluffing, for this was the man who had crossed the floor of the House of Commons in 1938 to strike a

223

Tory MP, Commander Bower, when he shouted to Shinwell the misguided racist remark, 'Go back to Poland.' Barbara Castle came to speak at Stratford Town Hall, red haired and glamorous, her northern accent strangely harsh to the ears of a cockney audience. As for the content of her speech, it roused the Labour faithful, but we detected signs of her future move towards the right of the Labour Party. Bevan arrived at West Ham baths, silver haired, head high, chin jutting defiance, ostensibly to speak on the Rent Act, only to deliver a blistering attack on German rearmament. They were days when politicians could fill a hall with hundreds, even when there was no election to be fought.

Study of *The British Road to Socialism* was a duty for every Party member, and the branch organised a series of five classes which were taken by Jim Horth, a leading comrade and a member of the West Ham Trades Council. Jim was a scientific worker, an educated and thoughtful Communist, well qualified for the role of tutor. He took us patiently through the main points in the programme, explaining the idea of people's democracy as the path to socialism and discussing the Party programme for nationalisation and plans for the social services. Scientists have a popular reputation for being coldly detached in their approach to problems. Jim Horth was a scientific socialist, well able to explain Marxist theory, but he was also filled with compassion for his less fortunate fellows. Unlike some comrades, his love of socialism was not subordinated to his hatred of capitalism. One day, prior to the classes, as I was travelling home from work by bus, I was reading Oscar Wilde's *De Profundis* when Jim boarded the bus and noticed the book. He leaned across to comment that it was a very moving human document, words I had not expected. At one of his study groups, I remember him making a point by explaining that socialism was about a worker being able to have a clean shirt to wear three times a week. In the class were some, who like many manual workers at that time, had to make a shirt last for six days, with a clean shirt saved for Sundays. I was more fortunate, owning three shirts, worn from Monday to Wednesday, Thursday to Saturday, and a Sunday best. Jim Horth, the neat and well dressed professional worker, who no doubt had a clean shirt every day, understood the need of people for human dignity, and was prepared to fight for that right.

Central to our work and lives as Communists was the *Daily Worker*. It was our paper, a national daily newspaper held in a special affection by its readers, and fervently supported by thousands of Communists who sold the paper at factory gates, railway stations, markets and street corners throughout the land. The *Daily Worker* gave us more than news, it brought solidarity, linking us as part of a growing world-wide movement, recording the advances made by our comrades in other countries. The paper had emerged from the Second World War, strengthened by the goodwill of the British workers towards the Soviet Union, reflecting the crucial role that the Red Army had played in the defeat of fascism. In formerly Nazi-occupied Europe, Communist-led resistance had enhanced the reputation of the Party, which emerged from the war with more than 800,000 members in France, and a colossal 1,700,000 membership in Italy, the Communist newspapers, *L'Humanité* and *L'Unita* counting their circulations in millions. By comparison, the circulation of the *Daily Worker* was small, not more than a hundred thousand during its post-war peak, with special Saturday issues for major events boosting the figure to double that number. For the May Day issue of 1948, sales exceeded a quarter of a million, but that was to remain as a record, never to be broken. Statistics, however, do not reveal the loyalty of its readers and staff, and the sacrifices they made to sustain the paper, while larger circulation papers of the capitalist press collapsed in the face of press monopoly. The *Worker* was to outlive the *Daily Herald, News Chronicle, Reynold's News*, and more reactionary papers, like *The Empire Sunday News, Daily Sketch* and *The Daily Graphic*, as well as the London evening papers, *The Evening News* and *The Star*.

The post-war *Daily Worker* was a co-operative venture, owned by its readers, who invested modest sums in the People's Press Printing Society, a maximum holding of two hundred pounds guarding against any dominating financial interest. Subscribers included a host of distinguished names, embracing scientists, actors, writers and trade union leaders, but the vast majority of shareholders were thousands of ordinary working people. I subscribed to our branch scheme, whereby members bought a one pound share at the rate of a shilling a week.

We were inordinately proud of the *Daily Worker*, which commanded an allegiance among its readers unmatched by any other British newspaper since the days of the old *Daily Herald*. A regular fighting fund appeal, with daily exhortation by Barbara Niven, brought in thousands of pounds each month, with pennies and pounds collected in factories, offices, and trade union branches. Every Christmas saw scores of *Daily Worker* bazaars held

225

all over the country, where goods made and given by supporters were sold to raise funds for the paper. The paper survived in a state of constant financial crisis, but was kept solvent by the energy and determination of its readers.

The names of the regular correspondents were as familiar to us as old friends, comrades we trusted to report the news that the capitalist press choose to ignore or distort. Wherever there were strikes, the *Daily Worker* could be relied upon to present first hand reports, giving workers a voice denied to them by the rest of the media. For trade union news, it was unsurpassed, giving more column inches to the TUC annual conference than any other paper. No industrial dispute or organised working class action was too small to be ignored. Supplementing the staff reporters was an irregular corps of reporters, the workers themselves, supplying information and news of working class action wherever it took place. The paper had a good arts page, and its features attracted famous writers, Sean O'Casey, Bernard Shaw, and Arnold Zweig among them. The *Worker's* cartoonist, Gabriel, was among the best, surpassed only by Low and Vicky. Its scoops, and there were many of them, exposed the duplicity of the British ruling class. The publication of photographs of British marine commandos posing with the heads and hands of freedom fighters, severed by Dyak head-hunters in the Malayan jungle, invoked the wrath of Tory MPs who howled 'fake', but forced ministerial admission of their authenticity. In its reporting of events concerning the royal family, it kept a sense of socialist proportion, giving a mere couple of factual lines to the birth of another prince, in complete contrast to the fawning columns in the national press, including *The Daily Mirror*, supposedly the voice of Labour.

In 1948, the *Daily Worker* had changed its size from a tabloid to a broadsheet, and I would proudly spread its wide pages for all to see when reading on bus or train. At the end of a journey, the paper diligently studied, I would carefully leave it on the seat for another passenger, always hopeful of winning a new reader. In 1954, the *Daily Worker* was chosen together with *The Times* for the annual Newspaper Design Award, an award it was to win outright just two years later, a tribute to the typographical skills of Allen Hutt, the *Worker's* chief sub-editor. Housed in a functional modern building in Farringdon Road, surmounted with the *Daily Worker* name glowing in red neon, it was a beacon of socialism, a paper of which we were justly proud.

Selling the *Daily Worker* was a yardstick to measure commitment, 'How many *Daily Workers* did you sell today, comrade?' was a rhetorical question that ended many a theoretical argument. Fortunately, I found selling the paper a less onerous task than some other obligations. I took my part in selling the paper on Saturday afternoons in Stratford Broadway, where I faced unexpected meetings with neighbours and old schoolfriends, and canvassed the paper from door-to-door, as did Pamela, sound training for any salesperson. Paul Weiss was our *Daily Worker* organiser, and for a short period my allotted task was to sell the paper at Stratford Railway Works, a sprawling industrial plant, with foundries, machine shops, and a host of ancillary services. The workers operated on shifts around the clock, and I would arrive at the works entrance gate in Angel Lane, opposite the Railway Tavern, at quarter to six in the morning to catch the men leaving the night shift. The pub was open, and I might sell a dozen copies to the railwaymen as they stopped for a quick pint before going home for dinner at breakfast time. At six-thirty I would leave to catch the bus from Maryland Point to go to work.

Factories were considered to be a vital base for building the Communist Party, and factory gate sales of the *Daily Worker* were a crucial part of our political activities. One of the largest factories in our ward was Crockett's leathercloth factory in Abbey Road, a Victorian Bastille with the bleak brick drabness of a workhouse. A rota of comrades, including myself, covered the works entrance for early morning sales, and for months we distributed leaflets and did our best to persuade the workers to buy the paper. The workers at the leathercloth factory were low paid and unorganised, their work hard and dirty. They were a dispirited lot, exploited and cowed, in complete contrast to the unionised, skilled and independent railwaymen. The leathercloth workers would hurry past us, heads down, as though afraid to meet our eyes. We made no progress, often failing to sell a single paper, and eventually we gave up our efforts to politicise the workforce as a waste of our limited resources.

Once a year there was a gathering of the faithful for a *Daily Worker* rally, at the Empress Hall or Harringay Arena, a family occasion, with thousands of supporters singing and cheering with revivalist fervour to a programme of spectacle and rousing political speeches. In 1951, at my first rally, veterans of the International Brigades marched in with their banners, a massed

227

choir conducted by Alan Bush sang *The Red Flag*, and greetings were read from the international Communist press, including the Chinese *People's Daily*, our new and powerful ally. Following a pageant, came the hard politics, with speeches by the editor of the *Daily Worker*, Johnny Campbell, the 'Red Dean of Canterbury' Hewlett Johnson, and finally the Secretary of the Communist Party, Harry Pollitt. All were received with what the Party was fond of describing as 'prolonged and tumultuous applause.' We gave more than we could afford to a collection appeal made by Barbara Niven, then stood *en masse* to sing *The Internationale*, and I never doubted the import of the words, 'Then comrades come rally, and the last fight let us face' for the evening rang with inspiration, the messages from socialist lands, from the Soviet Union to China, reinforcing my conviction that the ultimate goal of world socialism would come in our time.

Of all the issues on which we campaigned, none was more emotive and controversial than the fight against German rearmament. To draw public attention to the threat of the Western powers to create a new German army of forty-eight divisions, the Party organised a number of publicity stunts. Among the most eye catching was when two ex-service comrades, dressed in the full uniform of jack-booted Nazi officers, strode around London's West End with shuddering effect, handing out leaflets to astonished passers-by. At my studio in Dalston, I produced a giant post-card, three feet by two feet in size, complete with a huge replica postage stamp, addressed to the Prime Minister, Winston Churchill. On the message side of the card, was printed a statement of opposition to German rearmament from the people of West Ham, London's most bombed borough. The following Saturday afternoon we took the card to Stratford Broadway, moving among the shoppers and collecting hundreds of signatures on the card in support of the opposition message. We filled the card in little time, for the shoppers, mostly women, had endured the blitz. When no more signatures could be squeezed onto the card, we asked our Member of Parliament, Arthur Lewis, to deliver the card to 10 Downing Street on behalf of his constituents.

Our campaign against German rearmament was sustained for some years, issuing leaflets, holding poster parades, collecting signatures to petitions, flyposting, and whitewashing the streets with slogans. I made some mobile exhibition panels, showing photographs of the Nazi concentration camps, which we displayed on waste ground opposite the Rex Cinema in Stratford High Street, while we sold the *Daily Worker* and gave out leaflets. More than once we were harassed by the police who tried to deny our right to set up the display, but we steadfastly refused to move, engaging them in discussion until we won grudging acceptance. I felt passionately that rearming the Germans was wrong, and it was on this issue that I first spoke on a public platform. The main speakers at the meeting in Stratford were George Matthews, the assistant general secretary of the Party, and Reuben Falber, the national organiser. It was my job to make the final speech and to appeal for a collection. I lay awake the night before, anxiously going over the words in my mind, again and again. At the meeting, I scarcely listened to the two national speakers, but silently rehearsed what I was going to say. When George Matthews introduced me, I rose, dry mouthed and nervous, my words emanating mechanically, as though from another body, as I tried to listen to what I was saying. I began with the standard Party opening, 'Comrades and friends', and was soon in full flow, speaking from the heart about the wartime bombing in the area, evoking memories of the death and destruction that had been part of all our lives. I recalled a rocket attack when some young children watching the steam trains go by from Hamfrith Road bridge had been killed. I said that my young son now stood at the same spot, waving to the engine drivers, and that I wanted him to grow up in peace and safety. Never again must we allow the Germans to re-arm. After I had finished the appeal for money, I sat down, oblivious of the applause, glad that the ordeal was over. As the collection was taken, Reuben Falber passed me a note, which read, 'That was the best appeal I have ever heard.'

On a directive from the London District Committee of the Party, our branch was amalgamated with the Stratford High Street Ward, to form the West Ham North branch, with Wally Barnes appointed as secretary. Wally, who had started work in a bakery at the age of fourteen, was of stocky build with a rosy cheeked chubby face, and lived with his wife and young daughter in a wartime Nissen hut in Mortham Street, not far from Stratford High Road. He had overcome a poor education to become a fluent public speaker and an inspirational leader. The membership, for which I was now organiser, was boosted from about thirty to sixty or seventy. With active campaigning, we were to reach a target figure of one hundred paid-up members, and I was elected to the Borough Committee of the Party. By then there were a dozen dues collectors working under my control, and with a hard core of cadres, we considered our branch to be a formidable political force in a key industrial borough.

Party activity was conducted at a frenetic pace. Looking back at a Branch News Letter from 1954, 'Notes for your diary' lists flyposting, distribution of leaflets, poster parade, dance and social, loud speaker tour, whitewashing, public meeting, branch meeting, jumble sale and an AGM, all within the space of two weeks. In the midst of all this comes an 'Emergency Call' to 'support the striking portworkers!' Full time Party officials from the area, or London District, would descend on us like commissars to rally the troops for emergency causes, sweeping aside all protests that there was simply no time to add another cause to an already crammed programme. I recall a full time organiser, Charlie Findlay, arriving one evening to ask the branch committee if we had acted on a call in that morning's *Daily Worker* for the support of a pensioners' lobby of MPs at the House of Commons. 'How many comrades will be going on the lobby tomorrow,' he asked. 'None', we replied, He looked dismayed. 'But when you read the *Worker* this morning, were you not immediately galvanised into action.' 'No,' was the shamefaced reply, we were not, for the simple reason that we all had to go to work.

The workload imposed tremendous strains on family life, as men abandoned their wives and children for evenings and weekends to meet the demands of the Party. As Communists, we stood solidly for the equality of women, often explaining with pride that in the Soviet Union there were women sea captains, aeroplane pilots, engineers, scientists and road sweepers, but too often the role of our Party women was relegated to domestic support of their husbands. Pamela and our young son would often accompany me on weekend activity, but evenings would see her minding the baby at home, while I worked overtime or went out on the never ending round of Party activity, limiting her political work to selling the *Daily Worker*, booking the school for meetings, and typing the Branch News Letter. When Party meetings were held in the homes of comrades, it was usually the woman of the house who was called upon to make the tea. At one time, a Womens' Group was formed, but shamefully floundered because of the prior commitments of the men.

Fund raising for the Party took many forms, from raffle tickets to socials, but it was jumble sales that came as a lesson in abject poverty. Collecting old clothes and bric-a-brac from comrades and friends who wore their clothes until they were threadbare and used things until they wore out, produced a motley collection of tatty and dated clothing and battered household effects. Viewing the assembled ragbag collection of garments and junk, I could not believe that it would be possible to give it away, let alone sell it. Spread out on trestle tables in a school room, the poorest of the poor jostled each other to rummage through the heaps of discarded clothing, snatching at worn jackets, baggy trousers and shapeless frocks. It was children's clothes that sold the quickest, as shabbily dressed mums snapped up shoes, pullovers and coats as sixpenny bargains. Old men looked for overcoats and sorted among the stalls for scratched gramophone records, old bicycle parts and miscellaneous cutlery. People actually bought dull and dented tablespoons, blunt knives with bone handles that were yellow with age, and odd size forks with bent prongs. 'How much is this?' cried a woman over the bedlam of bargaining, holding up a tweed winter coat that was a fashion rage in 1940. 'A shilling', I said, but my eyes met her disappointment, I saw in her face the drawn look of penury and dropped the price to threepence, a political decision that deprived the party of ninepence. The three coppers were fished from her purse and I still felt as if I were robbing her. For a moment I hesitated, should I give her the coat for nothing? The large round pennies were in my hand. 'Thanks, I hope it keeps you warm', and she stepped aside and was lost in the crowd. I have often regretted not giving her that coat.

With the daily struggle to keep my business solvent, and my spare time taken up with political work, there was little time for recreation beyond that shared within the Party. Pamela, housekeeping on my minimum wage, looking after our baby in one small room, while sharing the facilities for cooking and washing, one small gas cooker and a single cold tap, decided that we needed a holiday. To pay for it, she would take in homework, a decision I did not accept with any grace, for I knew that homework was an exploitative system that took advantage of the poorest section of the community, invariably women. Despite my misgivings, Pamela, who is quietly independent, answered an advertisement in a newspaper for home typing. The advertiser proved to be the *Readers' Digest*, and she was asked to attend an office at St Paul's for an interview. When she arrived, the waiting room was packed with other young women desperate for the work; there was to be no bargaining over the price to be paid.

Pamela was one of the successful applicants, and promptly borrowed ten pounds to buy a second hand typewriter, a black, heavy, upright LC Smith office machine, with large round keys.

The job was all that I feared, and worse. The work entailed typing names and addresses onto direct mail cards, copying the details from a telephone directory for fifteen shillings (75p) a thousand. To collect the cards, Pamela had to travel to the *Readers' Digest* first floor office at St Paul's, taking with her the baby, push-chair and a suitcase. The woman in charge of the office would allocate the work to an anxious group of penny-pinched women, as she played the role of Lady Bountiful. Pamela would pack the thousand cards into her suitcase, and start her journey home by getting the pushchair, baby and card-stuffed suitcase down the narrow stairs. Cardboard is a heavy as the timber from which it is made, and I will never know how she managed the stairs, escalators and the long walk from the station to our house, encumbered as she was. Night after night, when our baby was asleep, she would pound the keys until her fingers ached with the strain and her eyes developed conjunctivitis. I resented that rich American publishing company, more and more, with every card that was typed. As a Communist, I understood that we were providing rent-free office space, light, heating, machinery, transport and labour, in exchange for non-union wages. When the cards were typed, the cycle of humping the suitcase and baby to and from St Paul's began all over again. They were pleased with her work, for it was accurate and Pamela was reliable, and offered her additional work, sticking postage stamps on the cards at ten shillings a thousand. Pamela considered it a bonus, for sticking stamps was easier than typing.

In time, Pamela paid for the typewriter and accumulated another ten pounds, with which she paid for the hire of a caravan for a week at Hayling Island, and had enough left over for the coach fare. This was to be the first real holiday of my life. As much as I loathed the homework, the holiday was a week of blissful freedom, away from the pressures of work and the Party. For Pamela, it was break from domestic life in a cramped living room and the strain of sharing a scullery with her mother-in-law. We spent every day on the beach, for we had no transport, and little to spend, but we enjoyed every minute together as a family and wished that we could spend the rest of our days as beachcombers. They were golden days, earned for us by Pamela's work and resolution, but to this day, I wince whenever a packet of direct mail from that wretched magazine drops through our letterbox.

Whenever possible, we tried to share activities as a family. When May Day came, we would assemble at Stepney Green behind Communist Party banners, with our son in his pushchair, to perambulate the route to Trafalgar Square. It helped to show onlookers along the way that not all Communists were lone revolutionaries, but ordinary working class families. The Stepney branch was one of the strongest in London, with a fine record of anti-fascist struggle and a history of militancy on rents and housing. I always felt a sense of pride when we joined in with the Stepney branch, I was also envious of their branch banner, a professionally made colour of deep red silk, emblazoned with a golden hammer and sickle. By contrast, ours was a simple linen affair, painted in my studio with the slogan, 'Stratford Workers March For Peace And Socialism.' Nevertheless, Joe Edkins and myself would proudly hoist our banner on its broomstick-handle poles, Pamela and John alongside, as we set off on the march.

As we passed the great newspaper offices in Fleet Street, the heartland of 'the capitalist press' any weariness was shaken off, for we could see the citadels of the enemy. The glossy black fortress of the *Daily Express* would always provoke a response, our banners were raised higher, the *Red Flag* sung *con mucho gusto*, and copies of the *Daily Worker* brandished in defiance. Along The Strand, when we passed American servicemen in uniform, and there were plenty of them to be seen in the West End, we would greet them with a song sung to the tune of a Sunday School hymn:

Go home Yankee Yankee, go home
We don't want you any more,
For the way of life you sell
Doesn't suit us very well
And we'll never, never fight your Yankee war.

Entering Trafalgar Square we would exuberantly sing *The Internationale* and greet those already assembled with clenched fist salutes. The air was filled with the boom of loudspeakers announcing the arrival of each new group of marchers, and we would join in the cheering as they added to the throng. We drew strength from the thousands of comrades, the swirling red flags and lofted portraits of Marx, Engels, Lenin, Stalin and Harry Pollitt. May Day demonstrations were joyous peaceful pageants.

Coming into the square from all points would flow the

streaming colours of the trades unions, banners as large as mainsails, ablaze with silver, gold and red, resplendent with the emblems of their crafts. The banners of dockers, furniture workers, coppersmiths, boilermakers, transport workers and engineers, mingled with the banners of Unity Theatre, the *Daily Worker*, the London Trades Council and other progressive organisations. In the main column, which marched from the Embankment, there would be elaborate tableaux, effigies of the ogres of capitalism. At the peak of the struggle against German rearmament, a giant head of Eisenhower was paraded, flanked by German generals, leading Churchill by a chain. Adding to the colour would be organised groups of dancers, girls with red skirts swirling, red scarves waving, singing socialist songs, accompanied by floats with bands from the Musicians' Union. The square became a place of reunion as we greeted comrades last seen at some other rally, moving among the throng, signing yet another petition, or buying the latest pamphlets. As we listened to the speeches, we were elated, throbbing with a sense of working class power, for May Day belonged to us, to the working class.

One Sunday morning, towards the end of 1952, Wally Barnes and a few comrades were canvassing in Livingstone Road, just one of the verminous turnings close to the factory area around Carpenters Road. The street was a terrace of ramshackle houses, many of them with bulging walls supported by huge timbers. Relics of the industrialisation of the area, some of the houses had been condemned as unfit for habitation before the war. Wally borrowed a chair, set it on the street corner and began one of his regular stump speeches. A few people gathered as he urged them to unite to demand that the council should take action to enforce the repair of their dilapidated houses. 'It don't matter any more,' shouted a woman, 'the council have told us that we will all be rehoused by Christmas.' Wally, an accomplished outdoor orator with a sharp cockney wit, replied as quick as a flash, 'Have they told you which Christmas?' There followed some good humoured banter, and Wally promised that he would be back in the New Year. Christmas came and so did the New Year, but the people remained in their slums. Wally and some comrades returned, and this time the people came out of their homes to stand and listen. Some of the houses were owned by the West Ham council, and the tenants had been fobbed off for years with promises of repairs and rehousing. Wally said the time had come to unite and fight, and promised the support of the Communist Party.

By invitation, Wally returned a few evenings later to a meeting in the kitchen of an end-of-terrace house, to form a Tenants' Defence League. He later related how men and women had crammed into the little room, and that the meeting, sustained with endless cups of tea had lasted until midnight. The house in question was shored up to stop the end wall from collapsing, and incredibly, one of the timbers protruded through the wall into the kitchen, so that moving around the room meant a continual circumnavigation of the buttress timber. Someone said that if they took it down, the whole street would collapse like a pack of toppling cards. The women told harrowing tales of their constant fight with dust, dirt, mildew, damp and vermin, while struggling to clean, cook and bring up their children in houses that were a danger to health and limb. Some of the houses lacked electricity, and one family had to do all their cooking on a single gas ring, the chimney of their coal-burning kitchener being blocked solid with rubble. The houses looked grim enough from the outside, but it was only when you went in that the true state of the wretched living conditions were revealed. Taken on a tour of the houses, by the newly formed tenants' committee, we were shown bedrooms where daylight could be seen through the ceilings, walls that bulged, rotten floorboards patched with plywood to cover the holes and plaster that crumbled to the touch. The men had made gallant efforts to patch up the decaying dwellings, but they were fighting a losing battle, the houses were ripe for demolition.

The perceived idea of the Communist Party as a disciplined, efficient and dedicated force that could mobilise for action within hours, was largely a myth, but there is no doubt that the Party could bring experience, organisation, energy and flair to any campaign in which it engaged. The plight of the tenants in Livingstone and Stanley Roads offered us an opportunity to lead a mass struggle. Led by the Party, councillors were lobbied by the tenants, mums and kids invading the Town Hall, the Public Health Department was badgered, compelling sanitary inspectors to visit the houses, leaflets distributed, banners painted, a council meeting harangued from the public gallery and a deputation sent to the *Stratford Express*. Reporters and photographers came to cover the story, and pressure on the council to demolish the houses grew. At one council meeting that was lobbied, a councillor conceded that the houses should be demolished, but said hopelessly, 'We have nowhere to rehouse the people.'

To increase pressure upon the council and to draw public attention to the shocking conditions demanded something dramatic, a stunt which would shake the complacency of the council to its core. Wally came up with an imaginative idea that would expose the horror of Livingstone and Stanley Roads in a way that could not be ignored. The proposal, simple but brilliant in conception, was that the tenants should hold an Ideal Home Exhibition, a parody of the popular annual exhibition that was sponsored by the *Daily Mail*. The tenants would throw open their homes, inviting the labour movement to see for themselves the appalling state of the houses and the shocking conditions in which the people were compelled to live. The women responded magnificently, readily agreeing to show parties of visitors the dilapidated state of their homes. Party members were instructed to extend the open invitation at their trade union branch meetings, and organise coach-loads of trade unionists to pour into Stratford to tour the houses and help to shame the Labour council into rehousing the unfortunate inhabitants. Livingstone and Stanley roads, were plastered with posters, some of the slogans displaying resilient working class humour in the face of adversity: 'Ceiling tastes good, with Yorkshire pud', proclaimed one poster in a house where lumps of ceiling plaster had dropped onto the kitchen table. Every evening for a week people came, respectfully and carefully edging their way in and out of the tiny homes, leaving to pledge support for the tenants' demands to be rehoused. My father toured the houses as part as a delegation from the West Ham Trades Council, and considered the conditions a disgrace. I had often heard him assert that it was a first charge upon a nation to house its people, and failure to do so was a failure of government.

Trade union branches, and the West Ham Trades Council passed resolutions condemning the houses as unfit for habitation, and called for the urgent rehousing of the tenants. The West Ham Borough Council was bombarded with protests, and as a result of the campaign, twenty families were rehoused within two months, all found alternative accommodation by the end of the year and the houses subsequently demolished. It was an outstanding victory for the tenants, a tribute to Wally Barnes' political leadership, and a morale boosting success for the Party.

During 1953, the Tory government had drafted proposals for a Housing, Rents and Repairs Bill, a landlords' charter to raise rents and threaten the security of tenure of millions of working class families. With the momentum gained from the campaign on Livingstone and Stanley Roads, we launched a campaign to rally people to oppose the new legislation. Biggerstaff Road, not far from Livingstone and Stanley roads, was our next scene of direct action. A bomb damaged turning of old terraced houses, surrounded by railway lines, factories and a canal where two children from the street had drowned, the houses were prime examples of slum landlordism and conditions were so bad that the people said that they should be paid to live there. The houses were overcrowded. One home was shared by grandparents, their married children and grandchildren, crammed into tiny rooms where the children slept head to toe, four in a bed, in the same room as their parents. To add to the hardship, the houses were plagued with rats from the nearby canal. Rats gnawed through cupboards to get at food, and a horrifying story was told of a child awakening to stroke the cat on her bed, only to find that it was a rat. Leaking roofs added to the misery, bowls and buckets spread around the bedrooms each time that it rained to catch the dripping water. Wallpaper peeled from the damp walls and mould spread as if it was growing on cheese. The landlord had ignored all pleas for repairs for years, but he never forgot to collect the rent.

Encouraged by the recent success in Livingstone and Stanley roads, the tenants agreed to form a tenants' association to fight the Rents Bill and battle for repairs to their homes. A committee of men and women was formed and once again Wally was leading tenants to the council, demanding that they should use their powers to carry out the repairs and compel the landlord to pay the bill. The council prevaricated and when the housing committee refused to meet a deputation from the tenants, it was proposed that the people of Biggerstaff Road should start an immediate rent strike. In the midst of the campaign, the Rent Act was passed by the government, and our opposition to the Bill now became a demand for the repeal of the Act. In my studio at Dalston, a long banner was painted to string across Biggerstaff Road, emblazoned with the slogan being promoted by the Party in opposition to the Rent Act, 'Not a penny on the rent.' Once again I put my studio at the disposal of the tenants, and we printed hundreds of posters for flyposting. In addition, the people themselves made individual posters, and every house carried a demand for repairs. The tenants' committee of Biggerstaff Road endorsed the proposal for a rent strike, and when the rent collector called, two of the tenants' leaders, Jimmy Glover and Mrs Nunney, followed him from house to house, urging the people not to pay. As the rent collector made his way, he was followed by a group of women and children, singing, 'There he goes, Twinkletoes, nothing to spend on repairs I suppose'. The tenants were solid in refusing to pay rent to the landlord. Instead, they paid it to the committee, who deposited it with the local vicar for safekeeping.

The rent strike attracted considerable publicity in the local press, and we kept up the pressure on the council by threatening a mass march of tenants to the Town Hall at the next council meeting. Weekly meetings were held at Carpenters Road school and the tenants' association grew, recruiting supporters from neighbouring turnings, Jupp Road, Gibbons Road and Grace Road, all of whom had their share of slum property. We mounted a regular Saturday morning canvass of the streets, selling the *Daily Worker*, and several of the tenants joined the Party, including the secretary of the tenants' association, Jimmy Glover. He was a thin faced man with lanky hair, short in stature, but wiry and tough, proud of his new responsibility. Regular meetings were held, planning further action to strengthen the fight and broaden public debate on the whole question of rents and housing. The sustained campaign forced visits from council officials, and success in the local dispute came with the issuing of twenty-three Certificates of Disrepair for houses in Biggerstaff Road, allowing the tenants to legally deduct rent until the repairs had been made. The women of Biggerstaff Road returned from the Town Hall, triumphantly waving their certificates, a demonstration of the power of unity and direct action. A photographer from the *Daily Worker* captured the scene for a front page picture, the women standing in the street beneath their banner. Where were the men? Like myself, they were all at work, but the women were capable of fighting on their own.

Our branch maintained a continuous level of activity on the issues of rents and housing, and in our Branch News Letter for August 1954, I was able to report under the heading 'Our branch and the mass movement', that 'The High Street Ward Tenants' Association have called a public meeting at Stratford Town Hall against the Housing, Rents and Repairs Act. They are having 400 hundred posters printed, 15,000 leaflets distributed, and are having banners made for the meeting. It is intended that tenants from other parts of east London will arrive at the meeting in lorries decorated with slogans.' Reading the newsletter again is a reminder of the enthusiasm and energy with which the Communist Party in West Ham fought on local issues, rallying people to oppose anti-working class legislation.

The tenants' movement spread throughout the borough, organisations being formed in Canning Town, Tidal Basin and Plaistow. I took the initiative in calling a meeting of tenants from our street, which was held in my mother's kitchen, an indication of just how small that first meeting was. I was well known in the street as a Communist, and most of the neighbours regarded the meeting with some suspicion. However, my mother made tea, and the half a dozen that attended agreed to form a tenants' association, my father, a well respected figure in the street, being elected as secretary. Our fight was not for repairs, for the houses were in fair condition, but opposition to our private landlord who threatened increases in rent and changes to our security of tenure. We held weekly meetings in the kitchens or front rooms of the committee members, taking it in turns to provide the venue and the inevitable cups of tea, generating a spirit of resistance to the landlord which was evocative of the togetherness that we had felt during the war.

I printed posters, 'Repeal the Rent Act', and 'Not a penny on the rent', and gradually the front room windows along the street became dotted with red splashes of colour as our neighbours joined the association. We issued leaflets, lobbied our councillors and won support from the local Labour Party who agreed to arrange for a Labour and Co-operative Member of Parliament to speak to us on the legal implications of the Rent Act. Jimmy Glover agreed to be another of the speakers, with my father as chairman. I considered the composition of the platform to be a political triumph, one Communist, a Labour MP and a representative of the West Ham Trades Council united in attacking the Tory Rent Act. I booked St James school for the meeting, a decision which came close to farce. My childhood memory of the school hall was of a vast, high vaulted space, which proved on the night to have been relative to my infant size. To my dismay, the audience was obliged to squeeze into what was no more than a good size room and sit uncomfortably on chairs made for children. The room was so crowded that some people had to stand outside in the playground and listen through the open windows.

In my efforts to politicise the committee, I loaned them in turn my copy of *Trouble in Porter Street* by John Sommerfield, a fictional but inspirational account of a pre-war rent strike. The whole committee read the book, each one in turn signing the flyleaf, the names of Reilly, West, Cook, Howard, Davis, Macaree, Magill and my father, inscribed as a momento of our struggle against the landlord. We affiliated to the West Ham Tenants' Campaign Committee, a co-ordinating body formed by the Party, and I started a regular canvass of the *Daily Worker*, but met with little success. A few members of the committee became readers, but for the most part I was met with the familiar and polite refusal, 'not today, thank you.'

When we finally received notices of a rent increase, the St James Road committee were ready to agree that I should lead a deputation to our landlord, the Land and Property Company, at their offices in Victoria. I took a morning off from work and we met with a director, a city-suited gent who sat in a leather-covered chair at a solid oak desk. He defended the right of his company to raise our rents under the terms of the new legislation, talking of the need to earn money for his shareholders. I disputed his use of the word 'earn', saying that they were 'making' money from us, but not earning it. The meeting became acrimonious but we remained resolute, telling him bluntly that we would refuse to pay any increase, though privately I doubted if support for a rent strike would go far beyond members of the committee. In the event, the committee rejected the idea of a rent strike, preferring to remain within the law.

Our Party work was dominated by the struggle on housing, and the council elections of May, 1955, were seen as an opportunity to combine the campaign with an attempt to get our branch secretary, Wally Barnes, elected as a Communist councillor. Night after night we canvassed the High Street Ward, holding street corner meetings, touring with a loudspeaker perilously tied to the top of a small van, saturating the ward with leaflets, flyposting derelict property, whitewashing our message in the roads and knocking on every door for support. It was my first involvement in a local election, and I entered the hustings with passionate enthusiasm, speaking in the streets, arguing on the doorsteps, printing election posters and distributing leaflets. We would meet in Ben's, a workmen's caff in the High Street which was owned by a Party member, Ben Todd. He strewed his tables with copies of the *Daily Worker* and *Soviet Weekly*, making no attempt to hide his allegiance from his customers. Over steaming mugs we would analyse our work and plan the next bout of furious activity.

On election night, I was a scrutineer during the counting of the votes at Stratford Town Hall, and watched as the votes piled high for Labour. Victory for the Labour candidate was inevitable, for despite growing support for the Communist Party, and the high regard in which Wally Barnes was held by many people in the ward, when it came to the vote, loyalty to Labour was unshakeable. The Labour candidate polled just over a thousand votes to Wally's one hundred and seventy-one, but we were not downhearted, for our vote offered the promise of a greatly increased membership of the Party, and we had not come bottom of the poll. That distinction was left for the Conservative, who could muster only sixty-five of the electorate to vote for him.

Whilst battling on behalf of tenants, Pamela and myself had to consider our own position with regard to housing, for our son was growing and had to share our one bedroom. We had put our names on the council housing list as soon as we had married, a roll which ran to sixteen thousand, with another twelve thousand on the priority list. In the past year, the council had built just four hundred homes, and I calculated that at that rate, I would be retired before we were allocated a council house. We had tried flat-hunting outside of the borough, only to be offered slum accommodation by private landlords for which extortionate key money was demanded. House purchase among the working class was rare, and although we would have preferred to rent a council house, there seemed no alternative but to buy a house. As a socialist, I had no principled objection to people owning their own home, but I was bitterly opposed to landlordism, the private ownership of other peoples homes. We had been scrimping to save ten shillings a week for a couple of years, putting the money into our Co-op savings account. Recently, with business improving, I had boosted our savings to a total of two hundred pounds, the bare deposit for a two thousand pound house. Pamela would avidly read the *Stratford Express* each week searching the estate columns for an affordable house, and one week she spotted a house for sale at Chadwell Heath for two thousand, one hundred pounds. The area was the traditional route out of London for working class East Londoners, who were given to migrating to Seven Kings, Romford, or even as far afield as Gidea Park or Upminster. We would never had dreamed of going 'over the water', for we regarded South London as foreign parts. We viewed the house one Saturday morning, a solid 1930s terrace in a quiet street which smacked of lower middle class respectability. We walked through the empty rooms, examined the kitchen with its mysterious Ideal boiler for heating the water, looked with anticipation at the bath room and could already imagine our son playing in the safe and grassy garden. Within an hour, we had paid a five pound deposit to the agent and committed ourselves to a two-hundred pound down payment and a future mortgage of thirteen pounds a month for the next twenty-five years.

Within a few weeks we moved, plucked from the growing struggle by circumstance, to leave parents and neighbours, comrades and friends, and the street which had been my life.

CHAPTER 14
Exodus

We left St James Road, jammed into the oily cab of a British Road Services' lorry. Joe Edkins, who worked as a long distance lorry driver, was a solid figure, tall and broad, with most of his front teeth missing, a single 'pickle stabber' hanging like a lone stalactite in the centre of his upper gums. Joe had hired his vehicle for Saturday morning at the concessionary rate of four pounds, to move us to our new home. The long, open, flat-backed lorry was large enough to have moved the furniture from a half a dozen homes, and our motley jumble of household goods looked pitifully lost, perched on the tail. I was glad when Joe finally hid them under a travel-stained tarpaulin. Amid excitement and good wishes from passing neighbours, we had loaded a bed given to us by my parents, three upright chairs, two small easy chairs, a bookcase, miscellaneous crockery and domestic items packed into a solitary tea-chest, a few clothes, books and a heap of toys. There was nothing else, no carpets, and not even a table, because the table we had used was a folding contraption designed to make space in our little room, and was fixed to the wall. Joe crashed into first gear, swung the huge steering wheel with his massive red forearms, and we pulled away to shouts of 'good luck' and the waved farewells of family and neighbours, as if we were emigrating.

Our new home was not in a street or road, for we had moved to a gardens, Christie Gardens, a terraced row of identical houses with gabled roofs, facing the open playing fields of a girls' school. We had our own small front garden with a wooden gate, a straggly privet hedge and a single hydrangea. The front door, glazed with a leaded-light window incorporating a hideous galleon design, opened into a wide hallway which led through the kitchen to a long garden at the rear of the house. With its unkempt lawn and a couple of small trees, it was paradise.

Joe helped us carry in our belongings, eyed by curious peeping neighbours, eager to assess the newcomers. It did not take long to dump the few pieces of furniture on the bare boards and Joe said with a laugh that he and Jenny would be round for tea that afternoon. I thought that he was joking, but told him that if they came, they would have to bring their own chairs. I had solved the problem of the table by bringing an old kitchen table from my factory, where it had been in use as a colour mixing bench. The deal top had been kept covered and was clean, but the legs were splattered with more colours than Joseph had in his coat. At four o' clock there was a knock on the door, and our first visitors had arrived, Joe and Jenny, each clutching a chair. We sat around the table drinking tea and eating sandwiches for an hour or more, and when they left, they made us a present of the chairs. We were on our own at last.

Our neighbours were friendly enough, mostly older people who had bought their houses for five hundred pounds, when they were newly built, before the war. They were quietly respectable, trimmed their privets and painted their houses and tended to keep themselves to themselves. A few had cars which they parked outside their houses and religiously polished every Sunday morning. Being out at work each day, I did not see much of them, but Pamela said that they were obviously intrigued by us, living as we did in a house with bare boards and make-shift curtains. Although our neighbours were working class, many considered themselves a cut above the industrial working class, most of them being white collar workers who worked shorter hours than manual workers. It was an assumption of superiority without economic foundation, for production and wages were rising rapidly, and most of them were little better off than the skilled car workers who lived on the vast council estate at Dagenham.

As we settled in, I soon made contact with the nearest branch of the Communist Party, which was at Ilford, a few miles away, for I was anxious to resume work for the Party. The secretary was Phil Joseph, a young and thoughtful pipe smoker. Both he and his wife Madelaine were Canadians, and were to become our very good friends. The branch covered a wide area, although political activity was concentrated mainly on Ilford, with supportive forays into Dagenham where the Ford workers were our point of contact with industrial workers.

After the frenetic pace of political activity in West Ham, Party work appeared to be spasmodic rather than sustained, and there were no Party members living in my immediate vicinity. The one regular activity was a Sunday morning canvass with the *Daily Worker* on the Dagenham estate, where sales among the unionised car workers from Ford's were steady. Anxious to build the Party in Chadwell Heath, I astonished our neighbours by standing at the bus stop in Chadwell Heath High Road each morning attempting to sell the *Daily Worker*, before catching a trolley bus on the first stage of my long trek to work.

My efforts to win support for the Communist Party from the inhabitants of the sprucely painted houses in streets with blossoming trees, were singularly unsuccessful. After a while, I abandoned my lone vigil with the *Worker*, and concentrated on working with the branch at Ilford. We engaged in supporting the key campaigns of the Party, mustering a coachload of comrades to join a mass lobby of parliament against German rearmament, holding poster parades in Ilford High Street, supporting local council tenants in a fight against rent increases, and building sales of the *Daily Worker* among the workers in Dagenham.

Within our new home, life was happy but far from easy. We lived in rooms without lino or carpets, every sound amplified by the hollow rooms, especially when we clumped up and down the stairs. Although we had the luxury of hot water on tap, there was no central heating. In winter, the bedrooms were like refrigerators, with ice forming on the insides of the windows, and at nights we would spread my business overcoat on the bed for additional warmth. In the mornings, I would rise early to light a coal fire in the dining room in readiness for Pamela and John coming down to breakfast. Gradually, we began to acquire single pieces of furniture, buying on hire purchase from the Harrison Gibson store at Ilford. We rejected the idea of buying second-hand, for we wanted furnishings that were 'contemporary', the current vogue for the post Festival of Britain designs which gripped the young. Bright curtains with geometric designs and G-Plan furniture with splayed legs marked us as the new generation. Pamela bought a bicycle, fitted a basket to the handlebars and a small seat behind the saddle so that she could take John shopping with her. As a luxury, we bought an electric gramophone, gradually collecting long playing records, ranging from Paul Robeson and Ewan MacColl to Prokofiev and Lonnie Donegan. We had no television, but enjoyed listening to the wireless, especially plays on the Third Programme, a BBC programme considered highbrow. For evenings out we went back to Stratford, to Theatre Workshop, where Joan Littlewood was producing plays by writers as diverse as Shakespeare, and Brendan Behan. We sat on wooden forms, up in the gods, for the price of a shilling.

It was on a sunny Sunday morning at breakfast time, in June 1956, when my unbounded faith in Soviet communism was severely shaken. The Sunday newspapers, *Reynold's News* and *The Observer* had dropped through the letterbox, and I settled to scan them as I ate my only bacon and egg breakfast of the week. The headline of *The Observer* jumped from the page, 'Russia's twenty years of terror.' With unprecedented coverage for a single news story, *The Observer* devoted eight of its fourteen pages to an account of a six hour speech made by Khrushchev at a secret session of the 20th Congress of the Communist Party of the Soviet Union, held in Moscow earlier that year. I had previously read the Party report of the congress, with its condemnation of the cult of the individual in oblique references to Stalin, and mention of past 'mistakes', but accepted the supremacy of the collective leadership of the Party as a welcome sign of the growing strength of the Party, emerging under the leadership of Khrushchev to renounce past injustices and to consolidate the building of socialism. There had been no mention of the secret session from which foreign Communist Parties had been excluded.

The report of the Central Committee to the secret session of Soviet delegates revealed the horror of the limitless power that Stalin had ruthlessly acquired since the death of Lenin. The account given by Khrushchev was damning. The statistics numbed. Of 139 members and candidates for the Central Committee of the Party to the 17th Congress in 1934, no less than 98 had been subsequently shot as enemies of the people. From the 1,966 delegates, 1,108 had been arrested and charged with anti-revolutionary activities. Within the Party, it was a hideous tale of the imprisonment and murder of old Bolsheviks. Individual stories were chilling, the loyal and old revolutionary Kedrov writing to Stalin, "I am calling to you from a gloomy cell in the Lefortsky prison. Let my cry of horror reach your ears.' Until his lonely death, he could not believe that Stalin knew what was happening. From the murder of Kirov in 1934, Khrushchev catalogued Stalin's reign of duplicity, purges, torture and murder of his comrades. Seeking convictions against the group of doctors accused in 1953 of an alleged plot to murder him, Stalin had reputedly told the Minister of State Security, 'If you do not obtain confessions from the doctors, we will shorten you by a head.' For non-Party Soviet citizens, it was a story of repression on a gigantic scale, from the liquidation of the Kulaks to the deportation of whole peoples, of forced labour and mass murder. Stalinism, Khrushchev had said, was 'rule by terror.'

Khrushchev also announced the rehabilitation of tens of thousands wrongly accused of being spies, saboteurs and enemies of the state, exposing the show trials of Trotskyites, Zinovievites and Bukharinites in the 1930s as a sham, with confessions forced by torture and coercion. Towards the end of his life, Stalin's paranoia was said to have reached a pitch where even Vorishilov, the President of the USSR, was under suspicion of being an English agent.

For loyal Communists, the report was a nightmare, for it confirmed with exactitude the allegations made for years by critics of Soviet rule. I read and re-read every word that *The Observer* had printed until I felt ill with the realisation of the extent of the horror and the deception. I was so engrossed that I was almost late for the usual Sunday morning rendezvous for the door-to-door selling of the *Daily Worker*, dashing from the house, leaving Pamela to read the revelations for herself. When I arrived, I immediately questioned Phil Joseph, who said that he had not seen *The Observer*. As I recounted the salient features of Khrushchev's speech, he interrupted, saying, 'Comrade, don't believe all that you read in the capitalist press.' It was a familiar response to anti-Soviet press stories, and not without some justification, for since the October Revolution the enemies of socialism had spread disinformation about the workers' state. This time, however, I had no doubt as to the veracity of the news, and suggested that we should abandon the canvass, buy a copy of *The Observer*, and discuss the matter. Phil, as Party secretary, insisted that we should work as usual and wait until the Executive Committee of the Communist Party of Great Britain issued a reply before rushing to judgement. After some argument, I accepted the decision, but my enthusiasm for selling the *Daily Worker* had gone. I knocked on doors in a state of shock, not caring if I sold the paper or not. It was a charade.

The name of Stalin had first become known to me during the

war, as the leader of the Soviet people in their fight against the Nazi invader, our common foe. He was Joe Stalin, the avuncular, mustachioed, pipe-smoking symbol of working class resistance to fascism. It was the name chalked on British tanks as they poured out of the Midlands factories, where Communist shop stewards on Joint Production Committees helped to boost output to record levels; 'one more for Uncle Joe.' It was the name scrawled on guns and munitions loaded onto British convoys for the dreadful frozen journey to Murmansk. Stalin was the name to bring immediate applause when local dignitaries with mayoral chains spoke in town squares urging support for an Aid to Russia Week. When the Red Army was shown in action on cinema newsreels, the audience would break into applause, but when Stalin appeared, the applause doubled. The resistance of the Soviet people was legendary, and as the Red Army began its great fight back from the outskirts of Moscow, I had become familiar with the names of Russian generals, of Zhukov, Rokossovsky, Koniev and Timoshenko, but it was Stalin who was portrayed in the British as well as the Soviet press as the quiet strategic genius behind the victories, his very name synonymous with Stalingrad, the hero city and the graveyard of an entire German army. The Red Army drove relentlessly across Eastern Europe, welcomed as an army of liberation, to be finally greeted with hugs and handshakes by their British and American allies on the banks of the Elbe. Throughout the liberated countries of formerly Nazi occupied Europe, Communist leaders of the resistance emerged as heroes. When the war ended, we had decorated our street in celebration of final victory, the hammer and sickle displayed alongside the union jacks and the stars and stripes. Uncle Joe was as popular as Monty.

Upon joining the Communist Party, I was introduced to a new image of Stalin. He was still the war hero, now bearing the exalted title of Generalissimo, but that was secondary to his position as General Secretary of the Communist Party of the Soviet Union (Bolsheviks) and his status as a revolutionary, the master builder of socialism. Stalin was a comrade, a fellow member of the Party, our leader and mentor.

In 1950, I had bought a short biography of Stalin, a joint compilation produced by the Marx-Engels-Lenin Institute in Moscow, a book now denounced by Khruschev as a sycophantic eulogy written under the guidance of Stalin himself. But what else should I have read, accounts penned by enemies of the Party? I had found the early life of Joseph Vissarionovich Djugashvili as gripping as an adventure story, laced with revolution. Here was the young hero, leading an illegal May Day demonstration, arrested, exiled, working underground, addressing workers, leading a strike, re-arrested and imprisoned, released, back into the struggle, arrested and exiled again, always on the run from the police. It was the story of the forging of a young rebel into the 'man of steel', Stalin.

My favourite photograph of him was not the familiar image of an airbrushed, wrinkle-free Generalissimo of official Soviet photographs, it was a profile picture which appears in the biography, showing him as a handsome, young, bearded agitator, a photograph taken of him by the Okhrana, the Czarist secret police, when he was just twenty. Taken by the image, I was to grow a similar beard. By the time I joined the Party, Stalin was approaching deification, his pronouncements on any subject, from linguistics to the growing of wheat, accepted as a received truth. He was a man in total control, and we saw him as the supreme planner, quietly giving orders for the diversion of a river or the planting of a forest, changing the climate of an entire region, altering nature to comply with a greater Soviet plan, building Communism.

The adulation of Stalin had reached its zenith with the extravagant celebration of his seventieth birthday in 1949. As world Communist leaders gathered in Moscow to pay tribute, gifts poured into the Soviet Union by the trainload. Writers, artists, poets and musicians created special works to his praise, while factory workers in the Peoples' Democracies worked 'voluntary' overtime to pay for gifts ranging from portraits to coal-cutting machinery. As streets were renamed in his honour and statues erected in towns and villages throughout the USSR, the British Communist Party made its own contribution to the exaltation of Stalin. On his birthday, the *Daily Worker* headline read, 'The world acclaims Stalin.' Celebratory meetings were held, and Party branches organised their own gifts and greetings. Telegrams were sent by the hundreds, and if we could not match the largesse of our Parisian comrades who sent a lathe, a group of London comrades trooped to Dunhill's to buy a suitable pipe, 'To uncle Joe on his seventieth birthday. Long live Comrade Stalin, the great leader of progressive peoples.'

Pamela never accepted the glorification of Stalin. To her, Stalin worship was contrary to the egalitarian spirit of the Party, where all were equal as comrades in the socialist cause. For myself, Stalin was a hero figure, his authority as the world's leading Marxist unquestioned. In 1952, the collected works of Stalin, published in Moscow and running to thirteen volumes, became available in Britain at five shillings a volume. Like many other Party members, I collected them at the rate of one a month. I studied them diligently, marking the significant passages, finding accord with my own views as a revolutionary. Stalin had the ability to communicate complex ideas in simple terms, bringing the intellectual reasoning of Lenin to millions who would never grapple with his volumes of closely argued theory. Stalin was regarded by Communists as the true disciple of Lenin, guardian of the faith, eternally vigilant for any signs of deviation. His style of speech was said to be unassuming, choosing his words with thought, patiently listening, taking 'concrete decisions' – a favourite expression among Party members – unhurried in reaching those decisions, but quietly seeing that they were carried out as planned. For countless Communists, Stalin became a role model, and we tried to think and act as we imagined Stalin would have done. To my shame, I remember visiting a railway worker in Stratford who had failed to carry out some small task for the Party. He made a feeble excuse and I was furious at his lack of Party commitment, demanding of him, 'What would Comrade Stalin have done?' My arrogance was shattered when he meekly replied that he was only a railway worker and that he had no idea what Stalin would have done. In the Communist Party of the 1950s, we were all Stalinists in the sense that we believed that whatever he said was indisputable. To quote Stalin gave the speaker unanswerable authority. 'As Stalin said' would end any contentious discussion.

The death of Stalin in 1953 saw the virtual canonisation of Stalin by the Communist Party. While his embalmed body lay in state, to be enshrined with Lenin in the mausoleum in Red Square, the *Daily Worker* proclaimed 'The architect of socialism is dead.' At a memorial meeting in West Ham, Wally Barnes asked us to stand for a minute in silence, and ingrained in my memory is the sight of tears rolling down the face of a shabbily dressed comrade who might have been a Soviet artist's model for the depiction of an oppressed worker. There was no shame, for he was not alone. Throughout the world, working people of all races and from all countries, including the Soviet Union, wept for the loss of Stalin. On the day that his death was announced, I paid my own tribute, selling fifty copies of the *Daily Worker* in Stratford

Broadway in less than half an hour before selling out. Curiosity apart, the death of Stalin touched an old wartime memory of affection among the British public.

After the Khruschev denouncement, I entered a period of torment as I struggled with my conscience. Socialism for me was about the freedom and dignity of working people, a concept of emancipation, a release from the tyranny of industrial capitalism, providing the opportunity for all people, regardless of race or sex to live lives of equal opportunity and fulfilment, a social system that cared for all its people, including the young, the old and the infirm. How could I continue to be a member of a party that had been instrumental in building a society based on fear and oppression? Yet, I did not resign. Pamela allowed her membership to lapse, and Lionel had already distanced himself from the Party, but I grasped at the positive side of Communism, whilst rejecting the evil. I could not agree with comrades who persisted in describing the blood-letting in the Soviet Union over the past thirty years as 'mistakes', arising from the attempt to build socialism in a hostile capitalist world, but neither could I bring myself to join those who immediately rejected the Party as being totally corrupt. My fellow Communists were self-sacrificing, decent people, who devoted their lives to the betterment of the working class. Two of my personal friends, Wally Barnes from Stratford and Sid Brown from East Ham, had suffered imprisonment for their Party activities. The record of international Communism was filled with the names of those who had suffered incarceration, exile and death in the cause of socialism, victims of fascism and capitalism.

Rejecting the cult of Stalinism as foreign to the spirit of Marxism-Leninism, Khrushchev had said that 'We are absolutely certain that our Party, armed with the historical resolution of the Twentieth Congress will lead the Soviet people along the Leninist path to new successes, new victories.' I accepted the reaffirmation of Leninism in good faith. The reign of Stalin had been a criminal offence against civilisation, a hi-jacking of working class power, but with the open admission of past tyranny, there was hope that the socialist countries could move back onto course, to build a new revolution that would realise the hopes of working people throughout the world. The alternative was submission to American monopoly capitalism with its goal of world domination by finance capital and the continued exploitation of the working class and the colonial peoples.

The monolithic role of the Soviet Communist Party, whose authority among international Communist parties had been tacitly accepted because it had been the first Communist Party to win power, had been increasingly questioned since the death of Stalin. Now, the debate among fraternal communist parties was open and international. The powerful Italian Communist Party, led by Togliatti, attacked the Soviet leadership, asking them to explain what errors in the Soviet system had allowed Stalin to become a tyrant. Others, more cogently asked if it was possible for one man alone to have been responsible for government by terror? In the British Communist Party debate raged fiercely in every Party branch, and letters poured into *Daily Worker* and King Street from comrades who were sickened by our leadership which would not face the reality of Stalin's crimes, nor question any aspect of the Soviet line on increasing unrest within the Peoples' Democracies. Two Communist historians, John Saville and E P Thompson launched an heretical journal, *The Reasoner*, and were promptly told by the Party executive to cease publication. They refused, were suspended from the Party and responded by joining the growing numbers of disillusioned comrades by resigning. The level of discussion within our branch may not have matched the intellectual standard of debate among Marxist scholars, but it was sincere and deeply searching. These were rank and file workers who daily confronted the problems of trade union organisation, jobs, wages, housing, and saw the Party torn between those who were inextricably bound by loyalty to the Soviet Union, right or wrong, and those who sought to question the continued supremacy and infallibility of the Soviet Party.

For the first time in seven years, my Party activities dwindled to attending branch meetings, to participation in unresolved discussion, without action. Privately, I argued with comrades for hours, listening with growing incredulity as some blamed the growing dissent among the peoples of Eastern Europe on the activities of the CIA, the Catholic Church and right wing deviationists. I sought out my old comrade and friend, Joe Edkins, to voice my misgivings, but he remained steadfast in his support for the Party line. I had no illusions that the church, former monarchists, dispossessed landowners and right wing groups were receiving financial aid from Western agencies anxious for the restoration of capitalism, but I could not blindly reject the flow of evidence that popular support for the Party within the Peoples' Democracies had collapsed under regimes that were both corrupt and oppressive. It was as though I had become a bystander to the slow disintegration of a monument, watching it crumble under the constant chipping of a seething force locked within, encouraged by an outside group who never wanted it built in the first place. The Twentieth Congress had accepted that the head did not conform to the original design, but promises to rebuild were foundering as the base itself crumbled.

There were months of agonising as Stalinists in Poland and Hungary strove to hold back the rising demands from students, workers, intellectuals and not a few honest Communists within those countries, for greater democracy and independence from the Soviet Union. In the midst of my soul searching, there was a flurry of political activity as our government, led by Anthony Eden, prepared for war against Egypt, ostensibly because the Egyptians had the audacity to nationalise the Suez canal. On a Saturday in mid-September, the Party called for support of a Labour Party demonstration in Trafalgar Square to protest at Eden's war plans. There seemed to be a new militant spirit within the Labour Party, raising my hopes for holding common ground with the Labour Party in opposition to an imperialist war, but for the first time in years I did not take part. Filled with an inner conflict, I spent the day quietly in Hainault Forest with my wife and son.

Within weeks, the Hungarian people took to the streets, demanding the end of Soviet occupation and the abolition of the AVH, the Hungarian secret police. Soon after, Britain attacked Egypt, by which time the Communist Party of Great Britain had embarked on the road to self destruction.

At first, the situation in Hungary was confused, the Hungarian government and Moscow blaming the uprising on counter revolutionaries funded and armed by the Americans. The *Daily Worker* reminded us that 'the class enemy never gives up' and called for Labour Party branches, Communist Party branches, trade unions and Labour MPs to send telegrams to the Hungarian government condemning the counter revolutionary violence and standing by the government and people in their efforts to build socialism. It was a forlorn appeal from a Party leadership that had lost its credibility. Like thousands of fellow Communists I was sceptical, balancing accounts of the uprising which filled the media with the official Party line, expounded in the *Daily Worker*.

On 5 November, 1956, as the *Daily Worker* splashed its front page with pictures and reports of a great Labour demonstration in London against the invasion of Egypt, the news came that Soviet tanks were roaring into Hungary. I was walking through Ilford with Pamela and John when we saw the placards and heard the newspaper seller shouting the headline, 'Russia invades Hungary.' It was news that cut deep. Ours was the Party that had so often called upon armies to refuse to shoot workers. Our own venerated Communist and trade union leader, the late Tom Mann, had gone to prison for a 'Don't shoot' speech directed to British troops following the use of military force against strikers. His famous appeal, printed as a leaflet, was framed and hanging in my studio: 'You are working men's sons. When we go on strike to better our lot, which is the lot also of your fathers, mothers, brothers and sisters, YOU are called upon by your officers to MURDER us. Don't do it.' It was an appeal for class solidarity, fundamental to every Communist, but now the Red Army, the workers' army, was shooting down students and workers on the streets of Budapest. The Soviet government claimed, and it was a claim to be repeated in the *Daily Worker*, that they were defending socialism from fascist insurgents and counter revolutionaries, yet they could find no Hungarians to fight alongside them.

The news from Hungary, following the revelations of the secret session of the Twentieth Congress and the turmoil engulfing the socialist countries, finally undermined my faith in the leadership of the Communist Party. All that we had believed in, the principles of working class solidarity, the spirit of proletarian internationalism, the basic goodness of socialism, was being crushed by tanks, ordered into action by a brutal bureaucracy that had distorted and degraded the very meaning of socialism. Pamela was devastated by the armed intervention of the Soviet forces, and irrevocably renounced the Party for its betrayal of the working class. I hesitated, avidly following the news, desperately hoping that our Party leadership would listen to its membership and condemn the outrage. It was not to be, for the Party system of democratic centralism, by which the lower organisations of the Party accepted the decisions of the higher organisations of the Party, was in effect bureaucratic centralism, with the executive following the line of the Soviet Communist Party.

For myself, the final act of treachery came from our own paper, the *Daily Worker*. That it stood solidly behind the Soviet line in stating that the issue in Hungary was a choice between fascist dictatorship and socialism, may have been predictable, and for some, proved persuasive. However, rumours, soon to be confirmed, that reports from our own correspondent in Budapest, Peter Fryer, were being suppressed because they contradicted the Party line was shattering. This was our paper, a newspaper owned by its readers, a socialist newspaper committed to espousing the cause of the working class in all countries. We used to sing a song about our paper, with a chorus that ran, 'No matter what they say, the truth is here to stay, because we'll fight for the *Worker* till we die.' In Hungary, workers were dying, but the *Daily Worker* could not face the truth as to why they were dying. Truth, as ever, became a casualty of the conflict.

Peter Fryer, who had been with the *Daily Worker* for nine years, resigned from the paper, as did a quarter of its staff, respected and familiar names vanishing from its pages, journalists like Malcolm MacEwan, and the cartoonist Gabriel among them. The effect of the Soviet armed intervention and the perfidy of the *Daily Worker* ripped through the Communist Party. Unable to stomach the Executive Committee of the Party with its abject support for the Soviet line, seven thousand comrades resigned from the Party, a fifth of the membership, including many who had been stalwart members from the earliest days. I lay awake at nights in mental anguish, battling with my loyalty and my conscience. To resign would be to walk into the wilderness. For seven years I had fought for the Communist corner in every political argument, with my friends and family, on hundreds of doorsteps, on street corners and schoolrooms, at bar and table. The Party had been my life, consuming me with a passion that shaped my work, reading, moral attitudes and political action. Communism had provided a base from which to judge every issue, to tackle every problem. Above all, it had offered the hope of a better world.

On 12 November, a week after the Soviet invasion, I wrote to the General Secretary of the Party, John Gollan, tendering my resignation, the most difficult letter that I have ever had to write, forcing every word. His reply was brief, referring me to statements already made by the Executive Committee. Of the comrades like myself who resigned, Gollan was later to say, 'They are not our best comrades, otherwise they would not have left.' It was a statement of Stalinist contempt for thousands of good comrades who had given years of selfless service to the Party, intellectuals, national trade union leaders and rank and file workers swept aside with a few words as worthless.

Resignation from the Party was a trauma, like the breaking of a solemn vow. I was not alone, for I knew comrades, well known comrades, who became physically ill as a result of breaking with the Party. Men and women who had organised thousands of workers, addressed mass meetings, people who were articulate, capable, self confident and filled with revolutionary zeal were broken by the scale of the treachery and carnage wrought by Soviet Communism. If I had any lingering doubts, they were dispelled by the Soviet abduction and murder of Imry Nagy, the Hungarian premier, after pledges by the Soviet commander and the Soviet government that he would be allowed to leave unharmed.

On the evening of my resignation I felt saddened, angry, and depressed, while my mind was filled with questions and reflections on my past years in the Party. What had gone wrong with a revolution that had brought hope to millions of working people, that had unleashed creative talent in the arts and sciences, proclaimed equality and internationalism, offering bread, peace and security in place of war, hunger and poverty, only to degenerate into a dictatorship, not of the proletariat, but a party of apparatchiks led by a paranoid tyrant?

How was it that so many of us were unaware that the reality of life under Soviet Communism, mocked the ideals of socialism? Why did we reject all criticism as anti-Soviet propaganda? I tried to draw some consolation from the knowledge that I was not alone in having been deceived. From the earliest days of the Russian revolution, well known individuals had journeyed to the Soviet Union to see for themselves the construction of a socialist society. Bernard Shaw, H G Wells, the Webbs and the gentle Christian socialist, George Lansbury, had been welcomed on official visits. Shaw returned to put a photograph of Stalin on his mantlepiece, the Webbs to write *Soviet Communism: A new Civilisation?*, and they were soon to drop the query. Visits by well known figures were usually followed by publication of the 'What I saw in Russia' genre, which, if not always fulsome in praise, were seldom unfavourable, pointing to the progress being made in health, education, housing and production. During my years in the Party, trade union delegations from Britain made frequent tours to the Soviet Union, bringing back accounts of former palaces used as trade union sanatoria, the construction of giant dams for hydro electric power, the fulfilment of yet another five year plan and consequent rise in the standard of living. Abe Woolf, a local Labour councillor, talked to us of his visit as a member of an official delegation, regaling us with details of a gargantuan feast on a collective farm, and a spectacular evening at the Bolshoi ballet in Moscow.

Why was it, I asked myself in retrospect, that instead of reading accounts of increased production at Russian tractor plants, I never studied the writings of former Communists like Koestler, Ignazio Silone or Louis Fischer? The simple truth was that their heart searching accounts of disillusionment with the Party were rejected without study as the literature of defectors. Against those intellectuals who deserted the Party, were the many who rebutted their arguments and remained loyal.

Throughout the world, there were famous Party members, and friends of the Soviet Union to be found in every walk of artistic, scientific, and intellectual life. Picasso, Leger, Professors Joliet Curie, Bernal, Haldane, and the poet Pablo Neruda, all held Party cards. In the universities, there were Marxist historians, mathematicians, physicists and philosophers. Folk singers, composers, film directors, actors, musicians, writers, lawyers and architects, all offered international names that were committed to the cause of Communism. In conversation, when a famous name was mentioned, I was on many occasions and to the astonishment of others, able to say with pride, that he or she was a Party member. Within the British trade union movement, the names of Communists rang as a role call of Labour history: Tom Mann, Arthur Horner, Will Paynter, Abe Moffat – their names could fill a book.

The *Daily Worker* maintained a permanent correspondent in Moscow, but there had been no reports of rule by terror. British Communist leaders like Harry Pollitt, and Willie Gallacher, men I trusted implicitly, who had been to prison for the cause, made frequent visits to Moscow and had meetings with Stalin. Were they deceived, or were they guilty of suppressing the truth? Did they know nothing of the Gulag, or if they had knowledge, how much did they know, and why did they remain silent?

In leaving the Party, I felt as though I was cast into a political void, cut off from my comrades who remained within the Party, and racked with guilt at having broken the bonds, despite an inner conviction that there was no honourable alternative. Many of my old comrades were to remain as good friends, but some never quite forgave. Ten years after my resignation, when researching material for my first book, *Banner Bright*, I made an appointment to visit the Communist Party archives in King

Street. I was greeted by the librarian, Frank Jackson, a veteran Communist, with a single word, 'Renegade.'

Reflecting on my years in the Party, I wondered if they were wasted years. There was some self recrimination, but few lasting regrets. I thought of my Communist friends Ken Sprague and Ray Bernard, who had joined volunteer work brigades after the Second World War to help with the reconstruction of socialist Yugoslavia. They had helped to build the Unity and Brotherhood Road from Zagreb to Belgrade. Was their socialist idealism misguided? I looked back on the work that we did in opposing German re-armament, supporting the co-operative and trade union movement, opposing the 1954 Rent Act, fighting for decent housing, campaigning for a ban on atomic weapons, opposing the siting of American bomber bases in Britain, supporting the struggles of council tenants and old age pensioners. Was that too misguided?

In the Party, I had found the comradeship that is built when a group of people are banded together against a common enemy, the romance of struggle against great odds. They were good days, the late night meetings in the homes of friends, the colour and excitement of great marches and demonstrations, the challenge of street work, of shared hardships and the education that comes with political struggle. My shame was for the extent to which I had been gullible in my adulation of Stalin and my unquestioning support for Soviet Communism, when so many were its innocent victims.

Looking back on that now distant period of my life in Stratford, it is easy to be critical of my impatient youth, the revolutionary fervour that burned for social change, grasping at Communism as a world-wide force for liberation. Harry Pollitt used to talk of the 'gleam of socialism', and it was a vision I shared, a goal born of a passion fed by anger at the unfairness of capitalism, where those who did the hard, dirty and productive work lived in poverty, while the indolent rich lived upon that labour.

My father died in 1984. In his last years he had taken to writing poetry, and his last poem was written in support of the miners' strike of that same year. The West Ham Trades Council hosted the launch of the publication of a little book of his poems as a final tribute, and it remains as a testament to his love of humanity. My mother, now in her late eighties, still lives in St James Road in the house where I grew up. When I visit her I see that the street has changed. The large and gloomy church, where the congregation had diminished to a handful, has been demolished, to be replaced with a little prefabricated church at the other end of the road. The vicarage is gone, so too is the little Church of England school and the rag and bone yard that was opposite. All that is left of the Sick Home is a brick facade, but there is no new hospital. At the Forest Lane end of the street, there are two new signs, one announcing the 'Hibiscus Caribbean Elderly Group', the other banning lorries from overnight parking. Parked cars line the kerbs on both sides of the street, television aerials dot the rooftops and telephone wires radiate from the telegraph poles like spiders' webs.

The children still play, but on the pavements, not in the road, and many of them are black. The old lamp-posts have gone, replaced by tall, slender standards of polished steel, smooth enough to defy climbing and without a bar to swing on. The corner shop is still there, owned by an Asian family, but the enamel advertising signs have gone, and they no longer sell the strips of toffee I knew as 'farthing golliwogs.' The women who used to stand and chat to each other as they swept their fronts and whitened their doorsteps have been replaced by a generation that go out to work. It is two wage economy to pay for the car, video, telephone, and, for most, the mortgage, in a struggle to buy houses that have already been paid for a hundred times over. With the young women at work all day, the sense of community has been weakened, but not entirely destroyed. Some of the old neighbours still live in the houses they occupied when I was born. Others are the children and grandchildren of names that are familiar from my youth. A neighbour takes my mother's rent to be paid each month, for the rent collector no longer calls. Another neighbour knocks on her door each morning to check that all is well, while others offer to do her weekly shopping. Her Asian neighbours treat her as part of their extended family, their children giving her the respect commanded by her years.

The changes that sadden are the Neighbourhood Watch stickers, and the notice my mother now has pinned inside her front door, 'Check identity', for three times she has been robbed of her pension by men posing as officials to gain entry to her home. No longer do people hang their door key from string to dangle behind the letterbox as they did when I was a child, for the homes of working people are burgled as often as the homes of the wealthy.

As I write, at our home in Epping Forest, where I live with Pamela, I ponder how little the economic structure of our society has really changed. Capitalism is once more in a cyclical state of economic depression and the British working class are again the victims of mass unemployment. Trade unions are circumscribed by draconian laws, drafted to make solidarity illegal. The rich grow richer purveying the necessities of life, including the water that runs from our taps. If they could bottle the very air we breathe, they would sell it for profit. The world has millions of hungry people, yet I can see fields that lie fallow, our farmers paid not to grow food. The world is torn with wars for power, profit and religious supremacy, to which is added the curse of divisive nationalism. Our society is torn by violence, greed, racial intolerance and the pursuit of private wealth, with minimal concern for community or the very earth on which we live. There has to be a better way, and that way surely lies in a society based upon co-operation, not competition. Within me, the gleam of socialism remains undimmed.

FORTHCOMING TITLES
FROM CALIBAN BOOKS:

Children of the Dead End
Patrick MacGill
(Introduction by Professor John Burnett)
First published in 1914, *Children of the Dead End* is Patrick MacGill's fictionalised autobiography. The book starts with an account of his childhood in Ireland at the end of the nineteenth century, and includes a detailed narrative of the poverty and hand-to-mouth existence common in Ireland at the time. As an adult, MacGill migrated to Scotland with a number of fellow Irishmen, and the book describes in both a humorous and moving way the life of a navvy in Scotland and England at the beginning of the century. The songs, sayings and life of an itinerant navvy are revealed in their full colour by this evocative autobiography.

"Has that freshness and force which is the mark of true literature . . . the structure is perfect. I heartily recommend it." – *Irish Press*

"Splendid . . . a superb account of its time." – *Irish Times*

Reprinted edition 1995.
ISBN 0904573745   Paperback   320 pages

Maureen
Patrick MacGill
This biographical novel by Patrick MacGill, set in the area of Glenties, County Donegal, covers the events of the war of the Irish against the British colonial administration, and details the personalities and actions of the local Sinn Fein movement. The major part of the book is a love story, and MacGill, by setting this in its context, vividly evokes the life of an Irish community in the early 1920s.

ISBN 1850660123   Paperback   320 pages

Life Of William Hutton
William Hutton
One of the earliest working class autobiographies to appear in print, Hutton's memoirs were first published in 1816. Written in the form of an annual diary, the book covers the period from Hutton's birth in 1723 to the year of his death in 1815. It also includes a history of the Hutton family between the years 1570 and 1798, giving genealogical and personal details of family members. Hutton presents an account of his life as a child worker in a Derby silk mill and in a stocking knitting factory in the East Midlands, as well as his eventual rise to success as an eminent businessman and owner of property. The book includes material on the social life of the eighteenth century, covering topics such as family life, courtship, elections, and the political and religious riots of 1791.

ISBN 1850660239   Hardback   432 pages

The Autobiography Of William Farish:
The Struggles Of A Hand-Loom Weaver
William Farish
(With an introduction by Dr Owen Ashton and Dr Steven Roberts) Born at Carlisle in 1818, William Farish first started work as a bobbin wheel operative at the age of eight, graduating to the loom two years later. His autobiography was privately printed in 1889, and includes an account of the hardship and poverty of his childhood, associated with the decline of the hand-loom weaving industry. As well as working as a weaver, Farish engaged in a number of other occupations, including clerk to a railway construction company and teacher at a local evening institute. The book is central for an understanding of the culture and politics of the period, the author being a leading member of the temperance and Chartist movements, both of which are described in full. The introduction by Dr Owen Ashton and Dr Stephen Roberts will discuss the life of William Farish in the context of the latest research on Chartism.

ISBN 1850660247   Hardback   208 pages

The Life Of William Mabey
William Mabey
Previously unpublished, the manuscript of this autobiography was written in 1930, a year before the author's death. Born in 1848, Mabey spent most of his life in Dorsetshire, and this book vividly depicts both the harshness and pleasures of nineteenth century rural society. The son of a master carpenter, Mabey describes his childhood and adult life, which included working as farm boy, apprentice shoemaker, innkeeper's assistant, itinerant salesman, journeyman carpenter, and eventually successful master builder. The author covers a number of areas of social life: schooling, leisure activities (including cockfighting and bull-baiting), public hangings, poaching, crime, superstitions, health, medicine, diet and food prices. The book recreates the cultural world of nineteenth century Dorsetshire, which was the background to Hardy's Wessex novels.

ISBN 1850660190   Hardback   240 pages

Proletarian Pilgrimage: An Autobiography
John Paton
Born in Scotland in 1886, John Paton was raised in the tenements of Aberdeen, and after a variety of occupations, became a full-time organiser and eventually a Member of Parliament for the Independent Labour Party. In this autobiography he writes of Scottish working class life at the end of the last century, covering street lore, school, church, leisure and working life. The book's focus is on Paton's increasing involvement with the newly-created socialist movement – the Clarion Club, the I.L.P. and other labour groups – and he describes his encounters with and recollections of all the leading early socialists, including Edward Aveling, Keir Hardie, Jim Larkin, Philip Snowden, Emmanuel Shinwell, and Jowett, Arthur Henderson and Ramsay MacDonald. Paton gives a first-hand account of the development of the Labour Party and its membership, creating a central text for the study of working class and socialist history.

ISBN 1850660050   Hardback   336 pages   A reprinted edition